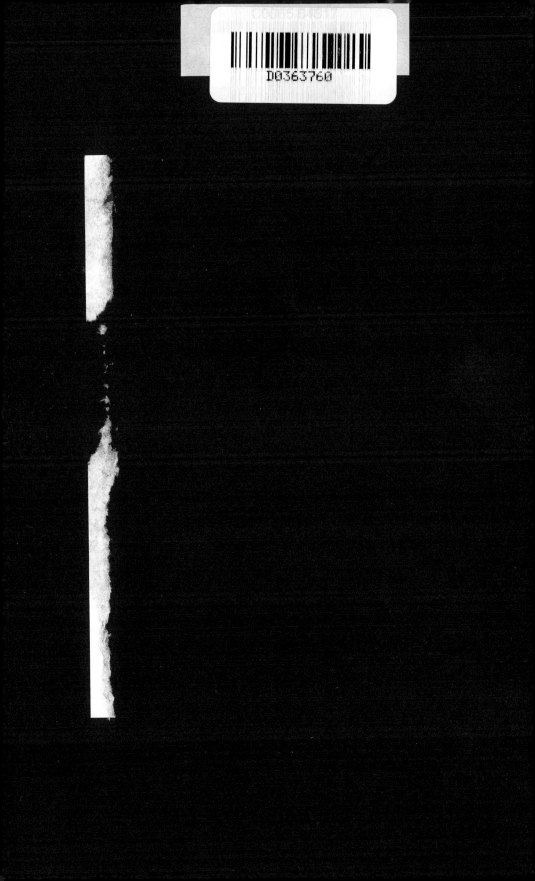

NOBODY'S VICTIM

NOBODY'S VICTIM

FIGHTING PSYCHOS, STALKERS, PERVS AND TROLLS

CARRIE GOLDBERG

with Jeannine Amber

virago

VIRAGO

First published in the United States in 2019 by Plume
First published in Great Britain in 2019 by Virago Press

1 3 5 7 9 10 8 6 4 2

The following names are pseudonyms:
Paul, Jerome, Becka, Macie, Sharon, Karl, Vanessa,
Destiny, Kai, Jennifer, Sarah, Arianne, Anna, and Jonetta.
In certain cases, identifying information was changed.

The information contained in this book is not legal advice.
This book is no substitute for obtaining independent
legal advice from a fabulous attorney.

While the author has made every effort to provide
accurate telephone numbers, internet addresses, and other contact information at the
time of publication, neither the publisher nor the author assumes any responsibility for errors
or for changes that occur after publication. Further, the publisher does not have any
control over and does not assume any responsibility for author or
third-party websites or their content.

A CIP catalogue record for this book is available from the British Library.

Hardback ISBN 978-0-349-01279-7
Trade paperback ISBN 978-0-349-01053-3

Printed and bound in Great Britain by Clays Ltd, Elcograf S.p.A.

Papers used by Virago are from well-managed forests
and other responsible sources.

Virago Press
An imprint of
Little, Brown Book Group
Carmelite House
50 Victoria Embankment
London EC4Y 0DZ

An Hachette UK Company
www.hachette.co.uk

www.virago.co.uk

For T.

For all the beautiful ways you've

changed my situation.

CONTENTS

INTRODUCTION

My name is Carrie Goldberg and I'm a victims' rights lawyer. Some people call me a "passionate advocate" or a "social justice warrior." I'd rather be called a ruthless motherfucker. I operate my firm, C.A. Goldberg, PLLC, with one fundamental rule: if one of my clients has been harmed, somebody must pay. It's as simple as that.

My clients—I represent everyone from successful businesspeople to struggling students—have endured unimaginable offenses. They've been assaulted, stalked, threatened, raped, and extorted. Their sexual privacy has been invaded, their reputations destroyed, and their lives put in danger. As a result of these crimes, some of my clients have lost their jobs or been forced to leave school, their entire lives and careers upended.

One of my first clients was a seventeen-year-old girl coerced into performing sex acts by a man she'd met online. She was so distraught I worried she might harm herself. Another client was being impersonated online by a vindictive boyfriend who posted multiple Craigslist ads with my client's phone number and work address promoting her as a sex worker and inviting men over for sex. Yet another client was doxed by an angry mob of trolls who bombarded her with death threats so vicious she fled her home in fear.

Before coming to see me, most of my clients have tried to help themselves. If they are students, they've gone to their school officials; if they are being harassed online, they've appealed to webmasters and platform administrators. Many have gone to the police—not once but repeatedly. One client sought help more than fifty times before he came to me. I meet people when they are desperate, traumatized, even suicidal, which is exactly what these offenders want. The attacks are meant to crush your soul. I know because it's happened to me.

———

I met my psycho ex on the dating site OkCupid. At the time, I was in my midthirties, newly divorced, and living in New York, working as the lead lawyer at the Guardianship Project at the Vera Institute of Justice. My job entailed advocating for mostly indigent, elderly, or mentally disabled adults unable to advocate for themselves and without suitable family to care for them. Courts had deemed our clients legally incapacitated and designated the Vera Institute their court-appointed guardian. I had the sobering responsibility of making decisions about every aspect of my clients' lives—from money and caretakers to housing and birth control. I didn't realize at the time how much I longed for someone to take care of me.

When my ex first messaged me, I was immediately intrigued. He was charming, smart, and creative. He'd graduated from the prestigious Wharton business school, he said, and had sometimes commuted there by helicopter. We texted and direct messaged for hours a day, talking about everything: past relationships, his missing turtle, fashion. Our connection was fun, playful, and deeply serious. When we finally met face-to-face, we became instantly inseparable. He chauffeured me around in his Mercedes SUV, bought me jewelry, and commissioned artwork for me—all within the first month. It was romantic and intoxicating. I trusted him with all my secrets. I felt protected and adored.

But then, a few weeks after we started dating, things began to change. He started checking up on me, texting me obsessively whenever I worked late: "Why aren't you home? Where are you? Who are you with?" Anytime I tried to hang out with friends or talk on the phone with family, he threw a fit. More than once I woke up in the middle of the night and found him sitting straight up, staring at me. He was insanely jealous and would fly into violent rages over imaginary cheating scenarios he refused to believe weren't true.

One night a friend invited me to a fund-raiser for her new play. The event was held in the basement of a community theater on the Lower East Side where I had no cell reception. Walking out, I checked my phone and saw more than two dozen missed calls from my ex and a string of frantic text messages demanding I respond. He called me a bitch, accused me of cheating on him, proclaimed we were "done," then insisted I call. He wrote: "Think you can betray me like this? I will fuckin END you." I was terrified.

I'd like to say I ended things right then. But it took a few months and more frightening incidents before I was finally able to summon the courage to leave the relationship for good. As soon as it was over, my ex started to attack in earnest. He flooded my phone and email with hundreds of threatening messages. He told me he was going to post intimate pictures of me online. He filed a false police report claiming I'd assaulted him. He even contacted my friends, family, and colleagues on Facebook, spreading lies about my having a sexually transmitted infection and being addicted to drugs. He said he hired three HIV-positive men to rape me. He told me this was "war."

For almost a year, my life was consumed by this battle. I filed a police report, obtained an order of protection, and begged a judge to restrain my ex from posting naked pictures and videos of me online. I spent $30,000 in legal fees and countless hours defending myself against my ex's false accusations before the charges were eventually dropped. I moved out of the co-op I loved and into an apartment with a doorman. Even then, I didn't feel safe. Walking down the street, out of the corner of my eye I would catch a glimpse of someone who looked vaguely like my ex and freeze. I thought there was no way I could ever escape his attacks and recover my life.

I was at my lowest point, in December 2013, when a friend invited me to go with her to Ireland, where she'd rented a vacation house. I jumped at the chance to get away. One afternoon we took a ferry to the Aran Islands. During a treacherous storm, I climbed a steep cliff overlooking Galway Bay. As the rain blew sideways, fogging up my glasses, I started replaying moments of what had been the most diffi-cult months of my life. I realized that through it all, the worst part was feeling completely alone. Neither the lawyers nor the judges nor the cops I'd turned to for assistance had ever made me feel protected. Instead, I'd been repeatedly told that there was nothing they could do. Then, standing on that cliff, I had an epiphany: as horrible as my experience had been, I couldn't possibly be the *only* one.

There had to be other people out there who had suffered the same kind of attack. It occurred to me that they were probably searching for the same kind of support I had longed for in my darkest days: a skilled fighter who could navigate both the law and the changing digital landscape; someone who understood the threat of privacy vio-lations and knew what to do when a psycho was spinning out of con-trol. In that moment, drenched in the pouring rain, I decided I was going to advocate for victims the way I wish somebody had fought for me. I would become the lawyer I'd needed when I was most desperate.

When I got home, I gave my two weeks' notice at work. My last day at the Vera Institute was January 23, 2014. I opened my own law firm the next day.

When I started my practice, I had little money, no staff, and zero idea of how to run a business. All I had was the fight. But that was enough. At first, I took any case I could find and often worked for free. I couldn't bring myself to say no to people who were in pain the way I'd been, and I wanted to learn how to fight on their behalf. I read everything I could about revenge porn, sextortion, rape, domestic violence, internet law, and First Amendment rights, and I studied state and federal criminal codes. I figured out how to get information removed from the internet, began establishing relationships with people at the major social media companies and search engines, and started working with other survivors, advocates, and lawmakers.

Soon I had more work than I could handle on my own. I hired an intern and then a receptionist. In five years, I grew my firm to a staff of thirteen, including six lawyers. In 2018, I was anointed by Law Firm 500 the fastest-growing law firm in the country.

———

My clients, many of whom I consider friends, are fierce and fearless warriors. No two are alike. I represent actors and activists, suburban moms, struggling artists, recent immigrants, celebutantes, the superrich—as in own-their-own-jet rich—and folks getting by on food stamps. But while my clients are special and unique, the offenders are not. They are as boring and predictable as they are dangerous.

I've spent years studying how the offenders who target my clients operate. I've catalogued their grooming and manipulation techniques, their strategies, methods, and intent. There are patterns and similarities in their behaviors that are hard to miss once you know what to look for. My staff and I have even developed a shorthand to describe the shitheads we see most often: psychos, who obsessively stalk, threaten, and intimidate their prey; assholes, who exploit or mistreat victims out of willful ignorance or arrogance or for their own financial gain; trolls, who terrorize victims under the cloak of internet anonymity; and pervs, who get off on overpowering victims into sex acts against their will. Frighteningly, these offenders are all around us, masquerading as regular people, just waiting to attack.

Psychos, pervs, assholes, and trolls hunt for targets on dating apps and social media. They lurk in bars and on college campuses. They teach in our schools, minister in our churches, and hold powerful positions in government, media, and tech. Some of the worst offenders victimize their own spouses and partners. These are the monsters my clients and I battle every day.

Of course, predators, stalkers, and abusers are nothing new. What's different now is that many of these offenders have harnessed the power and reach of the internet to facilitate their crimes. Armed with nothing but a laptop, and shielded by anonymity, a single bad actor can wreak unmitigated chaos and ruin the lives of countless victims. They stop only when we fight back.

————

In the first five years of its existence, my firm has secured more than one hundred orders of protection and removed more than 30,000 nonconsensual images and videos from the web. We've obtained millions of dollars in financial recoveries for our clients and had more than a dozen offenders arrested and thrown in jail. Working side by side with my clients, I've successfully sued major corporations and the mammoth New York City Department of Education.

Along with other advocates, we've also pushed for legislative change. Since day one, I've been getting in lawmakers' faces, email blasting, and sending letters and tweets about policy changes we need to implement to keep the public safe. I've helped craft more than a dozen states' revenge-porn laws and spoken at the White House, to Congress, and at think tanks and symposiums across the country.

My firm has made a difference in hundreds of clients' lives, and impacted countless others who've been protected by laws we've helped put in place. But I have not been fighting alone. Many of my clients have become powerful warriors in the wake of their attacks. Working with one of my youngest, a sweet girl who was assaulted near her middle school, we sued her entire city. Fighting back is a transformative act.

I'm proud of these victories. But this book is about more than my journey and the harrowing experiences of my clients who've agreed to let me share their stories here. This book is a call to arms.

As you will see in these pages, crimes of violence and violation—and the offenders who commit them—are not distinct and unrelated. They are all around us, connected like points on a web. Offenders are everywhere. What makes them so terrifying is that many of these unhinged men—and they are almost always men—are compelled by the same impulses that trigger other offenders to drive cars into groups of protesters and fire assault rifles into churches, synagogues, and schools. They are driven by rage and a thirst to strip victims of their agency and control. These offenders want to dominate, manipulate, and punish their victims. I refuse to let them win. And all of us have the power to fight back. We don't have to be victims. We can be the army to take these motherfuckers down.

CHAPTER 1

SLEEPING WITH THE ENEMY

Francesca Rossi stepped up to a microphone in a room on the eleventh floor of the US District Court in lower Manhattan. She placed a sheaf of papers—the carefully crafted victim impact statement we'd been working on for weeks—on the podium in front of her, and brushed a stray hair from her face. Glancing up at federal judge Kevin Castel, Francesca began in a clear and steady voice: "I stand here before you today grateful to be alive."

It was a windy morning in late December 2017. For more than a year, I'd been Francesca's lawyer. I'd spent countless hours working on her case, fielding calls, inventorying evidence, arguing with prosecutors, demanding meetings, and helping her keep sane and safe through a storm of vicious attacks. Finally, we'd arrived at the culmination of all our hard work: the sentencing hearing of the man who'd tried to destroy Francesca's life. "I feared for my life every day," Francesca continued, addressing the judge. "I'm not convinced that he still won't try to kill me."

Francesca wore a simple dark blazer to court that day. When we'd met at my office a few hours earlier, she'd slipped off her jacket to show me the T-shirt she wore underneath. On the front was a simple command, "Believe Women." Grinning, she turned around to show me the back, emblazoned with a picture of a dagger and the words "Or else." I loved that Francesca had armed herself like a warrior. But I knew she was a fighter from the first day we met.

Francesca, a social worker, had come to my Brooklyn office almost a year and a half earlier, in the spring of 2016, asking for advice. She was in her early thirties, dressed in leather boots and a motorcycle jacket, with a confident gaze and a deep, raspy voice. Settling into a chair in my conference room, she said she wanted to know what to do about "Paul," a guy she'd had a fling with years ago who now appeared to be using a half-naked photo of Francesca as his Facebook profile picture, without her consent. "I don't even remember sending him those pictures," she said, dismayed. The relationship had ended amicably, she added. "I don't know why he would do this."

Neither did I.

By the time I met Francesca, I'd worked on dozens of cases involving the nonconsensual distribution of sexual images and videos, also known as revenge porn. But the scenario Francesca was describing didn't fit the pattern I'd come to expect. Most instances of revenge porn happen shortly after, or during, a betrayal (real or imagined) or breakup. Typically a guy (it's almost always a guy) feels bad (as in jealous or humiliated), but instead of handling his emotions like a normal adult, he goes full asshole and posts his partner's private pictures on social media or a revenge porn website, and urges followers to harass his target because she's a "lying whore" or a "stupid cunt" or she "had it coming." It's vindictive and impulsive behavior, but it doesn't just happen out of the blue—and definitely not years after a relationship has ended. I suspected someone else was using Paul's name to create a phony account.

"Are you dating anyone now?" I asked.

Francesca nodded but said her boyfriend had been totally support-ive when she'd found the images of herself online. "It's definitely not him," she insisted.

Francesca wanted to know her options. I explained that sometimes in these types of cases we send a cease and desist letter to the offender, or we petition for an order of protection. Other times we negotiate our own brand of NDAs. (In our office the acronym often stands for "non-dissemination agreement.") But in Francesca's case I didn't think any of those options made sense. At her request I had done a little digging and discovered that Paul owned a home in Queens with his sister, had never missed a payment on his Honda Civic, and had worked the same job for half a decade. Most of the revenge porning exes I see can't hold down steady jobs. They are impulsive and unstable in every aspect of their lives. I was sure Paul was not the offender.

Plus, as I pointed out to Francesca, the Facebook account in Paul's name had apparently been created with the sole purpose of posting an intimate picture of Francesca and sending friend requests to her contacts. Dudes who use social media just to be assholes never use their real names on the fake accounts. "I doubt it's Paul," I said again as I walked Francesca to the elevator. "But definitely let us know if anything else happens."

Almost four months passed before I heard from Francesca again. She'd been calm and self-possessed during our initial consultation. The next time she called she was frantic. "I'm being sued!" she said.

Earlier that day, Francesca had received an email that purported to be from a process server, with a legal complaint attached. Written under a law firm's logo, the suit, seemingly brought by the wife of a former boyfriend, accused Francesca of sleeping with the plaintiff's husband and spreading a sexually transmitted infection to them both. I asked Francesca to forward me the email, but I knew before I even clicked open the attached PDF that the lawsuit was a fake. In New

York, process servers don't deliver lawsuits by email. Sure enough, when I called the lawyer listed on the document, she had never heard of the case.

I sat at my desk staring at the bogus lawsuit, wondering who might have sent it. I called across the office to my fresh-out-of-law-school associate, Adam Massey. "Hey," I said, "can you take a look at something?" I'd hired Adam as an intern not long after I'd opened my firm, in 2014. He'd impressed me by knowing more about revenge porn laws than most state lawmakers. He'd even written a paper about the topic while he was still in law school. Adam is brilliant and tech-savvy. It took him only a few minutes of digging around in the back end of the PDF to find the name of the person who had last edited the document: Juan Thompson.

We googled the name. At the top of the search results was a string of stories about a journalist who, earlier that year, had been fired from his job as a staff reporter at The Intercept. The editor-in-chief of The Intercept had posted a letter on the publication's website in February 2016, a few months before Francesca had first come to see me, informing readers that an internal investigation had uncovered that Thompson had engaged in "a pattern of deception." Thompson had been making up sources and fabricating quotes in an elaborate ruse to embellish his stories. Most notably, in his coverage of the 2015 massacre of nine African American parishioners who were killed while meeting for Bible study at the Emanuel African Methodist Episcopal Church in Charleston, South Carolina. Thompson claimed to have gained an exclusive interview with Scott Roof, the supposed cousin of the twenty-one-year-old shooter, Dylann Roof. According to Thompson, Scott described Dylann as upset that a woman he was interested in was dating a black man. The story was picked up by multiple news outlets then subsequently retracted when Intercept editors could find no evidence that Scott Roof existed. Thompson also created multiple fake email accounts to impersonate people and deceive his editors, the letter said.

I'd also found a video of a guy named Juan Thompson on the admissions website of my alma mater, Vassar. He was handsome, with a broad smile. But he oozed a slick charm that put my Spidey sense on high alert. "This guy's a con artist," I said to Adam. I picked up the phone and called Francesca on her landline at work. "Does the name Juan Thompson mean anything to you?" I asked.

"He's my boyfriend," Francesca replied. "Why?"

I took a breath and said in a calm yet insistent tone, "You need to come to my office as soon as possible. I think we have some answers. Don't discuss this with anybody," I added. "Especially not Juan."

A few hours later, Adam, Francesca, and I were seated at the oval table in my conference room. Francesca clasped her hands in her lap and looked at us expectantly. I nodded at Adam and he slid across the table a printout of the phony lawsuit, with Thompson listed as the editor. "If this is your boyfriend," I said to Francesca, "he's impersonated a process server, a lawyer, and a plaintiff. He's created this fake lawsuit, obviously to torment you. This is very sadistic behavior." Francesca's face grew pale. Later she'd tell me that it felt as though the ground had fallen out from beneath her feet.

———

For hours, Francesca sat in my conference room trying to make sense of the news. Haltingly, she recalled for Adam and me a string of bizarre incidents from the previous year, like the dozens of harassing emails and texts she suddenly started receiving right around the same time she learned of the Facebook profile featuring her semi-naked image. There were multiple messages from a string of ex-boyfriends or their current partners accusing her of having herpes. Some messages contained personal details and suggested she was being watched. One time, a woman claiming to be the current girlfriend of a guy Francesca once dated texted a naked picture of Francesca and warned her to "stay away." Another time Francesca received a text on her work cell phone—a number only a handful of people knew—that appeared to be from "Jerome," a guy she'd dated briefly a year earlier. Francesca had stopped seeing Jerome when she found out he had a criminal past. The text said he was coming to see her and knew where she lived. Jerome sent so many messages that Francesca grew alarmed and called the police.

At the time, the torrent of strange messages made Francesca feel like she was going crazy. Meanwhile, Thompson seemed to thrive on his girlfriend's distress. He would spend hours helping Francesca process the strange attacks, and guiding her to deconstruct the "mistakes" she'd made in her past relationships. Discussing the harassment became central to their relationship. Again and again, Thompson would point out how lucky Francesca was to have broken the cycle by being with him.

"I was so paranoid I even went into therapy to try and figure out what I'd done in my past to attract these horrible men. . . ." Francesca said, trailing off. "Oh my God," she said suddenly, her voice pinched in despair. "I can't believe it was him."

———

The more Francesca revealed about Thompson, the more convinced I became that his behavior fit the pattern of some of the most dangerous criminals we see at my firm. Thompson exhibited the telltale signs of offenders we call "psycho stalkers." He was deceptive, manipulative, and ruthless in his attacks. But more of a giveaway than anything else, Thompson, like every psycho I've ever encountered, was a master of charm and charisma. That's how he'd swept Francesca off her feet.

All my clients who've been targeted by psychos describe the early days of their relationships in the same breathless way: as a whirlwind romance that progressed at lightning speed and felt like nothing they'd ever experienced before. One client described her relationship as an "insta-marriage"; another marveled at the way her psycho ex "wifed" her from day one. Another said, "It was so intense, right away it felt like me and him against the world." Francesca's story is not much different.

The pair first connected in late 2014, on the dating site OkCupid, the same site where I'd met my psycho ex. After some easy banter online, they agreed to meet for dinner. Thompson was charismatic, with a sharp intellect. He told Francesca about his work as a reporter. He shared that he'd recently covered the protests that had erupted in Ferguson, Missouri, in the wake of the police shooting of unarmed African American teen Michael Brown. Brown's death had ignited the #BlackLivesMatter movement and Thompson had been reporting on it from the start. Francesca was impressed. She describes her politics as "pretty radical," and everything she cared about—race, gender, social justice—Thompson was passionate about, too.

Five months into the relationship, Thompson surprised Francesca with a romantic trip to Rome. They rode bikes on cobblestone streets and lay in their hotel bed talking late into the night. He started calling her his "muse." With that single word, repeated over and over, he conferred upon Francesca the power of a goddess, reflecting back to her everything she wanted to be. By the time they came home, she was convinced this was the man she was going to have kids with, grow old with. Francesca said she'd been in relationships before, but nothing felt like this.

Thompson was following the psycho playbook to a T. He'd captivated Francesca with his stellar conversation and flattered her with fantasy. He'd muse aloud about the wonderful life they'd have together changing the world, and write her over-the-top love letters claiming his undying devotion. "I feel at this very moment that I have nothing to declare more proudly than my love for you," he insisted in an email.

He also engaged in a signature psycho tactic I call "strategic over-sharing." He'd tell Francesca tragic stories of his difficult childhood, urging her to open up as well. Normally guarded, Francesca found herself telling Thompson all her secrets; she confided in him about her insecurities and deepest fears. Little did she know he was hoarding this information like an arsenal of weapons to ultimately use against her.

Thompson moved in with Francesca in January 2016, a few weeks after he was fired from his job. Thompson, who is African American, insisted he'd been let go because of racism. Francesca knew Thompson was one of the only reporters of color at The Intercept, and the explanation jibed with her worldview that racism and bigotry are everywhere. She was outraged on his behalf.

In my conference room seven months later, Francesca read the multiple press reports about Thompson's firing that Adam had printed out. Thompson's deceptive practices and made-up quotes had been a mini scandal in the journalism world. "I never googled why he'd lost his job," Francesca said. "It didn't occur to me that he was lying."

But Thompson's bad behavior with Francesca went much further than secrets and lies. As Francesca reflected on the history of their relationship, it occurred to her that sometime after he moved in, Thompson had likely hacked into her devices. It appeared that he had been monitoring her texts and emails, spying on her social media accounts, and reading her digital diary. That would explain the string of weird and harassing messages. It also explained why, on multiple occasions, Thompson had dropped into conversation the names of men from Francesca's past that she'd never told him about. He claimed to be doing a story about one guy; he told her another was a salesperson who helped him buy a phone. At the time, these seemed only like more weird coincidences in a year when everything in her life seemed off.

Francesca was clearly shaken. "What do I do now?" she asked.

I needed to be reassuring and firm. "I think you know what to do," I answered. "He's stalking you. This is incredibly dangerous."

Francesca nodded slowly and took a breath: "I have to end this relationship now."

———

There's a misconception I often encounter whenever I mention the word "stalker." People imagine victims are stalked by deranged strangers or people they barely know. In fact, the most common stalking scenarios I see with my clients are within the context of intimate relationships. Stalking is a pernicious and largely unacknowledged form of partner abuse. Even in instances in which the stalker is an ex-boyfriend or ex-husband, often the stalking began well before the couple broke up. Stalkers monitor their victims' movements, actions, and private communications. They'll install keylogging software on your computer and spyware on your phone. They'll know where you are, what you're doing, and anyone you've been communicating with. They'll use this information to threaten and control you. Stalking can go on for months, even years, after the relationship ends. According to the National Center for Victims of Crime, 11 percent of victims have been stalked for five years or more.

Stalking is one of the most effective ways for an offender to intimidate, terrorize, and manipulate a victim. And these offenders are often violent. More than 80 percent of women stalked by a current or former partner have also been physically assaulted by that same man, according to the National Coalition Against Domestic Violence.

For months Thompson had been surveilling Francesca, learning everything he could about his girlfriend, stockpiling intimate details of her life. He'd used this intel to bring chaos and confusion into Francesca's world. He was just getting started.

————

Although legislation varies from state to state, stalking is generally defined as a course of conduct directed at a specific individual that causes the person to feel intimidated, or in fear for their life. The crime is illegal in all fifty states. But it took a high-profile tragedy for lawmakers to pay attention and get these laws on the books. In the summer of 1989, Rebecca Schaeffer was a twenty-one-year-old actress with a promising career ahead of her. She'd just completed her second season starring in the CBS sitcom *My Sister Sam*, and was up for a role in director Francis Ford Coppola's latest movie, *The Godfather: Part III*. Schaeffer, who had big brown eyes and a mane of wild curls that she sometimes wore in a side pony, lived in an apartment in a two-story adobe home on a tree-lined street in West Hollywood.

Meanwhile, hundreds of miles away, in Tucson, Arizona, nineteen-year-old high school dropout Robert John Bardo was nurturing his growing obsession with the actress. For years, Bardo had been stalking Schaeffer. He'd sent her fan mail and had traveled to the set to try to meet her in person only to get turned away by a security guard. He even paid an Arizona private investigator $300 for Schaeffer's home address. On the morning of July 18, Bardo showed up at Schaeffer's door. By Bardo's account, the two exchanged a few words and he left. But he returned a few minutes later.

Schaeffer opened her door. She'd been expecting a courier delivering the script for her audition with Coppola the next day. Instead, she found Bardo wielding a .357 Magnum. He fired a single shot and struck Schaeffer in the chest. She died on her doorstep.

Years later, former deputy district attorney of Los Angeles County Marcia Clark, who prosecuted Bardo, called Schaeffer's murder at the hands of a deranged stalker the "epitome of tragedy." Bardo was sentenced to life in prison, with no chance of parole.

At the time of Schaeffer's murder, stalking was not considered a crime. Even if a man hunted you down, threatened to hurt you, and knew where you lived, there was nothing the police could do. At a Senate Judiciary Committee hearing in 1992, three years after Schaeffer's murder, stalking victim Jane McAllister recounted how a man she barely knew started following and telephoning her repeatedly. He showed up at her house and left her bizarre notes. One time while she was out walking, he tailed her in his truck and yelled obscenities at her. He threatened to wait for her to die, she said, so he could dig up her body and "have her." McAllister testified: "The police were not insensitive, but they were stymied. The man violated almost every area of my life, but had broken no law . . . there was nothing they could do until an assault occurred. I changed my routine, I lived in constant fear of an attack . . . It was clear that this man, who was apparently crazy, was not going to let up and that the authorities were powerless to stop him. Though he was free to move about, I was living in a state of siege."

Schaeffer's murder changed everything. Her story made national headlines. Stalking victims were invited on daytime TV and radio talk shows. California was the first state to enact anti-stalking legislation in 1990. By 1996, forty-nine states and the District of Columbia had adopted laws making stalking a crime.

Stalkers are terrifying. But when stalking happens within the context of an intimate relationship, the danger is especially acute. Studies indicate a high correlation between partner stalking and physical violence or even homicide. In fact, according to a 2010 study supported by the National Institute of Justice, a history of stalking has been reported in more than three-quarters of actual or attempted murders of female partners.

Intimate partner stalking often exists as part of a constellation of misogynist and violent behavior. And that aggression can extend, in concentric circles, beyond the victim to include her family, friends, coworkers, and even complete strangers. Many of the deadliest mass shootings in America were committed by men with documented histories of domestic violence, stalking, or deep antipathy toward women, including Omar Mateen, who murdered forty-nine and wounded fifty-three at an Orlando nightclub in 2016; Devin P. Kelley, who, in 2017, entered a church in Sutherland Springs, Texas, and massacred twenty-six people, most of them children; and Nikolas Cruz, who opened fire in Marjory Stoneman Douglas High School in Parkland, Florida, in 2018, killing seventeen students, teachers, and staff. After the shooting, it was reported that nineteen-year-old Cruz had a history of stalking a female student at the school.

Writing about the relationship between intimate partner violence and mass murder, Soraya Chemaly, director of the Women's Media Center Speech Project and author of the brilliant *Rage Becomes Her: The Power of Women's Anger*, noted in the *Village Voice* in 2017: "A domestic violence felony conviction is the strongest predictor of male-perpetrated violent crime. Men who feel free to hurt the people they know develop a sense of entitlement to hurt those they don't."

As we'd soon find out, Thompson, who dedicated months to stalking and tormenting Francesca, whom he claimed to love, had no reservations about inflicting pain on anyone else.

———

It's not easy for a victim to exit a relationship with a psycho. These guys thrive on intense engagement with their targets. If a psycho feels his partner pulling away, he'll do anything to make her stay.

The first time I tried to end things with my psycho ex, after he'd blown up at me for not returning his calls, he showed up at my apartment and started banging on my door. He refused to leave until I called 9-1-1 and was gone by the time the cops arrived. But when I left for work the next morning, he was waiting outside my building, crying. He followed me to my office and sent me roses and chocolate-covered strawberries. He convinced me I owed him the opportunity to talk things out. My biggest mistake was saying okay.

We spent an entire weekend holed up in my apartment, where he proceeded to break me down with some jiu-jitsu-level mind games. He called me "disloyal" for calling the cops and accused me of cheating. He insisted the relationship was crashing and burning all because of me. He talked circles around me, blaming, shaming, and making me feel guilty for what I'd done to *him*. Within hours, I was tearfully begging for forgiveness and promising to do better.

This is typical psycho behavior. These guys are master manipulators, skilled at gaslighting and distorting the truth. It's the number one reason I advise all my clients under psycho attack to make a clean break when they are trying to get away. "If you are ready to end the relationship," I told Francesca that day in my conference room, "please remember you don't owe him an explanation, or a face-to-face meeting. He will only use that opportunity to try to rope you back in."

She nodded in agreement.

"You'll have more control over the situation if you send him an email telling him it's over," I continued. "And don't engage in any back-and-forth. We'll arrange for a police escort for you to go to your apartment and get some things. Our immediate priority is your safety. I promise you, we'll figure out the rest."

Francesca left my office that afternoon with a plan to stay at a friend's house and instructions to call me the second anything happened. Sure enough, within hours of the breakup, Thompson started spiraling out of control.

At first he flooded Francesca with emails, declaring his eternal love and telling her a bunch of lies. He insisted he'd been framed by some-body who hated interracial couples. He contacted Francesca's mom, telling her the same thing. He composed fake emails from phony ac-counts masquerading as various "friends," imploring Francesca to give him a second chance. At the same time, he was also conspiring to get Francesca fired from her job. He emailed her boss and accused Franc-esca of sleeping with and buying drugs from her vulnerable clients. He sent pictures of guns to the human resources department, insisting the weapons belonged to Francesca, and sent similar accusations to the professional social work board under which Francesca is licensed, triggering an investigation that could have jeopardized her career.

Thompson targeted Francesca's friends and family, too. He sent an email to her mother with an image of a bull's-eye target superimposed on a photo of Francesca's face. He also wrote to Francesca's aunt threatening to release pornographic videos of her niece online. Fran-cesca's friends received emails referring to her as a "slutty cunt." In all, Francesca counted forty-seven different people who received suspi-cious and harassing emails in the months after she broke up with Thompson, including her ninety-two-year-old grandmother.

For weeks while Francesca was fielding concerned calls from her family and friends, Thompson continued his direct assault on her, using burner phones and anonymous email accounts. "This bullet's for you slut," he wrote in one message. "Your life will be destroyed." Another time, she received an elaborate email supposedly from his brother telling her that Thompson had been shot and was in the hospital, on life support, close to death. When she didn't respond, Thompson posted a video on YouTube filled with lies about Francesca's sex life, which he then commented on, disguised as other people.

As his attacks escalated, I was in touch with Francesca almost ev-ery day, by phone, email, or text, offering support and reminding her that this storm would pass. I remember giving a talk at the National Network to End Domestic Violence in San Francisco and sneaking in a couple of encouraging texts to Francesca from the podium, during the Q&A. Adam and I helped Francesca obtain a temporary order of protection and showed her how to create a stalking log—a timeline of Thompson's bad behavior, which was vital as we built her case.

Meanwhile, I was doing everything in my power to have Thompson arrested. Most local police are neither trained nor equipped to handle digital forensics, especially if the perpetrator is skilled at masking his identity online, using fake accounts and burner phones. Francesca had gone to her local police to file complaints about Thompson's harassment and threats on ten separate occasions and was told repeatedly there was nothing law enforcement could do without some solid proof.

If we couldn't depend on assistance from local police, I knew our best chance at justice was to get the country's top crime fighters involved. The day Francesca broke up with Thompson, I called Mona Sedky, a senior trial attorney at the Department of Justice's Computer Crime and Intellectual Property Section (CCIPS), and requested she open a case against Thompson. It was well past business hours, and I was sitting in my office, in the dark, so distracted I'd neglected to turn on the lights.

"Juan Thompson, Juan Thompson, Juan Thompson," I repeated into the phone. "Remember his name." I was working on a different case with Mona at the time and admired her deeply. This was not how I normally spoke to her. But I was desperate. "If you guys don't open a case now, you will read Juan Thompson's name in the paper. It may be next month, next year, or five years from now. But it will be for some awful reason. He's going to do something terrible. Remember that you could have stopped him now." For weeks, I persisted with more phone calls and emails until finally CCIPS opened an investigation into Thompson's abuse.

By then, Thompson had left New York and moved back to his hometown, St. Louis, Missouri. From there, he continued his assaults. He sent messages to Francesca claiming to have sex tapes that he threatened to expose, causing Francesca to fear that he had secretly recorded her. He created imposter accounts to harass and defame her on OkCupid, Tumblr, YouTube, Venmo, Twitter, Facebook, and Instagram. He portrayed her as an anti-Semite, a pedophile, and a racist, and accused her of spreading STIs. On 8chan, an online message board notorious for attracting users who advocate violence against women, Thompson posted Francesca's photo and home and work addresses and urged 8chan users to harass her. He claimed Francesca was best friends with Zoë Quinn, the woman at the center of Gamergate and a favorite target of 8chan trolls. I call this tactic "harassment by proxy." With a few clicks on his keyboard, Thompson recruited hundreds of foot soldiers to join in his attack.

It's hard to believe that Thompson, who was actively under investigation, could not be stopped. But the same technology he was using to carry out his attacks also enabled him to disguise his identity, creating endless roadblocks for the investigators trying to collect the evidence they needed to arrest him. Thompson used virtual private networks (VPNs) to mask his computer's IP address, a TOR browser to conceal his internet activity, and Tutanota, a Germany-based encrypted email server. Nothing except for the bogus lawsuit and one of the impersonating voicemails left on Francesca's office phone were traceable to Thompson. We had FBI investigators and the power of the Department of Justice on our side, and yet Thompson was still walking free, able to commit his crimes with impunity. In fact, his behavior was getting worse.

In October 2016, Thompson began a new wave of attacks. This

time his goal was clearly to get Francesca arrested, or worse. He contacted a Brooklyn police station, claiming Francesca was planning to "shoot up" the precinct. He also emailed a news station implicating Francesca in a death threat against the New York City chief of police and reported that Francesca had a stockpile of guns. Thompson also sent an anonymous tip to the National Center for Missing and Exploited Children, claiming Francesca had child porn on her phone. On five separate occasions, police officers showed up at Francesca's home or work to investigate her. Francesca would put them in contact with me and I'd explain to the cops that Francesca was a victim and not a suspect. The police would eventually leave without charging her. But I wasn't sure how long her luck would hold out. When my psycho ex used this tactic with me, I ended up in jail.

———

It happened a few weeks after I'd ended the relationship for good. I'd gone to the police to report that my ex was threatening and stalking me and that he'd tried to break into my apartment. Almost a month later, he was arrested, and I was called to the police station to identify him. "He's out of control," the precinct detective said, leading me to a tiny room with a one-way mirror covered by a venetian blind. "I don't know what you were doing with a guy like that."

I didn't bother to respond.

The detective raised the blinds. I gasped when I saw my ex glaring back at me. "He can't see you," the detective reassured me. "We just need an affirmative ID."

"That's him," I said, desperately wanting to get out of there. As I gathered my things to leave, another detective entered the room holding a manila folder. Matter-of-factly he explained that my ex had made his own police report, accusing me of assault. Then he told me: "You're under arrest."

I was so stunned I could barely speak as the detective cuffed my hands behind my back and guided me through the precinct to get my fingerprints taken. When we passed by the men's holding tank, I caught a glimpse of my ex clutching the bars of the cell.

Officers confiscated my phone, wallet, and bag. I had no pockets in my dress, so I put my ID inside my bra. They took me to a holding cell in the basement, where I met my cellmate, Becka. She had a wide, friendly smile and long orange ombré hair, and was dressed in jean shorts and a loose crop top. Becka had been arrested for shoplifting. "I didn't even want that purse," she said, shaking her head. "I already have a Coach purse! I don't know why I did it."

This wasn't Becka's first time in detention, and she took it upon herself to school me on the basics. She pulled a ten-dollar bill out of her pocket and hollered to the officer sitting watch at the end of the hall to get her some quarters and some snacks from the vending machine. "Salty ones," she said. She offered me some potato chips and told me I should eat before I got moved to central booking because all they have there is nasty-ass bologna sandwiches. Then she gave me a few quarters for the pay phone. I thanked her and added them to my bra. Becka was surprised to hear a lawyer could be arrested. I started telling her about my job, but she dozed off midconversation. Becka was the highlight of my time behind bars. The rest of the experience was like a bad movie.

Later that afternoon, I was questioned again, this time by a pair of investigators who introduced themselves as NYPD Intelligence. They wanted to know more about the allegations my ex had made. He'd told them I was part of a sex-for-favors scheme that involved my sleeping with judges in exchange for favorable outcomes for my cases. I explained that I worked for a nonprofit dealing with incapacitated elderly people, hardly the setting for a sex-and-corruption scandal.

Satisfied, the investigators said I could be transported from the precinct. I was put in a van, along with a handful of other detainees, and driven four blocks to Kings County central booking. I was ushered from line to line—for a mug shot, pat-down, fingerprints, and more questions—before I was taken to the female holding cell with half a dozen other women. On the way, we passed the locked-up men. My ex was already there and apparently had told his cellmates about me. They hollered my name when I walked past. "Carrie! He still loves you!" one of them yelled.

Central booking is in downtown Brooklyn, two blocks from where I worked every day at the Vera Institute of Justice, and not far from my apartment. But I felt like I was on another planet. The holding cell was worse than anything I'd ever seen on TV, with a concrete floor, single pay phone, handful of blue gym mats, and a stainless steel toilet without a seat. Right there in the middle of everything.

Night court closes at one a.m. If you do not get summoned to see a judge for your arraignment before then, you have to spend the night in jail. I spent almost seven hours in that holding cell before my name was finally called, a little after midnight.

I was chained to a group of other detainees and led through a maze of underground corridors that let out into a fluorescent-lit courtroom. The court clerk read the charges against me—menacing in the third degree, harassment, and attempted assault. The prosecutor argued for me to be detained. A lawyer I had never met but who was seemingly representing me argued I was a "first-time offender" and should be released on my own recognizance. My lawyer prevailed. I was uncuffed and allowed to walk out the main doors. It took months—and tens of thousands of dollars in legal fees—before I finally got the bogus charges against me dropped.

I didn't tell Francesca any of this. She was frightened enough already. Her greatest fear was that Thompson might follow through on his worst threats, and she confided in me that she'd left copies of evidence that Thompson had been harassing her with several of her friends. "That way," Francesca explained, "they can tell the police who murdered me if my body is ever found."

———

Nine months after Francesca ended their relationship, Thompson still hadn't been arrested. With each new stunt—like the time he created an anti-Semitic Instagram account in Francesca's name, or the time he emailed me that he was being hunted by African terrorists who wanted to harm him and Francesca—we would call Mona and forward the evidence to our field agent. We were at an impasse. Thompson was so skilled at using anonymizing software it was almost impossible to trace the communication to him.

And then, in late February Thompson elevated his attacks to a terrifying new level. From his home in St. Louis, he opened his laptop and googled the email address for a Jewish community center in La Jolla, San Diego, where Francesca had once lived. It was only weeks after the inauguration of Donald Trump. Across the country, there had been a rash of anti-Semitic bomb threats and vandalism, and criticism that Trump had not done enough to condemn the attacks. Tension was high. Thompson began to type. Someone had planted a bomb at the center, he wrote. The bomber "hates Jewish people," he added, and wants "to kill as many Jews asap [sic]." He included in his threat the name of the alleged bomber: Francesca Rossi.

In a separate email to a Jewish school in Manhattan, Thompson threatened a "Jewish Newtown," invoking the 2012 massacre in which twenty first graders and six adults were gunned down in an elementary school in Newtown, Connecticut. In total, Thompson made at least twelve different bomb threats to JCCs around the country, implicating Francesca in all of them. Buildings were evacuated, and thousands of people were terrorized, including dozens of small children. They were all collateral damage in Thompson's mission to destroy Francesca's life.

By then I'd helped Francesca develop a script for dealing with the local police when they showed up to investigate one of Thompson's fake reports—she would direct them to our contact at the DOJ, who would explain that Francesca was the victim, not the perpetrator. But bomb threats trigger a different type of response. In many jurisdictions, reports of serious threats are answered by paramilitary-style SWAT teams, who arrive on the scene with guns drawn.

Making fake reports of potentially deadly crimes, aka "swatting," is the ultimate harassment by proxy, a tactic popularized by gamers, sometimes with deadly results. After a dispute over *Call of Duty: WWII*, in December 2017, a Los Angeles man made a 9-1-1 call falsely reporting an armed hostage situation at a residence in Wichita, Kansas. Police were dispatched to the home of Andrew Finch, a twenty-eight-year-old father of two. When Finch opened his front door, an officer shot him dead.

On February 28, 2017, two armed FBI agents showed up at Francesca's apartment. With her heart pounding in her chest, she opened the door. The officers asked her about the bomb threats. "It's not me," she said, quickly handing the officers her stalking log—by now thirty-one pages long—chronicling nine months of Thompson's harassment and threats. "This is the guy you're looking for." Thompson had evaded arrest for months. But that was when he was focusing his attacks solely on Francesca, her friends, and her family. Bomb threats and threats to national security prompt the kind of urgent response from law enforcement that a lone woman in crisis does not.

Less than a week later, on March 3, Thompson, then thirty-one, was finally arrested. He was taken into custody in St. Louis and extradited to the Southern District of New York, where he ultimately pleaded guilty to one count of cyberstalking and one count of making hoax bomb threats, both federal crimes. When the police searched Thompson's home, they confiscated twenty-five digital devices he'd been using in his attacks, including cell phones, tablets, and laptop computers.

———

Judges weigh several factors when handing down sentences to convicted criminals, including the impact of the crimes on the victims. Francesca and I had worked on her victim impact statement for weeks to make sure that her words captured the anguish of being under attack. Her friends and family weighed in, too. For more than a year, Thompson had devoted his life to tormenting Francesca, but standing at a podium in front of Judge Castel on that brisk December day, the power belonged to her.

In vivid detail Francesca described how Thompson invaded her privacy, tormented her family, attempted to get her fired, called in fake police reports, and upended her life. "Juan devoted an entire year to destroying my life," she said. "He painted me as an anti-Semite, a racist, a drunk, a drug dealer, a child pornographer, and a gun runner. He did everything he could to instill terror in my life. Computers, phones, and tablets became the apparatus for his abuse." As Francesca spoke, the handful of reporters assembled in the courthouse leaned forward in their seats, hanging on her every word. "My abuse was not legitimized until an entire community, and the country, was terrorized," she continued. "I urge you to not let there be a next time, don't let Juan do this to another woman, another community, or the country."

Judge Castel thanked Francesca as she made her way back to her seat. "That was the most eloquent presentation I've ever heard in my courtroom," he said. Then he turned his attention to Thompson, who was seated at a long wooden table, flanked by his court-appointed attorneys, dressed in prison khakis and shackled at the ankles. Glancing over, I noticed the way he casually shifted in his chair, lazily rubbing the back of his neck. I got the distinct impression that he thought he was going to be able to talk his way out of this courtroom. And indeed, he tried.

When given an opportunity to address the court, Thompson told the judge he'd recently learned a lot about the scourge of misogyny thanks to the Me Too movement. I had to swallow a groan. "I apologize to Miss Rossi for the harm, pain, and embarrassment I've caused her," Thompson said. "I screwed up royally."

The judge peered at Thompson over his glasses. "This was not a mistake," he said flatly. Castel admonished Thompson for his malicious intent, and the terror he inflicted on Francesca and countless others. In court, the prosecution recommended a sentence of forty-eight months for Thompson's crimes. But Castel, clearly impacted by Francesca's statement, added an additional year, sentencing Thompson to five years behind bars, the maximum allowed.

Despite everything she'd been through, Francesca was incredibly fortunate. She has a strong network of friends, family, and coworkers who support her, a dozen of whom had accompanied Francesca to court that day. She had a lawyer who knew how to handle a case like hers, and the force of the DOJ behind her. The reality is that too few victims have teams like this to bring their abusers to justice. Instead, they are often met with exasperated eye rolls from friends, family, and even police, who don't understand the seriousness of these crimes. I can't tell you how many clients I have who've been advised to "block and delete" their abusers, as though that will solve everything. Block-and-delete is a fine strategy if you're ghosting a sane individual. It's useless advice when dealing with an obsessed, tech-savvy psycho. There's no such thing as deleting a stalker. On the internet, a psycho stalker can find you no matter where you try to hide.

Part of the problem is easy to fix. Media reports need to describe these offenses as the serious crimes they are: stalking, partner abuse, terrorism. Instead, too often the prefix "cyber-" gets thrown into the mix, as in "cyberstalking" or "cyberharassment." I understand the impulse to draw a line between crimes that happen on the internet and those that take place in "real life." But anyone who's had his or her life turned upside down by a "cyber" attack will tell you there is no distinction; it's *all* real life.

Case in point: a few months after I started working with Francesca, a new client came to my door, an aspiring actor named Matthew. You may have heard of his case; it was all over the news and involved lies, betrayal, and more than a thousand sex-seeking men. Matthew's case, full of salacious details and badass legal maneuvers, led me deep into battle with a multimillion-dollar internet company and became one of the most important fights of my career.

CHAPTER 2

SWIPE RIGHT FOR STALKING

S tart at the beginning," I said, leaning forward in my chair. "Tell me what's going on."

It was an unseasonably warm sixty-four degrees in Brooklyn on the January afternoon when Matthew Herrick, then thirty-two, first came to my office. The city was sweaty and agitated, and the mood in my conference room was no different. Matthew, an actor/waiter/model with an attractive 1990s Seattle-grunge-meets-Tom-Ford look, slouched in his seat and sighed. Often clients come to my office hyped up, convinced I'll solve everything. But not Matthew. He seemed exhausted, almost to the point of defeat. "Go on," I said, encouraging him with a smile. "Tell me everything."

Matthew let out a slow exhale. It all started, he said, one evening in late October 2016, right before Halloween. He'd been sitting on the front stoop of his New York City apartment, smoking a cigarette, when a stranger called to Matthew from the sidewalk and started heading up the steps toward him. The stranger's tone was friendly and familiar. But Matthew had never met this guy before. "I'm sorry," he said. "Do I know you?"

The stranger raised his eyebrows and pulled his phone from his back pocket. "You were just texting to me, dude," he replied, holding out his phone for Matthew to see. On the screen was a profile from the gay dating app Grindr, featuring a shirtless photo of Matthew standing in his kitchen, smiling broadly. Matthew recognized the picture right away. He'd posted it on his Instagram account a few weeks earlier. But the Grindr profile wasn't his. "I wasn't talking to you," Matthew explained. "That's not my account."

They went back and forth for a while. The stranger kept holding up his phone, insisting Matthew had invited him over for sex. But Matthew knew the profile wasn't his. Finally, the stranger became exasperated and left. "Fucking liar!" he shouted in Matthew's direction as he walked away. "You're an asshole!"

Rattled, Matthew went back inside. A few minutes later, he heard his buzzer ring. It was another man insisting that he, too, had made a sex date with Matthew. Two more men showed up that day. And three others came calling the next. "Matt!" they'd holler from the sidewalk, or they'd lean on the buzzer expecting to be let in. At first the strangers only went to his apartment, but by the end of the week a steady stream of men was showing up at the restaurant where Matthew worked as well. Some were in their twenties, others much older. A few arrived in business suits, as though on the way to the office. Others were twitchy and sweaty, looking like they'd been up all night getting high. They'd stalk him at work and at home, all hours of the day and night, each one convinced Matthew had invited him over for sex.

In my conference room, Matthew told me he'd never heard of someone getting targeted like this, by a storm of horny strangers. But he was pretty sure he knew who was behind the attack: his ex, Oscar Juan Carlos Gutierrez.

The pair had met more than a year prior, on Grindr, and dated for eleven months. In the beginning, Matthew recalled, Gutierrez "was like a knight in shining armor." But as time wore on, he became increasingly jealous and clingy, accusing Matthew of cheating and doing things like showing up at Matthew's job and refusing to leave. Eventually, Matthew couldn't take it anymore; the pair broke up. The week after he ended his relationship with Gutierrez, strange men began showing up at Matthew's door.

In my office, Matthew reached into his backpack for a folder, and handed it to me. Inside were printouts he'd made of some of the imposter profiles bearing his image, which he'd found on Grindr and Scruff, another gay dating site. I leafed through the pages, noting the aggressive screen names—"Gang Bang Now!" "Raw Pig Bottom"—so at odds with the soft-spoken man in front of me. Several profiles advertised Matthew as HIV-positive, and into "rough," unprotected sex.

I'd actually seen this particularly vicious form of harassment by proxy before. In one of my earliest cases, a young mother with an infant son was impersonated online by the father of her child. After he posted fake Craigslist ads falsely promoting my client as a sex worker, dozens of men showed up at the pharmacy where she worked. My client was terrified she was going to get sexually assaulted. She had good reason to be afraid. In 2009, a Wyoming woman was viciously raped at knifepoint by a man responding to an ad her ex-boyfriend had posted on Craigslist, claiming she was seeking a "real aggressive man with no concern for women."

One Sunday morning, a man showed up at Matthew's restaurant during a busy brunch rush, responding to a message he'd received from one of the phony accounts inviting him for sex in the bathroom. When Matthew politely told the man to leave, the guy went ballistic, yelling in the packed restaurant, "You lying Grindr whore!" Another time, a guy trying to push his way into Matthew's apartment lunged at Matthew's roommate, who was blocking the door.

Matthew said sometimes, if the guy wasn't too creepy, he'd ask to see the direct messages that were coming from the imposter accounts. "They make me look like I'm a 'yes' man," Matthew said. "It's like 'yes' to rape fantasies, 'yes' to unprotected sex, 'yes' to crystal meth. It looks like there is nothing I won't do." Fake Matt eagerly invited men for fisting, orgies, and aggressive sex. Fake Matt instructed strangers to not take no for an answer. If he resisted, Fake Matt assured prospective sex partners, it was part of the fantasy. They should just play along.

It seemed clear to me that Gutierrez was endeavoring to do more than harass and frighten Matthew. He appeared to be trying to recruit unwitting accomplices to perpetrate sexual assaults. I asked Matthew what he was doing to keep safe. He shook his head and stared at the floor. "Sometimes I turn off the lights in the apartment so they can't see I'm home," he offered. "I'll just sit in my room in the dark, listening to the door buzzer going off, texting my roommate, like, 'Please come home . . .'" Matthew cleared his throat and glanced up at me. It was the first time he'd made direct eye contact all afternoon. "Literally, every minute of every day is like a new nightmare," he said. "I just want it to stop."

———

Like many of my clients, before coming to see me Matthew had tried everything he could to take care of the problem on his own. He filed more than a dozen complaints with his local police department. The officers dutifully took down his information but didn't seem to understand the danger he was in. "One guy rolled his eyes," Matthew recalled. "I think they figured since I'm a big guy, and I look like I should be able to take care of myself, that I should just go beat him up or something. I guess to them I don't look like a 'victim.'" Another officer suggested Matthew pack up his belongings and "find a new place to live."

Through a friend of a friend, Matthew was able to arrange an appointment with Jeanine Launay, deputy chief of the Domestic Violence Unit at the Manhattan District Attorney's Office. When Matthew described what was happening, Launay said his was one of the most extensive stalking cases she'd ever seen. She opened an investigation into Gutierrez's behavior but warned Matthew that it would take time to build a case against his ex.

Launay also put Matthew in touch with Sadie Holzman Diaz, a skilled attorney with the New York–based nonprofit organization Sanctuary for Families, which does extraordinary work assisting victims of intimate partner violence. Diaz helped Matthew secure a permanent order of protection against Gutierrez, which is critical for victims of stalkers. Matthew had what's called a "stay away" order. It stipulated that Gutierrez could have no contact with Matthew—not in person, by phone, or through a third party. Police may not take a complaint of stalking seriously enough to arrest the offender, but violating an order of protection is a separate crime, one police understand. One night, Matthew caught Gutierrez hiding in the bushes outside his apartment. Matthew called the cops; they arrested Gutierrez for violating the order.

Matthew also did everything he could to get the imposter profiles taken down. He contacted Grindr and Scruff directly and begged the companies to remove the fake profiles from their platforms. In their terms of service, both companies explicitly prohibit the use of their products to impersonate, stalk, harass, or threaten. Scruff, the smaller of the two companies, responded to Matthew immediately. They sent him a personal email expressing concern, took down the fake accounts, and blocked Gutierrez's IP address, effectively banning him from the app. When Gutierrez started impersonating Matthew on Jack'd, another gay dating app, that company also banned Gutierrez from using its platform to harass Matthew. But Grindr took a different approach: they did absolutely nothing.

"I emailed and called and begged them to do something," Matthew told me, the frustration rising in his voice. His family and friends also contacted Grindr about the fake profiles—in all, about fifty separate complaints were made to the company, either by Matthew or on his behalf. The only response the company ever sent was an automatically generated email: "Thank you for your report."

Grindr is a wildly successful company. In 2018, the dating app reportedly had more than three million users in 234 countries. Like most social media companies, Grindr operates, in large part, as an advertising platform. The free content and services these platforms provide—porn, photo sharing, direct messaging, emailing, shopping, news, dating—are just lures to get us to show up so they can collect data about what we buy, who we're friends with, where we're going, and use that information to advertise at us. Grindr prides itself on its state-of-the-art geo-locative feature, which can pinpoint a user's exact location, allowing users to match with others in their vicinity. This is how they rake in advertising revenue—by customizing the ads users see based on nearby businesses. Even though Grindr's terms of service state Grindr can remove any profile and deny anybody the use of their product at the company's discretion, no matter how many times Matthew emailed the company describing his crisis, they refused to help.

I'd never had a case in which a client was battling so many malevolent forces at once. Matthew was under attack by his psycho ex, who was hell-bent on destroying Matthew's life. He was also up against Grindr, a multimillion-dollar company that seemed at best uninterested, at worst willfully negligent. But Matthew was confronting an insidious force that few people outside the world of tech even know exists. Arguably, a decades-old legislation called Section 230 of the Communications Decency Act of 1996 was Matthew's greatest foe of all. This single law is the number one reason the internet is a safe space for peddlers of fake news, graphic death threats, conspiracy theories, Russian propaganda, racist slurs, Nazi hate speech, anti-LGBTQ vitriol, vivid promotions of violence against women, instructions for how to make your own bomb, and phony dating profiles offering sex in someone else's name. If you really want to get to the bottom of why Matthew's ex and countless other offenders are free to harass, terrorize, violate, impersonate, and threaten innocent people online, you need to understand this law.

———

Simply put, Section 230 of the CDA, as it's interpreted, protects internet companies from legal responsibility for any content users post to their platforms. Free speech purists and tech heads alike hail the legislation as instrumental in protecting the First Amendment online and laying the foundation for the thriving internet we have today. Without Section 230, they argue, we'd have no Facebook, Twitter, Yelp, or Reddit. But that's a wildly simplistic understanding of the law. I see things very differently.

I'm convinced Section 230—or, more specifically, the court's broad application of the law—is the enabler of every asshole, troll, psycho, and perv on the internet. From revenge porn websites to rapists using dating apps to hunt for prey, everything bad that happens online is allowed to happen because Section 230 of the CDA exists. The great irony here is that the Communications Decency Act was originally intended to keep the internet safe.

When the law first came into existence the internet was a very different place: there was no Google, Reddit, YouTube, or Twitter. Mark Zuckerberg was in middle school, and Amazon was an exciting new website that only sold books. Cell phones could only make phone calls, and two-thirds of Americans didn't even own one. Internet access was even scarcer; in 1997, only 18 percent of American households were connected to the web.

Even so, online companies offering information, shopping, news, and discussion groups were quickly gaining popularity. One of the most successful at the time, Prodigy Communications, featured rudimentary online news and weather reports, and popular "bulletin boards," arranged by topics, where users could post comments. In 1992, users posted more than forty million messages to the site. The company did its best to monitor this user-generated content and had a team of censors who screened for and deleted posts deemed offensive—for instance, profanity was banned; so, too, were comments disparaging advertisers—but the censors couldn't catch everything.

In 1994, an anonymous user posted a comment on one of Prodigy's most popular bulletin boards, Money Talk, criticizing Stratton Oakmont, a now-defunct Long Island–based financial institution, and accusing the firm of fraud. The poster claimed Stratton Oakmont was staffed by a "cult of brokers who either lie for a living or get fired." In fact, only two years later Stratton Oakmont was indeed expelled from the National Association of Securities Dealers for defrauding customers out of millions of dollars. (The firm's jaw-dropping corruption was the focus of Hollywood's 2013 blockbuster *The Wolf of Wall Street*.) Despite its guilt—or perhaps because of it—Stratton Oakmont did not take kindly to getting called out on the internet. In a move that sent shock waves through the burgeoning tech industry, Stratton Oakmont sued Prodigy for defamation in connection with the anonymous post.

Here's where things start to get complicated: Prodigy argued the company should not be held liable for user-generated content posted on their message boards. But in a 1995 ruling, a New York Supreme Court judge disagreed. The court determined that since Prodigy was monitoring and vetting user-generated content, it was behaving as a publisher. This is a critical distinction because publishers can be held legally responsible for content they release to the public. For example, if the *New York Times* prints a defamatory article, both the journalist who wrote the piece and the corporation that owns the newspaper may get hauled into court. But most internet companies driven by user content, like Facebook or Yelp, are not set up like print media; they don't have armies of editors, fact-checkers, and lawyers on hand to vet contributors' work. Furthermore, they aren't managing the work of only a few dozen contributors; there are potentially *millions* posting on the platforms.

After Prodigy issued a formal apology, Stratton Oakmont dropped their $200 million suit. But the court's ruling made clear that as long as interactive computer services like Prodigy were considered publishers, they could be liable for every defaming comment users posted on their sites. The only way to avoid legal jeopardy, it seemed, was to stop managing user-generated content. Instead of monitoring and deleting the most offensive comments, internet companies could relinquish their publisher duties and adopt a hands-off approach. They could simply distribute user-generated content on their platforms with no vetting at all.

Lawmakers immediately recognized they had a problem on their hands. They'd been slow to impose regulations governing content on the web. Instead, for years they'd relied on website operators to act as Good Samaritans and police user content themselves. But if internet companies were going to back away from vetting duties, elected officials realized they had to intervene. For lawmakers, this was about far more than protecting financial firms from disparaging comments or shielding tech companies from defamation lawsuits. What they worried about—and scrambled to enact legislation to address—was what they saw as a growing crisis of internet porn.

———

Today, porn is so ubiquitous online it's hard to believe that lawmakers ever tried to control it. But consider the political landscape at the time: in the mid-'90s, the country was in the midst of a cultural revolution. Republicans, including a contingent of far-right religious candidates, had swept the 1994 midterm elections. Almost overnight, the nation took a giant swing to the right. These newly elected officials had come into power with a clear mandate to reform taxes and the welfare system. But they also focused on social issues, or what they called "family values," like banning abortion and sex ed in schools. Not surprisingly, many conservatives also wanted to regulate the internet. In particular, they were concerned about the prospect of innocent children having access to porn.

Back then porn was a very big deal. It wasn't available for mass consumption like it is today. If you wanted it, you had to do some work. You could buy an "adult" magazine, which came wrapped in brown paper and was stored on the top rack at the newsstand, or you could rent an XXX-rated film from the back room of a video store. Most important, you couldn't get any of it without ID proving you were over eighteen. Porn was strictly off-limits for kids, save the dog-eared copy of *Juggs* that always seemed to find its way onto the middle school bus. But the internet changed everything.

In 1994, the same year Prodigy was sued for defamation, *Christianity Today*, an influential magazine among far-right conservatives, published a shocking article titled "Hard-Core Porn Technology Hits Home," sounding the alarm about the impending porn disaster. If the internet remained unregulated, the publication warned, there would be nothing to stop users from uploading, posting, and sharing tons of porn.

On Capitol Hill even the Senate chaplain took note. In 1995, the chaplain offered a prayer, which was read on the Senate floor by Nebraska senator James Exon: "Lord . . . guide the senators as they consider ways of controlling the pollution of computer communications and how to preserve one of our greatest resources: the minds of our children and the future moral strength of our nation." Senator Exon also introduced a possible solution to the porn problem. The Communications Decency Act, the first-ever federal bill aimed at censoring content on the web, proposed fines and prison time on anyone who sent or made available to minors "indecent" or "offensive" materials. To bolster his case, Exon asked a friend to download a collection of pornographic images from the internet—a veritable smut sampler—which he kept in a blue folder on his desk, inviting skeptical senators to check out the problem for themselves.

Exon's Blue Book, as it came to be known, was a bold move. But what really sealed the deal for lawmakers was the publication, the following month, of a salacious *Time* magazine cover story. "Cyberporn," blared the July 1995 issue on its front cover, along with a question "Can we protect our kids?" The article inside spared no detail, describing the internet as home to "a grab bag of 'deviant' material that includes images of bondage, sadomasochism, urination, defecation and sex acts with a barnyard full of animals." Never mind that the study on which the *Time* article was based was swiftly discredited; the damage had been done. The country went into a full-blown cybersex panic. The topic was discussed endlessly on daytime talk shows, as worried parents wrung their hands from coast to coast. Something had to be done. Seven months later, the Communications Decency Act, aimed at protecting children from porn, was signed into law. The legislation made it illegal to transmit on the internet "obscene" or "patently offensive" material that could be accessible to kids. The crime was punishable by up to two years in prison and up to $250,000 in fines.

But here's the crazy part: after all that, the Supreme Court ruled the CDA unconstitutional the very next year. The court decided that many provisions of the CDA violated the First Amendment. However, Section 230, a twenty-six-word provision embedded in the original bill, was spared. Drafted in direct response to the Prodigy ruling, Section 230 established that "no provider of an interactive computer service shall be treated as the publisher." And if a company is *not* a publisher, it is not liable for any content users post on its site. Some lawmakers thought that special immunity from litigation would actually *encourage* internet companies to continue monitoring their platforms for offensive content and removing it from the web. With the specter of a cyberporn apocalypse still looming in lawmakers' minds, anything that might prompt tech companies to police themselves seemed like a pretty good idea. What legislators did not anticipate was that Section 230 would actually give rise to the very problem it was supposed to prevent.

———

Section 230 was originally conceived to shield internet companies that ran online message boards—where the majority of user-generated content appeared online—from legal action traditionally lodged against publishers, like defamation and obscenity claims. But in the two decades since the legislation was enacted, the internet has ballooned into a many-tentacled behemoth, reaching into every corner of our lives. We turn to the web for everything from what to buy to whom to vote for. Tech companies today wield unimaginable power and influence. They create and control the algorithms that dictate our rankings when we google our name and influence our purchasing when we buy something on Amazon. They curate which posts we see on Facebook and Twitter and whom we connect with on Tinder and Bumble. They also offer services that didn't even exist when the CDA was passed, like direct messaging and geolocating.

You'd think there would be some sort of legislative course correction to account for this new reality. But that's not how the law works. Instead, courts have broadly applied the protections of this woefully outdated legislation to virtually every company that operates online today: from Facebook and Reddit to sites hosting revenge porn, neo-Nazi propaganda, or child sex trafficking.

Today internet companies not only use Section 230 to shield themselves from liability for anything users post on their platforms; they also think that immunity extends to cover any and all decisions they make about how their products operate—even if those decisions cause users harm. For instance, if a company receives multiple user reports that sex predators are using its platform to find victims, the company may choose to ignore those reports because it believes it is protected from litigation by Section 230 of the CDA. In other words, internet companies are not legally bound to protect their users, so many of them don't. Twitter, Facebook, and Reddit all have terms of service that prohibit various harassing behaviors, but these policies are not always enforced. Tech companies maintain Section 230 of the CDA protects them from having to comply with promises they make to their users in their own terms of service. Even worse, internet companies that exist for the *sole purpose* of disseminating material that violates people's privacy, damages their reputations, and puts lives at risk believe they too are protected by Section 230.

No other media entity—not Fox News, or the *New York Times* or even the *National Enquirer*—is allowed to operate as a vehicle for defamation, threats, or the promotion of hate crimes, nor can they legally facilitate the dissemination of nonconsensual porn. But thanks to Section 230 of the CDA, internet companies get a pass.

Decades ago, lawmakers had this pie-in-the-sky idea that internet companies would monitor content their users uploaded to protect the rest of us. What's become painfully apparent, and arguably should have been obvious, is that without the threat of legal liability hanging over their heads, companies like Grindr really don't give a shit about who gets hurt. This is what Matthew was up against.

———

I knew it might take months for the DA's office to collect the evidence they needed to indict Matthew's ex on serious charges. I suspected that, like Juan Thompson, Gutierrez was likely using multiple burner phones, IP addresses, and software to conceal his identity. But Matthew needed immediate relief. As long as his ex was able to use Grindr to impersonate him, Matthew was in danger. We had to get Grindr to take down the fake profiles to keep Matthew safe.

"I think I know how we can get Grindr to wake up and listen," I told Matthew that afternoon in my conference room. He looked at me expectantly. It was the first time since he'd arrived at my office that I saw a glimmer of hope. "We'll send them a message in a language I know they'll understand," I said. "Let's sue the motherfuckers."

———

Going up against Grindr, a global company reportedly valued at more than $245 million in 2018, was a total David-and-Goliath situation. At first it was just me and my associate Adam against Grindr's cadre of well-heeled lawyers from their marble-lobbied Manhattan firms. I knew they probably figured they could intimidate me with their Ivy League degrees and $2,000 Armani suits. But this wasn't my first rodeo. I'd taken on powerful defendants before. My secret advantage in cases like these is that I deal with victims entangled in stalking and sexually violent situations every day. Opposing counsel is almost always more at home with commercial contracts and intellectual property disputes. They blush at words like "dickpic," "fisting," and "gang bang." I wasn't worried about Grindr's lawyers. Thinking about Section 230 is what kept me up at night.

For internet companies facing litigation, Section 230 is like Teflon. Over the past decade, Facebook, Craigslist, Uber, Airbnb, Amazon, eBay, and OkCupid have all invoked the legislation when fighting lawsuits brought by users with serious, sometimes life-threatening complaints. In 2013, Mary Kay Beckman sued the online dating service Match.com for negligence and other claims after she was brutally attacked with a butcher knife by a man she met on the site. Beckman's attacker had previously been reported to Match.com by other women he'd assaulted. But the company failed to remove his profile or warn users of the danger. The case, and several others like it, was dismissed on grounds of CDA immunity.

In fact, until 2018, the courts' application of Section 230 of the CDA was so broad that even websites facilitating online child sex trafficking and exploitation were able to do business with impunity. Only after several lawsuits brought by trafficking victims against Backpage.com were dismissed because of the CDA did Congress pass the Stop Enabling Sex Traffickers Act, in March 2018. The bill created an exception to the protections offered by Section 230 and allows victims to sue websites that knowingly or inadvertently facilitate child sex trafficking. But this is a small carve-out to the otherwise sweeping immunity companies have claimed under the CDA.

I anticipated Grindr, too, would argue the CDA protected it from liability. I needed to launch a decisive attack. In January 2017, I filed our initial complaint in the New York State Supreme Court, arguing that Grindr had facilitated the "attempted rape and murder scheme" Gutierrez had initiated against Matthew. The complaint detailed Gutierrez's scorched-earth campaign to stalk and intimidate Matthew and destroy his reputation. I described Matthew's months of hell, his repeated efforts to contact Grindr about the offending accounts, and multiple examples of Gutierrez's attempts to orchestrate an assault. I included several of Gutierrez's imposter profiles, like one that he posted advertising Matthew as "waiting on all 4s with my ass lubed."

I also came up with an unconventional legal strategy to help keep

Matthew safe while our lawsuit made its way through the courts. Since Grindr had repeatedly ignored Matthew's requests to disable Gutierrez's imposter accounts, I did what I do in many of my domestic violence cases: I requested a same-day temporary restraining order. Of course, this TRO wasn't against an abusive ex—Matthew already had an order of protection against Gutierrez. This was against Grindr itself. To my delight, Judge Kathryn Freed issued the TRO ordering the company to stop letting Gutierrez use their product to stalk Matthew.

It wasn't long before Matthew's story got picked up by the press. *Wired* magazine did a full-length feature, "Spoofed Grindr Accounts Turned One Man's Life into a 'Living Hell'"; CNN, the *New York Post*, and a variety of national magazines followed. The story was picked up in Canada and the UK, too. At least one reporter reached out to Gutierrez for comment. He denied he'd done anything wrong. In truth, he was escalating his attacks, enabled by Grindr. The company was ignoring the court-ordered TRO and allowing Gutierrez to continue posting imposter accounts, even as Matthew's life was at risk.

Matthew would leave his apartment at six a.m. to walk his dog and find strange men waiting on his stoop. They'd hound him at work and wake him up in the middle of the night hollering his name from the sidewalk. One evening, four guys arrived at his door insisting Matthew had promised them a crystal-meth-fueled orgy. He posted a sign on the front door: "WARNING GRINDR USERS. Do Not Buzz or Enter Apt. FAKE PROFILE. REPORT to GRINDR." But it made no difference.

Gutierrez attacked Matthew in other ways, too. He called Matthew's bank and impersonated him over the phone, deactivating Matthew's debit card nine times in a week and a half. He transferred money from one of Matthew's accounts to another, causing Matthew to bounce his rent check (moving money, instead of stealing it outright, meant Gutierrez would avoid any possible criminal charges of theft). Gutierrez also falsely filed for an order of protection against Matthew and then made false reports of violation, causing Matthew to get arrested. One afternoon, Matthew's pregnant sister called him, hysterical. A man had shown up at her house looking to hook up with Matthew. Her eleven-year-old stepdaughter had been the one to answer the door.

In February, our case got moved to federal court. I fought for an extension of the temporary restraining order and threatened to hold the company in contempt for not complying with Judge Freed's original order. The federal judge denied the request, citing Grindr's protections under the CDA.

I was furious. And I simply refused to accept that a powerful and profitable internet company was above the law. During heated oral arguments in court, opposing counsel insisted that Grindr had no legal duty to take down imposter profiles. They also argued that the company didn't possess the ability to protect Matthew. They said they couldn't control their product or disable Gutierrez's phony accounts. This caught my attention immediately.

It was foreseeable by Grindr, even predictable, that their product, which facilitates millions of offline sexual encounters, would likely attract malicious users. Yet Grindr hadn't built into its platform ways to identify and block users who repeatedly abuse the product. Despite its sophistication, the company seemed more interested in creating "gaymojis" than implementing common safety protocols, such as user verification, IP and/or MAC address blocking, photo-hashing, or word and location recognition, to name a few. Grindr had no functional system in place for users to alert the company of a sexual assault or harassment. As a product, Grindr was very clearly flawed. It was defectively designed and released into the marketplace. In any other industry, a company could be sued for this kind of negligence. There was no reason Grindr should be exempt.

By this time, I'd brought in fearsome trial attorney Tor Ekeland to join the fight as co-counsel. Tor became an invaluable partner in the case. Together we composed a forty-two-page amendment to the complaint, a petition of blood, sweat, and tears. Grindr was liable for fourteen separate claims, we argued in our amendment, including deceptive business practices, negligent manufacturing and design, false advertising, and failure to warn. It was a radical suit, with the potential to completely change case law regarding the court's overly broad interpretation of the CDA. But even as our courtroom battle raged on, Gutierrez continued to attack.

———

By the time we filed our amended complaint on March 31, 2017, Gutierrez had directed more than eleven hundred men to Matthew's door. Tor and I told Matthew that the most important thing for him to focus on, next to his safety, was recording every incident in a stalking log. Just as it had been with Francesca, I knew this information would be vital for Matthew's criminal case against Gutierrez and the civil case against Grindr.

Every time a new guy showed up responding to the imposter profiles and expecting sex, Matthew would record detailed notes on his phone, then transfer the information to spreadsheets on his computer. He made lists of the phone numbers Gutierrez was using to contact him, and charted graphs and timelines. One Sunday afternoon while I was in Denver at a law firm policy and procedure conference, Gutierrez directed more than a dozen guys to Matthew's apartment. Matthew called me, frantic. One of the guys was outside his apartment, refusing to leave. I emailed Grindr's lawyers and pleaded with them to do something: "Our client is going to get killed," I wrote. The lawyers didn't get back to me for a few days. When they finally responded, they told me there was nothing they could do.

By September 2017, prosecutors finally felt they had the evidence they needed to charge Gutierrez with felony crimes. They subpoenaed records from Scruff, Grindr, AT&T, and Matthew's bank, and empaneled a grand jury to hear the case. As the complaining witness, Matthew was called to testify. By then, he'd recorded more than seven hundred pieces of evidence in his stalking log.

Grand jury hearings are nothing like trials you see on TV. There is no judge present, just a jury of up to twenty-three people, selected at random. Before prosecutors can arrest or indict a person for a federal crime, they have to present their case to a grand jury. The jury considers the evidence and interviews witnesses to determine if there is probable cause; only then can a prosecutor indict. The purpose is to prevent prosecutors from abusing their power and arresting anyone on a whim. Jurors are allowed to ask witnesses anything they like relating to the case. They can grill victims of assaults about the most intimate details of their attack. What happens in front of a grand jury stays completely secret. The only person who can talk about what happens during grand jury testimony is a witness.

Matthew says that during his sworn testimony, he held it together for more than two hours of questioning. Finally, a juror asked, "How has this affected you?" Matthew found himself suddenly overcome by the thought of trying to put into words the fear and anger that had dominated almost every minute of every day for the past eleven months of his life. His eyes filled with tears, and he could barely choke out an answer. How do you describe to a roomful of complete strangers what it feels like to drown?

In late October 2017, a full year after Gutierrez first launched his offensive, he was arrested at the construction company where he was working part-time. Investigators confiscated his computer, his cell phone, and the multiple burner phones he had stashed in a box behind his desk. He was indicted on seven felony charges and nine misdemeanors, including stalking, criminal impersonation, and identity theft. He was remanded to the Manhattan Detention Complex, where he was held on $250,000 bail.

———

A few months after Gutierrez's arrest, and a year from the date we first filed suit against Grindr, on January 25, 2018, US District Judge Valerie Caproni delivered a crushing blow. Caproni, an Obama appointee, dismissed all but one of our fourteen claims. She compared Matthew's hell to a simple case of "catfishing." In her decision, Caproni acknowledged that Matthew had endured a negative experience as a result of the fake profiles posted on Grindr, but concluded: "While the creation of the impersonating profiles may be sufficiently extreme and outrageous, Grindr did not create the profiles." She agreed with Grindr that Section 230 of the CDA "immunizes Grindr for content created by other users." Simply put, Grindr had enabled and facilitated Matthew's abuse. They knew it was happening. They could have stopped the strangers showing up at Matthew's door. But legally they didn't have to do anything to keep Matthew safe because of the fucking CDA.

Immediately, Tor and I wanted to appeal. But this was Matthew's case and his decision. With Gutierrez behind bars, Matthew was out of danger and free to move forward with his life. Appealing the Grindr decision would mean staying locked in a fight that might last for years. It would have been completely understandable if he wanted to put the ordeal behind him.

A few days after Caproni issued her decision, I picked up the phone and dialed Matthew's number. "This doesn't have to be over," I began.

"We can appeal." I'd barely gotten the words out of my mouth when Matthew jumped in to respond.

"I am not okay with what happened," he said. "I have my whole life to fight this. I am not walking away now." On the other end of the line, I broke into a happy-dance. Matthew, the man who'd come to see me a year earlier so beaten down he could barely look me in the eye, was focused and determined. He'd been transformed. As an attorney, this is what I live for.

———

When people discuss the human toll of violent crime, they often refer to "victims" and "survivors," as in "before" and "after." But to me, these describe passive states of being. I like to focus on the fight. When I'm battling alongside a client, we are in the trenches, strategizing, doing surveillance, and plotting our next attack. This is when I often see the change take hold. My clients become warriors. I watched it happen with Matthew, when he threw himself into plotting and charting his stalking log. He told me he felt as though he was imposing order over chaos, like he was taking back his control.

On May 24, 2018, we filed an appeal with the US Court of Appeals for the Second Circuit. More than twenty organizations, including privacy think tanks, consumer protection groups, domestic violence service providers, and policy experts from around the country, signed onto amicus briefs in support of our appeal. Some of the most powerful lobbyists for big tech filed amicus briefs in support of Grindr.

By October 2018, almost two years since Matthew first came to see me, our case had become one of the most closely watched in the country regarding Section 230. Law schools were teaching our case. And others were taking note, too. One day while at an airport, I picked up a copy of *Harper's* to read on the plane. I flipped open the pages, only to find that the magazine had published a portion of my complaint, right where a poem usually goes.

We had oral arguments in front of the Second Circuit on January 7, 2019. The courtroom was packed, with the overflow of spectators—journalists, law students, domestic violence advocates—huddled in an adjoining room to watch the proceedings on a closed-circuit monitor. Tor and I had prepared for months, hoping the appeals court, known for handling complex white-collar securities issues, would recognize that Caproni's decision was faulty. She'd not only ignored precedent, she also clearly misunderstood some of the key facts underlying the case.

Almost three months later, on March 27, 2019, we experienced another blow. The Second Circuit affirmed Caproni's decision. Matthew would not see justice and Grindr would face no liability.

The Second Circuit decision is not a defeat. We will ask the court to reconsider. If the court continues to choose the interest of a greedy company over the safety of vulnerable individuals, Congress must act.

This case is not only about justice for Matthew. We are fighting for future victims' rights to sue any tech company that knowingly, or recklessly, aids their abusers, and causes victims harm. We are putting tech companies on notice. For too long, dating apps and other digital products have been enabling stalkers, psychos, assholes, and pervs to commit heinous crimes that put us all at risk. It's time these companies are held accountable. They need to think differently about the responsibility they owe us all. Grindr and their ilk can try to shut me down with their battalion of fancy lawyers. But I've got an army of warriors, too. And we have a clear advantage. We are fighting on the side of right.

CHAPTER 3

ASSHOLES IN CHARGE

When I first opened my practice in 2014, I set up shop in the only place I could afford—a windowless, fifty-five-square-foot room with a desk in a shared workspace in Dumbo, a Brooklyn neighborhood filled with cobblestone streets and bearded hipsters. My office shared a glass wall with the space next door rented by some dude-bros working for a San Francisco–based start-up. They'd collected an impressive selection of empty cereal boxes and local beer bottles and even had a remote control robot operated by someone in their West Coast headquarters. Occasionally, the bros would have loud meetings, arguing with the robot as it careened around the room.

I logged a lot of hours in that cramped space working hard for the few paying clients I had. There was a woman whose psycho ex had tried to throw her from a moving car and pulled a knife on her as she held her young child, and a former reality star who was being impersonated on social media by an obsessed fan. I also represented a recent immigrant from the Philippines. Her ex had surreptitiously recorded her during sex, then inundated my client with hundreds of text messages demanding she meet him at a New Jersey hotel for a sexual encounter. He threatened if she didn't comply, he'd send the video to her new husband and post it on the internet, which he ultimately did. In one of my earliest victories, I was able to get this PoS (piece of shit) arrested and charged with harassment.

For almost a year, most of the clients I represented were battling psychos, like my ex, and psycho-adjacents—abusers, blackmailers, and con artists. That changed one cold January night when I received an email that introduced a new type of menace to the firm, one that often evades the law. I call these offenders "assholes." I realize the term "asshole" gets thrown around as a catchall for all kinds of bad actors. But in the Carrie Goldberg Offender Taxonomy I use the term in a very specific way: A basic tenet of human decency is that when someone is in pain, you do what you can to help. Assholes, by comparison, do the opposite. Some exploit desperate victims for their own financial gain; I call these greedy shits "a$$holes." Others act on the arrogant belief that it's their duty to teach someone—namely, the victim of a sexual violation—a "lesson." These assholes are ignorant, self-righteous fucks. They specialize in victim blaming and public shaming and are experts at making my clients' misery exponentially worse.

———

The email I received that chilly January night had been forwarded to me by my brilliant friend and colleague Annmarie Chiarini, the victims' coordinator at the Cyber Civil Rights Initiative (CCRI), an amazing organization devoted to combating nonconsensual porn. The original email was from a woman needing help for her seventeen-year-old daughter, who was in the midst of a crisis. The teenager, whom I'll call Macie, had shared intimate pictures with her then boyfriend. After they'd broken up, he'd distributed them to his friends without her consent.

Embarrassed and desperate for help, Macie reported the violation to her school's resource officer, who was also a police officer in her small Texas town. But instead of offering Macie assistance, he and the other school officials did the inconceivable. In true asshole form, they punished Macie, a star dancer on her school's elite squad, instead. The dance director demoted Macie from her position as team captain and pulled her from upcoming competitions. "The administration at [my daughter's] high school opted to punish my daughter but not the boy who distributed the photos," Macie's mother, "Sharon," wrote in her email. "She cries and cries and doesn't want to go to school. Please help."

I responded immediately:

> Dear Sharon,
> The treatment that Macie experienced first from the privacy betrayal, then from the school's seemingly punitive treatment toward her, and finally from the harsh and judgmental law enforcement is sickening and crazy-making. Please have faith that the two of you are the sane ones here. Let your daughter know, we will get her to the other side of this.

I hit "send." It was 1:04 in the morning. I barely slept that night. How could adults in charge punish a child whose naked pictures were everywhere? What made the situation even more galling was that Texas, where Macie lived, was one of the first states to institute legislation specifically aimed at addressing the growing phenomenon of teenagers texting nude selfies to one another. In other jurisdictions, underage couples caught sexting might face charges related to creating and distributing child pornography, felony offenses that can carry serious prison time and designation as a registered sex offender. But Texas, along with a few other states, quickly realized draconian punishments did not serve kids well.

In 2011, the state reduced the crime of underage sexting to a Class C misdemeanor for minors and developed a comprehensive "sexting reduction" education program that judges could require teens and their parents to complete. The online course "Before You Text" was created by the Texas School Safety Center of Texas State University and describes the impact of nonconsensual distribution of sexually explicit images. In other words, information was readily available and supported by state legislation. And yet the administrators at Macie's high school seemed totally oblivious. In fact, the more I dug into the specifics of Macie's case, the more convinced I became that the adults running her high school knew nothing about what it means to be a teen.

———

Macie started dating her boyfriend "Karl" in the fall of senior year. Karl "worshipped" Macie, Sharon recalled. Macie was two years older than he, pretty and popular. It didn't take long before Karl started pressuring Macie to send him a naked pic.

"I don't want to," Macie texted the first time he asked.

"C'mon," he begged.

"No."

Karl became more insistent. He said if Macie didn't send a pic, he'd end the relationship. He told her to use Snapchat, which meant the picture would disappear seconds after he'd viewed it. "It's not like anyone is gonna see it," he assured her. "It's only for me."

Unlike Instagram, which is filled with personal galleries of carefully curated photos filtered to perfection, Snapchat's primary allure is impermanence. The brainchild of a trio of Stanford University bros,

Snapchat was created in 2011 after one of the trio mused aloud that he wished he could make the pics he was texting to a girl disappear after she'd seen them. Put another way, the app is great for sexting. In fact, some dating experts credit Snapchat's vanishing pictures for revolutionizing dating, making sexting a normal, even expected, part of flirting for many adults. It should come as no surprise that teenagers use Snapchat for the exact same thing. By 2016, the app was the most popular social media platform for the under-twenty set.

Still, Macie was sure that if Karl tried something sneaky, like taking a screenshot of her naked photo, she'd know about it. One of Snapchat's features is to ping the sender if the recipient has captured and saved an image. What Macie *didn't* know was that Karl had discreetly installed another app on his phone specifically designed to circumvent the Snapchat alert. SnapCapture and other apps like it allow users to stealthily screenshot Snapchat images on their devices without the sender knowing.

Macie went into her bathroom, took a deep breath, and snapped a topless photo of herself. On the other end of the line, Karl saved the image to his phone.

———

There are a lot of reasons kids send one another naked pictures (aka nudes, noodz, or simply pics). As some experts point out, sending explicit texts is Generation Z's version of flirting. "[Teenagers] are testing their level of appeal," clinical psychologist Barbara Greenberg told *Time* magazine in 2014, back when adults were just beginning to catch on to the trend. Even Macie's mother notes matter-of-factly that teens have been playing "you show me yours and I'll show you mine" forever. "Boys manipulating girls into doing something they aren't ready for is also nothing new," she adds wryly.

For some sexting teens, a coyly posed topless snapshot might be intended to convey "I like you," or possibly "I want you to like me," or maybe a confident "I know you want this." The practice is incredibly common: one out of every four teenagers between the ages of eleven and seventeen has received a sext, and one in seven has sent one, according to a 2018 study published in *JAMA Pediatrics*.

That's a lot of nude pics flying back and forth. But here's something even more surprising: at least two separate studies on teen sexting report that the majority of kids who send explicit images say they've experienced *no negative consequences as a result*. In 2014, a Drexel University study found only 8 percent of teens said they'd endured damage to their reputation after sending explicit images, and less than 1 percent said they'd been bullied. Another study, authored by Bridge-water State University professor Elizabeth Englander, an expert in high-risk online behavior, found the same thing. An overwhelming majority of teens—92 percent, to be exact—who said they'd sexted voluntarily (that is, without being pressured, coerced, or blackmailed into it) reported zero negative impact.

At a glance, this might seem counterintuitive. If kids aren't experiencing post-sexting remorse then why do we keep hearing about kids getting bullied, shamed, and harassed over naked pics? It turns out—as with most things sexual—the real issue is consent. When a teenager voluntarily shares a nude with another teen and that other teen looks but *does not share the image* with anyone else, usually it's like—shrug emoji—not a big deal.

The problems arise when a teen feels as though she or he was pressured or coerced. Englander's research shows that almost a quarter of teens who've sexted under duress report experiencing negative fallout, including "excessive anxiety," most often in connection with the photos getting shared around school. In other words, when it comes to adolescents sending one another nudes, by far the most dangerous and damaging situations occur (A) when the sender is coerced, manipulated, blackmailed, or pressured into sharing the image and (B) when the images are subsequently distributed without the sender's knowledge or consent. Most important: (A) and (B) often go hand in hand. As in, the teenage piece of shit who thinks it's okay to badger someone into sending him nudes is the same PoS who will share that pic with all his friends. Englander also found that while boys and girls consensually sext at about the same rate, girls are twice as likely as boys to be coerced or pressured into it, most often by a dating partner. This is what happened to Macie.

Let's be clear: Coercing someone into sending an intimate picture and then distributing that image without consent isn't "sexting." It's a violation and a crime. And the first step to protecting young people from this kind of abuse is to teach about consent. I'm talking about no-holds-barred conversations with real-world examples of what pressure and coercion look like. As in, *Yes, asking a girl over and over again to send you a nude is PRESSURE.* And, *Someone threatening to dump you if you don't send a pic is COERCION.* And, *Sharing someone else's naked pics with all your friends without their consent in many states is a fucking CRIME.* Teaching sex ed to the digital generation is not only the responsibility of parents. Safe sexting should be taught in middle school, when most kids get their first phone (and also hit puberty). It should be woven into the plots of teen movies and disguised as listicles on BuzzFeed ("Ten Reasons to *Not* Send Your Friends That Nude Pic of Your Ex!"). This is an all-hands-on-deck situation.

The problem is most adults old enough to have adolescent children came of age way before sexting as foreplay became a thing. Many parents of teenagers don't know what to say about sexting, except "Don't do it!" More often than not, they leave it up to teens to figure it out themselves. Some kids possess the maturity to treat private images with care, but most have no clue. They handle nudes as casually as trading cards—collecting, swapping, and showing them off.

In 2015, one Colorado high school made headlines when it was discovered that more than three hundred images of naked students (about half of them boys) were being traded among students through secret password-protected vault apps on their phones. The apps hid the caches of illicit photos behind innocent-looking icons—like a calculator—so as not to raise suspicion. The students had assigned a point system to the photographs and were passing them back and forth. The kid who had the most nudes was admiringly dubbed "the pimp of pictures" by a classmate in an interview with the *New York Times*. One parent complained that the problems began well before the kids got to high school. She recounted finding images of naked classmates on her middle school–aged daughter's phone. When she reported it to the school's officials, she was told by school administrators that there was nothing they could do "because half the school was sexting."

———

When I was a teenager growing up in Aberdeen, Washington—a harbor-front city a couple of hours southwest of Seattle and the birth-place of my greatest teenage crush, Kurt Cobain—the most embarrassing thing that ever happened to me was when I gathered my nerve and, in a huge explosion of confidence, asked Adam Gamboa to the winter formal. Unfortunately, that lone act of courage depleted my reserves. I felt so shy afterward I couldn't talk to Adam at all, not even to make plans. I avoided him at school. I didn't even tell my mom or any of my friends I'd invited him. I had nothing to wear and had made no arrangements about whom we'd double date with or how we would get to the dance. The day before the formal, I forced myself to pick up the phone and dial Adam's number. "Hey," I said, trying to sound confident. "It's Carrie. We haven't talked. I guess we shouldn't go." He was like, "Okay." And that was it. I saw Adam again a few years ago, at our high school reunion. I laughed as I recalled how paralyzed I'd been by shyness. "That was the most embarrassing thing, *ever*!" I said. Adam looked at me blankly and shrugged. He didn't remember any of it.

Adolescence is not a fun time. I remember it as a state of perpetual mortification punctuated, occasionally, by despair. Many teens barely have the emotional fortitude to manage a bad test score or a rogue pimple. For kids whose sexual images are shared around their schools without their consent, the fallout of forced exposure—and the savage shaming that can follow—can be devastating. School administrators should know this. We've seen it happen before.

In 2008, Ohio high school senior Jessica Logan texted a naked photo of herself to her boyfriend. When they broke up, he shared the picture with other girls at the school, who then ruthlessly attacked Jessica, calling her a slut and a whore. She complained to her school guidance counselor and the local police, but the harassment continued. A few months after her picture was first shared, Jessica hanged herself in her bedroom closet.

Less than two years later, thirteen-year-old Florida teen Hope Witsell texted a picture of her breasts to her boyfriend. Another girl borrowed his phone, found the image, and texted it to several other students. The photo quickly made its way around six different middle schools. Hope was bullied relentlessly; one student even created a "Hope Hater" webpage devoted entirely to humiliating the already traumatized teen. In September 2009, Hope hanged herself from her canopy bed.

————

As soon as Macie discovered Karl had been sharing her private pictures, she reported the violation to her high school's on-campus police officer, who informed the principal, the vice principal, and the director of the dance team. Karl and his friends were rounded up and made to erase the images from their phones. Macie assumed the boys would also be punished, but the vice principal insisted it was impossible for him to know which boy was responsible for distributing the image. Instead the administrators focused their attention on Macie. The dance director maintained that Macie had violated the dance team's constitution, which prohibited "conduct unbecoming." Never mind that the vaguely worded prohibition neither defines "unbecoming" nor gives any examples of what this might mean. The message was clear: Macie had done something nice girls don't do.

Adolescent slut-shaming is often viewed as a teen-on-teen crime (and a clichéd subplot of many Hollywood high school flicks). But what I see more often are adults in positions of power shaming teen girls for displays of sexuality that make adults uncomfortable. Under the guise of being concerned, asshole school administrators routinely single out, shame, and even send home girls (some as young as elementary school!) for, among other infractions, dressing in a manner deemed "distracting" or "inappropriate." This judgment, usually issued under the pretense of dress-code violations, is highly subjective and frequently has more to do with a girl's body than her clothing—a distinction not lost on any student who has had the tops of her thighs or curves of her breasts scrutinized by a principal. Boys rarely receive this same "concern."

Macie's dance director told Macie that, as a consequence of her behavior, she would no longer be allowed to perform her center stage role in an upcoming performance at which college recruiters and professional dance companies scout for talent. Macie was devastated. The Texas dance community is small and tight-knit. She dreaded having to explain to other dancers, their parents, and regional coaches why she'd been removed from the choreography. As if that wasn't humiliating enough, Macie was also given five "demerit points." The only way to erase the demerits, per dance team policy, was for Macie to perform five hundred high kicks in front of the entire team. This went well beyond the scope of taking away her privileges; it was school-sanctioned public shaming. "The school administrators said as the captain of the team, Macie should be a role model," Sharon recalled, incredulously. "But my daughter stood up for what was right. Isn't that exactly what you want a role model to do? Instead the school is sending other girls a message: 'Don't report if you're a victim of a crime because you may be the one in trouble.'"

Sharon is one hundred percent right. But in many ways, the behavior of Macie's school administrators was emblematic of the entire legal system's misguided response to sexual privacy and minors.

As recently as 2017, prosecutors have used child pornography laws to adjudicate sexting teens—even if the pictures were shared consensually and not distributed beyond the intended recipient. Many of these laws were introduced in the mid-1980s, in response to the Meese Report, a sprawling, almost two-thousand-page opus on pornography conducted by the Office of the US Attorney General. The report paid special attention to the horrific emotional and physical impact of porn on children who'd been sexually exploited in its production and distribution. The resulting laws imposed serious penalties, not only on producers of child pornography but also on anyone found guilty of possessing the material. The aim was to target adult predators. Of course, lawmakers of the day couldn't possibly have anticipated the advent of smartphones, or what a generation of horny adolescents primed on internet porn and celebrity sex tapes might do with these devices.

Between 2009 and 2013, forty-two states considered bills specifically aimed at addressing teen sexting. Many of these proposals—not all of them passed—sought to reduce the offense, under specific circumstances, from a felony to a misdemeanor or to dismiss the crime altogether if the kid attends a one-day workshop about online civility. For instance, in Georgia it is now a misdemeanor for teens fourteen and older to send sexually explicit photographs to someone seventeen or younger, as long as the image was not meant to "harass, intimidate, or embarrass," or for commercial use. If a couple of teens get caught sexting in Georgia, they might receive a warning, fine, or more than a year behind bars. Before this change, the same teens might have faced felony child porn penalties of up to twenty years in prison.

But state laws vary widely. Some states focus on the age of the person in the image, others on the circumstances surrounding distribution. Still others are concerned primarily with education programs aimed at deterrence. With no legislative consensus, and overall confusion about the issue, all too often the response to underage sexting is determined by some asshole in charge.

In 2015, North Carolina authorities investigating a report of statutory rape looked through the phones of several high school students and discovered that a pair of sixteen-year-olds—a couple in a dating relationship—had consensually sent each other nudes. Neither teen was connected to the initial complaint of rape, but on discovering the naked selfies, the police charged the teens with creating and distributing child pornography. The girl faced two felony counts relating to sexually exploiting a minor (herself). The boy, a star football player, was charged with five felony counts, four of those charges stemming from two nude pictures he'd taken of himself and sent to his girlfriend; the fifth charge was for having a picture of his girlfriend on his phone. If found guilty, the boy faced up to ten years in prison. The arresting officer, Sergeant Sean Swain, insisted he was doing the kids a favor. "We don't know where these pictures are going to go," he told a reporter at the time. "We're more or less saving the kids from themselves because they're not seeing what's going to come down the road." After a public outcry and negative press, the charges against the teens were eventually downgraded to misdemeanors.

Still, I can't stress this enough: the confusion over how best to respond to sexting minors, and the indiscriminate application of child pornography laws, puts young people who've had their images distributed without their consent in a direct line of being re-victimized. In fact, in some instances the charges against victims can be much more severe than those against the offenders. For instance, if a minor takes a nude selfie, in theory she's produced child pornography. If she has it on her phone, she's in possession of child porn. If she sends the image to anyone else, she is guilty of distribution. If she sends it to one of her peers, that's another crime, distribution to a minor. By comparison, say she sent the image to her boyfriend, they break up, and he retaliates by forwarding the image to all his friends. In that case, he might face only one possible felony charge for distributing child porn, compared to the victim's four.

Amid all the confusion, one thing is clear: too often, people in positions of power—such as school administrators, police officers, judges, and lawmakers—are focusing their attention on kids who *create* the pictures. If anyone needs to be taught a lesson, it's the shithead teenagers who violate their peers' sexual privacy, or pressure or threaten other kids into sex. You'd have to be an asshole not to get it.

———

Macie wasn't the only girl at her school who'd had her naked picture shared without her consent. She knew of another girl on the dance team whose intimate pictures were circulated around the school. The other girl's parents accepted the school's discipline and grounded their daughter as well. But Macie's mom was different. Sharon was fired up and feministing in a way I hadn't expected from a mother living in a small Texas town. Her daughter had been mistreated, and Sharon wasn't having any of it.

The day after Macie was cut from the dance team, Sharon showed up at the school demanding an explanation. She said she was sure the school was in violation of Title IX, the federal law that stipulates schools that receive federal funding must investigate complaints of sexual harassment and violence, and protect victims from further abuse, including retaliation. But almost as soon as Sharon began speaking, it became clear that neither the principal nor the vice principal had any idea what the federal law mandated, nor did they seem to care. "Title seven, title eight, title nine . . ." Sharon remembers the vice principal saying, with a dismissive wave of his hand, like, *Whatever.* But the worst part of the meeting—and the thing Sharon couldn't get out of her head—was when the vice principal made it clear to Sharon that he had viewed naked images of Macie when he'd confiscated the boys' phones. To her horror, he tried to assure Sharon: "I won't treat your daughter any differently."

The day after her meeting with the vice principal, Sharon hand-delivered a formal Level 1 grievance to the school's district office, requesting the school cease disciplinary actions against Macie and instead "support her and protect her from further harm, not only from the perpetrators but also from the harm being inflicted by the disciplinary actions." As soon as she got home, Sharon contacted the Cyber Civil Rights Initiative, which put her in touch with me.

Sharon has the youthful voice of a college student and the energy to match. When the two of us spoke by phone, the day after I received her email, we immediately bonded over our outrage at Macie's school administration.

I drafted a five-page amendment for Sharon to attach to her original complaint. In it, I pointed out that Macie had been the victim of dating violence, bullying, and retaliation related to reporting the initial abuse. I also demanded an explanation for why an adult male administrator would find it appropriate or relevant to view naked images of an underage student. "This [situation] warrants very serious attention and investigation," I wrote.

The school's response was swift and infuriating. The administrators claimed the assistant principal had viewed Macie's photos "for confirmation purposes only" and denied our request to reinstate Macie's dance privileges. Immediately, we appealed the decision to the superintendent. I appeared remotely, via Skype, during the brief hearing arguing that Macie should be protected by the school, not disciplined by it. Again, we lost. And again, we appealed. This time, the complaint would be adjudicated by the district school board, including elected members of the community and the district superintendent. I flew to Texas for the meeting, which was held in the gymnasium of a middle school.

For more than two hours the board discussed assorted school business—the budget for the basketball team uniforms, the new director for the high school band—while I leaned against the cinder block wall waiting for Macie's case to be heard. Suddenly, Sharon leaned over and whispered in my ear: "Oh my God. He's here!"

She nodded in the direction of a tall, lanky boy dressed in a basketball uniform sauntering through the gym with a bunch of his friends. Furious that Karl would have the nerve to show up for no reason other than to intimidate Macie—seriously, when have you ever heard of a high school athlete showing up for a school board meeting?—I asked Macie and Sharon if they would mind if I had a word with him. They gave me two enthusiastic thumbs up.

I walked over to Karl and pointed my finger at his chest. He was only fifteen, but still a good foot taller than I was, even in my four-inch heels. "Don't you ever do that again," I hissed. "You should never be trusted with naked pictures. But if you ever do receive them, don't you *ever* distribute them."

I heard him mumble a vague defense as I made my way back to Sharon. It was clear from his stammer that he was shaken by our confrontation. At the very least, I was confident that this one boy had learned a lesson. I crossed my arms and smiled to myself, savoring this small victory.

Moments later a woman approached me, followed by the school board lawyer. "How dare you talk to my son!" she sputtered, enraged. I was tempted to point out that none of this would have happened if her son hadn't been such a supreme dickhead. But she had crazy eyes and I was afraid she might hit me. As she turned to leave, the lawyer called back to me: "That may be how you do things in Brooklyn, but not down here." I took a breath, straightened my back, and tried to act cool.

Finally, the board was ready to hear our case. Macie, her mother, and I were ushered into a blindingly bright windowless room for a closed-door meeting. Again, I argued vociferously that the school's own policies about dating violence and cyberbullying meant the school should have protected Macie. She was the *victim*; the school was in the wrong. The board then invited the school administrators into the small room for a closed-door meeting of their own. It was eleven p.m. before the board finally returned to the gym. They'd been deliberating for almost two hours. They took a vote and decided, five to four, to restore Macie to her position on the team.

The news was bittersweet. Although the school had capitulated, the months-long fight wasn't resolved until early May, when there were only a few weeks left in the school year. Macie had missed the most important performances of the season. She wasn't recruited by the dance company that earlier in the year had told her she was a "shoo-in." She also lost her chance at a dance scholarship for college.

And the board's decision did nothing to prevent the kids at Macie's school from continuing their harassment. They'd snicker and tease her relentlessly, calling her a slut. One day she found cockroaches in her pencil case. Sharon's distress at watching her child endure the humiliation was eclipsed only by her anger at the way Karl had been let off the hook. "That boy is a pig," she says. "What he did in saving and then disseminating that image is inexcusable. Not to mention the fact that he should never have pressured Macie into sharing it in the first place. What ever happened to 'no means no'?"

When I tell people about Macie's case, they sometimes shrug, like, *Doesn't this kind of thing happen all the time?* As though a high school dancer getting kicked off her squad isn't really that big a deal. But they are missing the point. Macie's case, like so many we handle at my firm, is about a system that fails victims while tacitly condoning exploitive, and even criminal, behavior. It's about the need to teach consent and refusal skills to kids, and about the messages we are giving young people about sexual privacy and agency and, ultimately, who is in control.

Macie's case was one of my first involving a school-aged client. I'd like to say it helped prepare me for the horrific case I would take on the very next year. But that's not true. Nothing could have prepared me for a client I'll call Vanessa. Working on her case changed my life.

CHAPTER 4

GIRLS' LIVES MATTER

The first time I met Vanessa, when she was only thirteen, she looked like a zombie. Her cheeks were sunken and her dark eyes vacant as she shuffled into my office with her mother and toddler half brother in tow. I extended my hand to welcome her, and Vanessa gave me the limpest handshake I've ever felt. She was there in body, but everything about her—the way she slumped in her chair and barely made eye contact—told me she wanted to disappear.

I opened with a few tween-friendly questions to help Vanessa feel more at ease. I learned she liked Ariana Grande, Beyoncé, and shopping at H&M. She did well in school, and science was her favorite subject. But home life hadn't always been easy. Vanessa shared that for more than a year the family had lived in homeless shelters after her mother had escaped a violent relationship. Vanessa's mother is Haitian and speaks very little English. It was up to Vanessa to translate as they moved from place to place, applying for benefits and housing vouchers, and searching for a landlord willing to take a government subsidy for rent. Life had been chaotic—one time, all their belongings were stolen from storage—but over the past few months, there'd been more stability. The family had settled into an apartment, and Vanessa had enrolled in eighth grade at Spring Creek Community School, a middle school in East New York, Brooklyn. She'd been there five months, the longest she'd attended any school in years. Only Vanessa hadn't been to class for a while, she told me. Not since the video of her attack had gone viral.

"Can you tell me what happened?" I asked.

Vanessa took a breath and stared at the floor. "It was on the last day of school before spring break," she began. A month and a half before she'd come to see me, on the afternoon of April 2, 2015, Vanessa had been waiting at a bus stop near her school. She was there later than usual that day. After her last class, Vanessa and some friends had gone on the hunt for one of the friends' missing cell phones, then stopped at a corner store for snacks. Her friends were headed home in a different direction, so they parted ways and Vanessa crossed the street to wait for her bus. She hadn't been standing there long when she noticed a boy walking in her direction. She recognized him from English class, but they weren't friendly, which made it all the more shocking when he approached her and announced that the two of them should go somewhere and have sex. Just like that, out of the blue.

Vanessa told him no, but he kept badgering her. Suddenly, he grabbed her by the arm and started dragging her toward a nearby alley, away from the view of oncoming cars. He undid her belt buckle and pulled down the blue pants of her school uniform. She tried to break free, but he told her to stop struggling unless she wanted to see what would happen if she didn't. Straddling her waist, he turned Vanessa onto her stomach, on the cold concrete, and sodomized her. The pain was excruciating; the boy kept telling her she wasn't doing it right. Then he flipped her over, tried to penetrate her vaginally, gave up, and demanded she perform oral sex. Again she told him no. He grabbed her by the head and shoved his penis in her mouth.

When he was done, the boy—who was thirteen at the time, like Vanessa—zipped up his pants and left her in the alley. She could hear him on his phone as he walked away telling someone on the other end, "Yeah, I got her to do it."

Vanessa pulled on her clothes and ran to the bus. She had eleven missed calls from her mother, who'd been expecting Vanessa to meet her at a hair salon. Vanessa cried the whole way there.

When Vanessa's mother saw her daughter, she asked why Vanessa was so disheveled. It would be weeks before Vanessa would tell her mother about the attack. She was afraid her devout mother, who'd warned Vanessa countless times to stay away from boys, would be angry. Even as Vanessa haltingly recounted the story of her sexual assault in my office, her mother repeatedly interjected to fret about Vanessa's virginity, wondering aloud if it could still be considered intact.

Spring break lasted ten days. The whole time, Vanessa barely left her bedroom. She couldn't eat or sleep. She lost six pounds from her already thin frame. Her mother kept asking what was wrong, but Vanessa couldn't bring herself to put into words what had happened in that alley. The attack was the most awful thing she'd ever experienced. Never in her life had she felt so ashamed. But when she went back to school things only got worse.

———

Every so often the news cycle is filled with horrific reports of a teacher charged with sexually assaulting his or her young student. The stories are sickening and inspire collective outrage over the abuse of power and violation of trust. But what many people don't realize is that the greatest threat of sexual assault among students in K-12 schools comes not from teachers, coaches, or administrators. On and around school grounds, students are most at risk of being sexually assaulted by their peers.

For every report of sexual violation committed by an adult on a child at school, there are seven incidents in which the perpetrator is another student, according to a groundbreaking analysis of state education records and federal crime statistics conducted by the Associated Press in 2017. In four years, between the fall of 2011 and the spring of 2015, there had been seventeen thousand incidents of peer-to-peer sexual assaults reported at US K-12 schools, according to the AP. These figures do not include consensual acts, the AP notes, or even incidents reported as "sexual harassment." These are the most serious violations, including rape, sodomy, rape with a foreign object, and forced groping.

While the vast majority of sexual assaults on children happen in their homes—with relatives, neighbors, stepparents, and family friends—the second most common place for sexual violations of children is in and around schools. These attacks happen in stairwells, lunchrooms, parking lots, school buses, and empty classrooms—anywhere kids are left unattended—and no school is immune. Student-on-student sexual assaults have been reported at wealthy suburban schools and under-resourced inner-city schools alike.

The impact of a sexual assault can be earth-shattering, especially for adolescents who may be too frightened or embarrassed to tell an adult, seek counseling, or find support. In addition to the psychological symptoms associated with trauma—depression, anxiety, guilt, shame, eating disorders, and suicidal thoughts—sexual assaults can also lead victims to engage in high-risk behavior such as binge drinking or self-medicating, which actually increases a victim's risk of further assault. Children who've experienced a rape or attempted rape as adolescents are fourteen times more likely to experience a rape or attempted rape in their first year of college, according to the National Center for Victims of Crime.

And no child is immune, no matter how young. Of the seventeen thousand incidents of student-on-student sexual assault reported by the AP, 5 percent happened to children as young as five or six years old. Forty percent of these youngest victims were boys. By the time kids reach middle school, the rate of peer-on-peer sexual assaults rises dramatically and girls are overwhelmingly the most frequent targets. Overall, eighty-five percent of all victims of these types of sexual violations are girls.

———

Vanessa dreaded going back to school when spring break was over. She worried she'd see her attacker and feared what he might say. She'd been back at school for a few days before she first heard the laughter.

Vanessa was in the lunchroom when she noticed a group of boys at the next table huddled around a phone. They were pointing at the screen and cracking up. One of them exclaimed, "Yo, she did *that*?" Another boy glanced up, noticed Vanessa, and snickered. He called her a thot (slang for "slut"), picked up the phone, and shoved it in her face. On the screen was a video of Vanessa getting raped. Vanessa had no idea her attacker had taped the assault. She fled to the bathroom, locked herself in a stall, and wept.

Vanessa's friends urged her to tell the guidance counselor about the assault and offered to go with her to the meeting. On April 15, three days after she'd returned to school, Vanessa and her friends went to report the crime. The counselor asked Vanessa if she'd agreed to the sex. She said she hadn't. The counselor suggested Vanessa try to put the incident behind her and move on with her life. But how could she?

Everywhere Vanessa went—in Spanish class, in math, in English— someone had something to say about the video. They pointed at her, laughed, and called her names. In the school hallways, twelve- and thirteen-year-old boys would pantomime sex acts, proposition her, make lewd gestures, and ask Vanessa details about the assault. One called out, "I wish it was me." She overheard another boy ask her attacker if he wore a condom and, if so, what brand. Vanessa had been sexually assaulted and filmed without her consent, but according to the unwritten rules of middle school, the boy who raped her was a hero and she was a ho. Vanessa spent more and more time hiding in the girls' bathroom.

On April 24, Vanessa was summoned to the principal's office. It had been more than three weeks since the assault. By then the video was circulating all over school. To Vanessa's horror, the video of her rape had also made its way to other middle and high schools in the city. Her friends' older siblings had seen it. In the principal's office, the school's resource officer met with Vanessa first. He'd seen the tape, he said, and asked Vanessa why she hadn't done more to fight off her attacker. "Have you ever been in a fight before?" he inquired. Vanessa said once she'd gotten into a scuffle with a girl from school. "Why didn't you fight him like that?" the officer wanted to know.

When the principal joined the meeting, she told Vanessa she'd also seen the tape and asked if the sex had been consensual. Vanessa told me she didn't remember giving the principal an answer. When she'd been asked, she said, she didn't even know what the word "consensual" meant.

Vanessa's mother was called to the school; so were the police. The cops took Vanessa and her mother to the 75th Precinct. When they arrived, the first person Vanessa saw was the boy who'd attacked her. He was already there with his parents. He looked up as Vanessa walked in and smirked. The officers asked Vanessa about the assault and warned her that if she pressed charges against the boy, there was a good chance that the boy's parents would press charges against her, too.

"For what?" she asked, confused.

"Underage sex," the officer said. Vanessa didn't understand what was going on. The officer was acting like *she* was the one in trouble. He kept pointing out that the boy was only thirteen and asking if she was *sure* the two of them weren't friends before the attack. Eventually, Vanessa and her mother went home.

A few days later, on April 27, Vanessa's mother returned to Spring Creek to ask about the possibility of Vanessa transferring to another school. The vice principal assured Vanessa's mother she would make arrangements for a safety transfer. In the meantime, she said, Vanessa should stay home since her presence at Spring Creek would only "make things worse."

"Wait," I interrupted, when Vanessa got to this part in the story. "Did anyone from your school refer you to counseling or legal services?"

"No," she answered.

"So you reported your assault," I said, slowly, "and then you were told not to come to school?"

Vanessa nodded yes. That's why she and her mother had come to see me, she explained. Her mother was confused by the bureaucracy and wanted help getting Vanessa back into school. But I was alarmed by what I was hearing: a child had been violently assaulted, then humiliated, bullied, and shamed by her classmates. In response, school administrators had effectively suspended her for reporting her abuse, denying her the right to an education. This is more than egregious treatment of a young victim of sexual assault; it's also against the law.

———

According to Title IX of the Education Amendments of 1972, when a student makes a report of sexual violence to a school administrator, a number of things are supposed to happen: the school is required to conduct a thorough and impartial investigation, protect the victim, and provide accommodations so the victim can continue his or her education in a safe environment. In addition, the school is supposed to take steps to prevent retaliation against the student for making the report.

When Title IX first became federal law, it wasn't intended to combat sexual misconduct at school. Originally, the goal of lawmakers was much more rudimentary. Title IX was a way to ensure that girls and women would not be discriminated against at schools because of their gender. Specifically, the thirty-seven-word clause mandates that women and girls must have equal access to education and programs offered at all schools that received federal funding, which includes K-12 public schools and most colleges and universities. In 1970, two years before Title IX was passed into law, only 8 percent of American women had college degrees, according to the US Department of Justice. Some colleges refused to admit female students; others had quotas, or higher admissions standards, for girls. Certain colleges and universities banned women from particular programs, like medicine, entirely. Title IX made these practices illegal, which changed everything. In 1972, men went to college at approximately twice the rate of women. By 2017, women were outpacing men on campus, making up more than 56 percent of students enrolled in colleges nationwide.

Title IX also ensured that girls and young women had access to the same athletic programs as their male counterparts, revolutionizing American sports. Between 1972 and 2011, the number of high school girls playing sports soared from less than three hundred thousand to more than three million. When Jackie Joyner-Kersee was a child, the only athletic program available to her was cheerleading. After Title IX passed, she was able to join her school's track team. She went on to compete in four consecutive Olympic games, breaking world records in the heptathlon and winning three gold medals, one silver, and two bronze. *Sports Illustrated* named Joyner-Kersee the greatest female athlete of the twentieth century.

Title IX was a game changer for women and girls. It made

available opportunities we now take for granted, like equal access to college or the right to play high school soccer on the same field as the boys. But it took more than two decades from the time Title IX was enacted before the Supreme Court, in two landmark decisions, determined that being sexually harassed, molested, or assaulted at school impacted girls' ability to access education, and therefore fell under the protection of Title IX. In 1999, the Supreme Court heard *Davis v. Monroe County Board of Education*, a case involving a fifth grader whose school repeatedly ignored reports that the girl was being sexually harassed by another student, creating a hostile and abusive environment. The court's ruling established that colleges, universities, and school districts receiving federal funding that respond to reports of sexual misconduct with "deliberate indifference" can be held responsible under Title IX and may be sued for damages.

Title IX became a powerful tool in combating sexual assault, especially on college campuses, leading to some notable legal actions. In 2007, for instance, a federal appeals court ruled that the University of Colorado Boulder (CU) could be held responsible for the 2001 rapes of two female students that took place during football recruitment season, following years of widely reported sexual misconduct involving the team. According to the ACLU, "The court held that . . . the risk of rape during recruiting visits was so obvious that CU violated Title IX by ignoring this risk." The school was sued and agreed to pay almost $3 million in damages to the victims.

Under Vice President Joe Biden's stewardship, during the Obama administration Title IX enforcement became a priority. The White House established the Task Force to Protect Students from Sexual Assault, offering colleges and universities resources and recommendations to combat sexual misconduct and comply with Title IX. In 2011, the US Department of Education's Office for Civil Rights (the agency that handles Title IX complaints) issued a nineteen-page

"Dear Colleague" letter reminding schools of the requirement to investigate and address reports of sexual assaults. The letter also detailed a variety of ways schools can respond to victims, such as connecting them to counseling, and noted that failure to comply with Title IX might cost a school its federal funding. In response, colleges spent millions of dollars putting in place Title IX coordinators, lawyers, investigators, caseworkers, survivor advocates, and other trained professionals to deal with complaints. In 2011, the Association of Title IX Administrators (ATIXA) did not exist. By 2016, the organization boasted five thousand members.

But while colleges attempted to adhere to Title IX regulations—with varying degrees of success—in many K-12 school districts across the country, administrators did the bare minimum when it came to compliance, if they paid any attention at all. In 2017, only eighteen states reported having any requirements for training K-12 teachers, school administrators, or students about peer-on-peer sexual violence, according to the Associated Press. Not surprisingly, the majority of high school guidance counselors reported feeling ill-equipped to address reports of abuse, according to Break the Cycle, a national organization aimed at reducing dating violence among teens.

Instead of offering students care and counseling, school administrators are often confounded by reports of sexual assault. They minimize, victim-blame, interrogate the victim in the presence of their alleged attacker, and dismiss accusations based on nothing more than a denial by the accused. Sometimes they deliberately try to cover up the crime. In an interview with the AP, Dr. Bill Howe, a former K-12 teacher who spent seventeen years overseeing Connecticut's compliance with Title IX, noted that, "no principal wants their school to be the rape school, to be listed in the newspaper as being investigated. Schools try to bury it."

Sometimes students who report sexual harassment and assault are deliberately pushed out of their schools. On a May 2017 episode of the *Reveal* podcast, AP reporter Emily Schmall, who worked on the news organization's yearlong investigation into peer-on-peer sexual violations in K-12 schools explained, "[Victims] are suspended or they're expelled or they're forced to transfer to another school, because the schools won't accommodate them in a way that allows them to go to school without being terrified of an assault happening again." This is exactly what happened to Vanessa.

Vanessa had been told by her principal to stay out of school until things calmed down. But there had been no follow-up. No one told Vanessa or her mother when she could return to school. They didn't even forward her any homework. By the time she and her mother came to see me, Vanessa had been out of school more than a week.

———

My first meeting with Vanessa and her mother lasted almost six hours. When they got up to leave, it was close to midnight. "I know this is hard," I told Vanessa as I walked her to the door. "I promise you won't feel like this forever. I'm going to do everything I can to help you. You aren't alone."

I stayed in my office until two a.m. trying to figure out a plan. This was my first sexual assault case, and Vanessa was my youngest client. I had never done anything like this before. All I knew for sure was that my client was in crisis. My first priority was getting her care.

Over the next week I filled an entire legal pad with notes. I called almost two dozen providers looking for a therapist who took Vanessa's mother's Medicaid and a trauma-informed pediatric gynecologist. I also made countless calls to the 75th police precinct to find out the status of the case. I learned the police had neither detained the boy nor charged him with a crime. Instead, they'd gone to his house for a "knock and talk," which is basically when cops try to scare the shit out of an offender with a stern warning. People often assume when police learn a crime has been committed and there's a suspect, they automatically make an arrest. But that's not how it works. Officers can use their discretion. And in this case, they thought giving the offender a good talking-to was an adequate response to a reported rape of a thirteen-year-old. This type of lackluster response on the part of law enforcement is shockingly common. According to federal crime data compiled by RAINN, the nation's foremost organization devoted to combating sexual assault, out of 230 reported rapes, only forty-six lead to an arrest. Only five of those cases result in a conviction.

I also sent Freedom of Information requests to the New York City Department of Education looking for any information relating to Vanessa's case and sent demand letters to DOE's lawyers insisting they preserve all related emails and internal writings. Meanwhile, I continued to work my way through the labyrinth of DOE requirements to get Vanessa enrolled in another school, which took a couple of weeks. It turned out her principal had not even initiated the process.

I also found Vanessa a therapist. But even after she began counseling, Vanessa confided to me that she frequently felt suicidal. I gave her my cell number and told her she could use it whenever she needed to talk. She'd text me sometimes, late at night, telling me she was having "bad thoughts." I'd call her right back. One time she was in the bathroom, fighting the urge to drink a bottle of bleach. "I can't take this anymore," she said, weeping. We talked a lot in those first few months, sometimes spending hours on the phone. If Vanessa was especially distraught, I would conference in the Suicide Prevention Lifeline so I could have an expert on the call.

Years after I'd started working her case, Vanessa texted "SOS" while I was in Los Angeles, in the writers' room for the Netflix teen drama *13 Reasons Why,* consulting about a revenge porn plotline. I excused myself and called her back. Vanessa was frantic. A girl at her new school was threatening to beat her up over a boy. The girl said she knew all about Vanessa's video. I returned to the meeting and delivered a diatribe about how teenagers can never escape a sexual assault. Even when they have doctors, lawyers, and therapists helping them, the kids at school won't let them move on.

It wasn't long after I found Vanessa a therapist that our legal strategy began to take shape. Of course we were going to sue the school in civil court. That was a given. But I thought we could strengthen our case by first lodging a complaint with the federal Department of Education Office for Civil Rights (DOE-OCR). Vanessa's case was such a clear violation of Title IX, I was sure they would rule in our favor, which would only bolster our position when we filed a civil suit down the road.

In November 2015, I filed our Title IX complaint with the DOE-OCR. I demanded an investigation into Vanessa's school and the school district's noncompliance with the federal law. I also included demands for systemic improvements that were very important to Vanessa. For instance, we required that all New York City schools be ordered to implement comprehensive policies for responding to students' reports of sexual misconduct, including the distribution of nonconsensual sexual images. "These policies and procedures must be such that they are likely to prevent future harassment and retaliation against complainants who report sexual abuse and harassment," I wrote in the complaint. Vanessa wanted to make sure that what happened to her didn't happen to anyone else.

I knew this couldn't have been easy for Vanessa. After a sexual assault, fighting back can feel like getting dragged into a war you didn't sign up for. And she wasn't battling only her attacker; she was going up against the largest public school system in the country. I was so proud of her. "You're a gladiator, a goddess, a warrior," I told her during one of our late-night calls. "What you are doing is so courageous. You're my hero."

On the other end of the line, Vanessa giggled: "Thanks, Ms. Carrie." She'd been a zombie when I first met her. Slowly Vanessa was coming back to life.

———

When I first started working on Vanessa's case, I assumed the way she'd been treated by her school's administration was an anomaly, an exception to how reports of serious sexual assaults are usually handled by public school administrators. But as months went by, I made a shocking discovery. Vanessa's mistreatment wasn't an outlier. What happened to her is part of an insidious pattern of punishing victims at New York City schools.

I first met "Destiny," a fifteen-year-old disabled student from Teachers Preparatory High School in Brownsville, Brooklyn, after her mother was referred to me by a law student at one of New York University School of Law's free legal clinics. Destiny has a severe developmental delay, loves chocolate chip cookies, and is fascinated by luxury cars, especially Mercedes. One afternoon in February 2016, Destiny was coaxed into an unsupervised stairwell at her school by a group of seven boys. Two of the boys forced Destiny to her knees and made her perform oral sex on them, while their friends watched and stood guard. A few days later, the boys told Destiny they were going to do it again. She complained to a school guidance counselor, who made a report of the incident. Destiny and one of the boys who'd watched the assault were called to the vice principal's office. The VP interviewed Destiny, and the boy, and determined that the behavior had been "consensual." He then suspended Destiny for engaging in sexual activity on campus, which is against school rules. It would be almost a month before her suspension was lifted.

Just like Vanessa's case, Destiny's assault was not properly investigated, no attempts were made to ensure she was safe from further attacks. Instead, she was effectively denied her education after she reported the assault.

After I took the case and sued the city, Destiny's assault was written about in the *New York Daily News*. Within days, another student's mother contacted me to share that her daughter had been sexually assaulted in that same stairwell, raped by a fellow student in 2010. In that case, the city had paid a $500,000 settlement to the victim, who for years suffered from PTSD as a result of the attack. I was infuriated to learn that the assault had happened under the same vice principal who was now punishing Destiny. I became convinced that the school's assertion that Destiny had engaged in "consensual sex" was actually an attempt to cover up that another assault had taken place in the same stairwell, in the same school, on the same administrator's watch. I immediately amended our suit to reflect that the school had been on notice that the unattended stairwell posed a risk to students prior to Destiny's assault. We doubled the amount of money we were demanding the city pay.

A few months after I started working with Destiny, I met "Kai," an eighth grader at Brooklyn's Middle School 584. In November of 2015, Kai had been tackled by two boys in a school hallway. One boy punched her in the vagina, then jumped on top of her and started simulating sex while the other boy slapped her in the head. One of her attackers was suspended for a month. When he returned to school, Kai was forced to see him during three classes and the lunch period they had in common. Kai started having anxiety attacks. Her mother requested a safety transfer to another school. But Kai was denied placement, a blatant violation of her Title IX rights for accommodations. It took Kai's mother almost two months traversing the bureaucratic maze of New York's public school system to find another school that would take her traumatized daughter.

Within one year, I was representing three clients between the ages of thirteen and fifteen, at three separate public schools in Brooklyn, all with similar stories of sexual assault followed by formal or informal school suspension after the victims reported the attacks. But that's not all my youngest clients have in common: Vanessa, Destiny, and Kai are all girls of color. These cases aren't only about gender discrimination; they are also about race.

———

In my line of work, it's impossible not to be aware of the impact of race on who gets considered an "innocent victim" and where we place our compassion and concern. Every day, I see the disparity play out in the way my clients and others are treated by law enforcement, school officials, the public, and the press. In sexual assault cases, for instance, white women are often seen as deserving protection in a way that women of color, in particular black women, are not. Even when racial biases are not openly acknowledged or spoken about, they exist below the surface, permeating our beliefs and behaviors. For decades, researchers have studied the effects of assumptions—also known as unconscious bias—we make about individuals based on their race, ethnicity, or other identities. One famous study showed that résumés from fictitious job applicants with white-sounding names (like "Conner," "Heather," or "Harrison") were offered follow-up interviews 50 percent more often than applicants with black-sounding names (like "Jamal," "Keisha," or "Shaquan"). Other research found medical professionals assumed black people were more likely to abuse pharmaceuticals and were less sensitive to pain than their white patients and routinely prescribed the patients less pain medication as a result, even when the patients were seriously ill children. A meta-analysis of forty-two studies on shooter bias found that individuals were quicker to shoot at targets depicting an armed black person than at those depicting an armed white person. And the US Government Accountability

Office found, in 2018, that teachers in K-12 schools were more likely to suspend black boys than white boys who committed the same infractions. This bias impacts children as soon as they enter the school system, according to the report. Black children make up 18 percent of preschool enrollment, but 48 percent of suspensions or expulsions.

When it comes to faulty assumptions adults levy against black girls, there is perhaps no study more elucidating than Georgetown Law Center on Poverty and Inequality's 2017 report *Girlhood Interrupted: The Erasure of Black Girls' Childhood*, which looked at adults' perceptions of black girls between the ages of five and fourteen. Researchers administered questionnaires to hundreds of adults from various backgrounds, ostensibly asking about child development in the twenty-first century. None of the participants knew the real purpose of the study. Instead, they were randomly assigned surveys that measured their attitudes about either white or black girls. Researchers found adults were more likely to view black girls as "more sexually mature" than their white peers, and also more knowledgeable about "adult topics." Adult respondents also regarded black girls as more "aggressive" and less in need of "nurturing, comfort and support." The study's authors note that adults ascribed to black girls supposed attributes of grown black women, features that are themselves rooted in racist stereotypes. For example, black girls are characterized as hypersexual—a toxic image of black women that has persisted since slavery—and, consequently, less childlike. The phenomenon, called "adultification," can have a profound effect on the way black girls are treated, especially by law enforcement and in schools.

"What we found is that adults see black girls as less innocent and less in need of protection as white girls of the same age," Rebecca Epstein, executive director of the Georgetown Law Center on Poverty and Inequality told the *Washington Post*. The compelling report describes adultification as "a form of dehumanizing," which the authors argue is "robbing black children of the very essence of what makes childhood distinct from other developmental periods: innocence."

Writing about the study in the *Washington Post*'s parenting blog, African American mother Jonita Davis noted wryly: "Any black mother could've told the researchers that, from the time they are talking and walking, little black girls are deemed 'fast,' a word synonymous with promiscuity."

When Destiny and Vanessa reported their assaults to school officials, there was no doubt the sex happened; no one ever suggested the girls were "making it up." The question in the minds of the administrators was about consent. In other words, maybe the girls had *wanted* it. The school's resource officer asked Vanessa repeatedly why, if the sex hadn't been consensual, she hadn't done more to fight off the boy? He was clearly skeptical of Vanessa's complaint.

After Destiny was assaulted in a stairwell at her school—an assault witnessed by multiple students—the vice principal of her high school not only deemed the act "consensual," he also sent a letter home to Destiny's mother, placing the blame squarely at her daughter's feet. "This behavior constitutes a danger to the health, safety, welfare and morals of your child and others at school," the letter read. The vice principal was holding Destiny—who has an IQ of 71—responsible for her own assault, and blaming her for being a bad influence on the entire student body. For the record, Destiny is unfailingly shy and had an unblemished school disciplinary record. Her best—and only— friend was her little brother.

The fear of being met with skepticism keeps many women from reporting their sexual assaults. For girls and women of color, the prospect of facing challenges to their credibility must feel insurmountable. Some experts estimate that for every black woman who reports her rape, at least fifteen stay silent about their assaults. This is three times as high as the nonreport rate among white women rape survivors. Other studies show that even when black women do step forward to report sexual assault, they are less likely to be believed than their white counterparts. And if the offender is brought to justice, the disparity is likely to continue. According to a review of relevant studies conducted by Brandeis University's Feminist Sexual Ethics Project, the adjudication of rape cases can vary significantly according to the race of the victim. Juries are more inclined to see black victims as less credible and their assaults as less serious. When presented with various rape crime scenarios, mock jurors were significantly more likely to find a defendant guilty when the victim was a white woman, compared to scenarios in which the victim was portrayed as black.

The lack of attention and care afforded to young black victims of sexual abuse and misconduct was brought into sharp focus in early 2019, when Lifetime aired a scathing six-part docuseries, *Surviving R. Kelly*. The series detailed the middle-aged R&B star's history of alleged serial predation and sexual abuse of underage black girls. Scores of victims, many of whom were first targeted by the singer while they were still in high school, shared anguished accounts of being groomed, manipulated, beaten, and sexually enslaved by Kelly. Almost as shocking as the scope of the abuse is the fact that Kelly's behavior had been allowed to continue, largely unchecked, for decades. Kelly's conduct had been the subject of credible press reports, was widely discussed in the music industry, and hotly debated among his fans. It was no secret. But where was the public outrage? In 2017, revelations about the gross sexual misconduct of dozens of powerful men, like Harvey Weinstein, Kevin Spacey, and Matt Lauer, led to widespread condemnation; the men were pushed out of their respective industries, fired, shunned, and canceled. Yet, somehow, Kelly evaded a #MeToo moment of his own. It wasn't until weeks after the docuseries aired that Sony Music, Kelly's record label, finally dropped the multiplatinum-selling artist from their roster. The obvious question—and one posed repeatedly in the wake of the Lifetime series—is would there have been more of an outcry if Kelly's young victims had been white?

In the final episode of *Surviving R. Kelly,* Tarana Burke, the founder of the Me Too movement, notes that the distraught parents of at least two of Kelly's victims had been trying to get the attention of media and law enforcement for years. "But [public perception is that] black girls don't matter," said Burke. "They don't matter enough." The Title IX cases I've brought on behalf of my clients against New York's Department of Education are about holding the city accountable for the value it places on black girls' lives.

In June 2016, six months after I filed Vanessa's Title IX complaint with the Department of Education's Office for Civil Rights, I filed two more complaints on behalf of Destiny and Kai. Since together these cases demonstrate a clear pattern of race-based neglect, I included race as another form of discrimination my clients had endured at school. I called on the federal Department of Justice, which has concurrent authority with the US Department of Education to enforce Title IX and conduct a joint investigation into the city's school system. "It is our strong belief that these incidents are indicative of institutionalized deliberate indifference to the needs of black female victims of sexual assault 'educated' by the New York City Department of Education," I wrote in my complaint. "Our clients' tortured experiences prove that the New York City Department of Education feels entitled to run a freewheeling bureaucracy exempt from state, federal, municipal, and administrative laws aimed at protecting our most vulnerable students."

In my demand for an investigation, I specifically requested the DOJ review New York City's Title IX resources, which were woefully inadequate. By federal law, all school districts, colleges, and universities receiving federal financial assistance must designate at least one employee to act as a Title IX coordinator, to oversee compliance with the law. As I noted in my complaint to the DOE-OCR, Harvard University has one Title IX employee for every 420 students. By comparison, New York City's Department of Education—which serves more than one million kids—has only one Title IX coordinator. One. Total.

When I opened my firm, the idea of representing clients who were still in middle school wasn't even on my radar. But by 2018 I'd filed seven Title IX complaints with the US Department of Education Office for Civil Rights, including five on behalf of middle and high school students who were sexually violated by their peers, then shamed and blamed by the school officials who were supposed to be protecting them.

———

Vanessa's case is one of the most meaningful I've handled at my firm. Not only because it put the entire New York City Department of Education on notice but also for a more personal reason: Vanessa helped save my firm.

Before we met, in May of 2015, I was teetering on the edge of financial ruin. I'd been in practice a little more than a year, and was running my business into the ground. Back then, I had a few clients, and I was representing almost all of them for free, including Vanessa. In the two months after taking her on as a client, I'd made less than $4,000 in revenue. My only advertising strategy, if you can call it that, consisted of tweeting feverishly about revenge porn and writing dazzling opinion pieces that ended up on my blog, which nobody read. In my free time, I created a map on my website that showed the revenge porn laws in every state, which I updated religiously. About a month after I opened my practice, *Brooklyn* magazine published an article in which I was described as a "revenge porn expert." I got a few clients after that. But not enough. Plus, I'd offered Adam, my intern at the time, a full-time job as soon as he passed the bar, which he was scheduled to take that July. I realized, with a knot in the pit of my stomach, there was no way I could pay him. I couldn't even pay myself.

And then there was the matter of office space. I held my first meeting with Vanessa and her mother in my tiny office in the shared workspace I rented in Dumbo. But by the end of that summer, it had become clear that I was going to have to move. At the time, I had an order of protection against my psycho ex, but it was about to expire, and I was scared. The building in Dumbo didn't feel safe. It was on a desolate street and the front door lock was always broken. Sometimes I'd still be working at two a.m. I felt exposed in an office with glass walls, where anyone could come in at any time of the night and find me all alone.

I hired a real estate agent and asked him to find me the cheapest office space in Brooklyn with twenty-four-hour security. He showed me a place on the twenty-fifth floor of a prewar building directly across the street from where I used to work at the Vera Institute of Justice. The space had huge windows with spectacular views of the Hudson River. Other than that, it was a dump, with dingy, low-slung ceiling tiles, peeling paint, and stained, puke-green carpeting. And it was way more than I could afford. But I had no choice; I had to feel safe. "I'll take it," I told my agent, with the caveat that the landlord agree to strip the paint, remove the carpet, and take down the ceiling tiles before I moved in. Then I went to the gym and took out my anxiety on a punching bag.

Looking back, I don't know what I was thinking. I was charging blindly ahead, fueled by Diet Mountain Dew and adrenaline, with no concrete plan for sustainability. Every meeting with Vanessa left me feeling guilty and ashamed because I knew my firm wasn't going to survive. I had to get my shit together, but I didn't even know where to start. They don't teach you how to run a business in law school.

Luckily for me, the landlord agreed to do the renovations, which bought me some time. In October, a few months before I was set to move into my new office, I attended the New York City Bar Association's annual conference for small law firms. There were a bunch of lectures on topics like social media for attorneys, and booths selling management software and malpractice insurance. I wasn't planning on getting much out of the conference. I'd gone with my best friend, Susan Crumiller, who was opening her own firm. Crumiller, P.C. would become a groundbreaking feminist law firm focusing on pregnancy discrimination, and a sister law firm fighting alongside us in many battles. But while at the conference, I attended a presentation led by a rep from a law firm management organization. He was gesticulating wildly and using decidedly unprofessional language, like "shit" and "asshole," which caught my attention in a good way. The rep was admonishing small law firm owners, like myself, for having a poverty mind-set. He said we acted like martyrs, in constant competition with one another over who put in the longest hours, got paid the least, and was the most miserable. Then he made an outrageous pronouncement: in a year and a half, he said, a law firm should be able to become a million-dollar company. It sounded preposterous, like some kind of scam. But the longer he spoke, the more excited I became. I was vibrating in my chair.

A few months later, Susan and I flew out to Malibu for our first law firm management conference. Over a weekend of back-to-back lectures on everything from cash flow projections to developing an owner mind-set, I absorbed the kind of life-changing lessons that make you wonder how you ever managed before. The first thing I learned is that I was doing my clients a horrible disservice. I was promising them a solution, without creating a business that would allow me to actually deliver. It seems obvious, but the realization hit me like a ton of bricks. I kept thinking about Vanessa. Who would I refer her to if I went out of business? Handing off her case wasn't an option; I had to keep my firm afloat.

I realized I had to be strategic, analytical, and disciplined. I had to think about sales, marketing, and financial controls. If my ultimate goal was to help as many people as possible, I had to grow my business and make it profitable so I could hire more attorneys. If I wanted to run a company, I had to be a boss.

I also learned it takes a certain confidence to turn a business around. You have to believe you're entitled to success. But that didn't come easily for me. Ever since I opened my firm, I'd felt like an imposter. I hadn't done particularly well in law school, and I guess I'd resigned myself to a life of professional mediocrity. I didn't think I could do Big Things. But then I met Vanessa. Her case was bigger than anything I could have imagined. We were fighting the entire fucking city of New York.

I came back from the conference and started to hustle. I devoured self-help books and small-business manuals. I learned how to write a business plan and a budget. I put systems into place and learned how to delegate work so I could hire more staff and not do every single thing myself. I learned how to work on my business and make it grow. Within a year, I'd hired a receptionist, another associate lawyer, and a marketing person. By 2016, I'd increased my revenue by 400 percent. In 2018, Law Firm 500 declared my firm the fastest growing in the country. In three years I'd increased my revenue by almost 2000 percent. I don't know if any of this would have happened if I hadn't been so scared of failing my youngest client. I got my shit together because I couldn't stand the thought of letting Vanessa down.

———

In February 2017, billionaire and Republican mega-donor Betsy De-Vos was confirmed as the Trump administration's secretary of education. One of DeVos's first acts of power was to rescind Obama's Title IX guidelines, which she called "a failed system." Survivor advocates are no fans of DeVos. But you know who loves her? Guys who've been accused of rape.

Shortly after taking office, DeVos met with various men's rights activists for guidance on how best to investigate sexual assaults on campus. Men's rights activists routinely argue that countless innocent young men's lives are being ruined by the scourge of false rape accusations plaguing our nation's colleges. (In fact, some experts estimate that false allegations account for less than 1 percent of reported rapes.) Arguably, a far greater problem is the vast majority of rapes that are never reported. Rape is the most underreported of all crimes, according to the National Sexual Violence Resource Center. On college campuses, more than 90 percent of sexual assault victims do not report the crime.

After almost two years in office, DeVos finally unveiled a proposal for a new set of Title IX guidelines. Her sweeping overhaul lessened liability for colleges and gave new rights to the accused, including the chance to cross-examine their accuser. Advocates, myself included, disagree vehemently with the notion that justice will be best served by allowing victims to be interrogated by their attackers. In fact, the initiative seems like a particularly cruel deterrent, designed to keep victims from coming forward and reporting their crimes.

Once DeVos took the helm at the DOE, I changed strategies. Instead of aggressively pursuing Title IX investigations, I turned my attention to filing civil suits on behalf of my clients without waiting for a finding from the DOE's Office for Civil Rights first. In January 2018, I filed a civil lawsuit against the city of New York on behalf of Destiny, my client who'd been sexually assaulted by a group of boys in her school stairwell. Six months later, on a gloriously sunny day in June, we reached a settlement; the city agreed to pay Destiny $950,000.

I know the money will never compensate for Destiny's pain. She may carry the weight of what happened to her in that stairwell forever. But the money will make her life more comfortable, which is what she deserves. After the judge awarded the settlement amount, Destiny and her mother came to my office for fancy cookies to celebrate. The money is going to be paid out to her over many years. It was enough for Destiny to take care of her family and get herself something nice, too. I asked her if she had anything special in mind. She beamed and told me she wanted to take her mother and brother to visit Disney World for the very first time.

———

In July 2018, on Vanessa's behalf, I filed a civil lawsuit against the city of New York, its Department of Education, the city's schools chancellor, and the principal of Vanessa's middle school. We are suing these entities and individuals for, among other infractions, violating Vanessa's right to education as stipulated in Title IX of the Education Amendments Act of 1972 and Title IV of the Civil Rights Act of 1964. We are also suing for their negligence in breaching their duty to protect a student in their care and intentional infliction of emotional distress. My client was harmed; someone needs to pay.

When Vanessa walked into my office three and a half years earlier, she had been a shattered child, as lifeless as a zombie. Fighting back helped her gain back control. Three months after we sued the city, Vanessa spoke publicly about her assault for the very first time. We were at a protest at City Hall organized by the Brooklyn-based advocacy group Girls for Gender Equity (Tarana Burke is the organization's senior director). I'd been working with GGE on their School Girls Deserve campaign to create safer school environments for girls of color by, among other things, calling on the city to hire more Title IX coordinators. There were several speakers, but I couldn't take my eyes off Vanessa. She shined like a star.

"Three and a half years ago, I went through a nightmare I thought I would never wake up from," she began in a bold, clear voice. "I felt like I was all alone in the cold, dark world. To women in the world who have been through this," she continued, "I want you to know you are not alone." Vanessa had come to me in need of help; now she was the one offering solace. It was one of the proudest moments of my life.

CHAPTER 5

GODWIN'S LAW

ave you ever heard of Godwin's law? It's not a real law, but an internet meme that says that if an online discussion goes on long enough, sooner or later somebody will interject with a comparison to Adolf Hitler or the Nazis. Well, we've come to that part of this book. I can't really talk about my motivation for becoming a lawyer, or my theories about justice for victims, without taking it back to the Holocaust.

In the summer of 1999, I moved to New York, a fresh graduate from Vassar College with a not-particularly-marketable English degree. For a couple of months, I fumbled around trying to find my way. I did a few shifts at a dessert restaurant near my tiny shared apartment, which was nestled between two hard-core gay sex shops on Christopher Street in the West Village. I worked for several months at the New York Foundation for Senior Citizens and for a few weeks as an assistant at an ad agency. Then I made a life-changing discovery.

An organization called Selfhelp was advertising in the *New York Times* for a caseworker for their Holocaust survivors program.

Selfhelp had been founded in the 1930s, when Jews escaping Hitler's Nazi regime first started pouring into New York. The organization was called Selfhelp because members would help one another adjust to the city and find jobs, apartments, and schools for their kids. I interviewed for the position in a tiny office in Washington Heights and was hired in the spring of 2000.

Selfhelp was like boot camp for learning how to work with people in extreme mental anguish. I'd taken the job because I am Jewish and it felt like a privilege to surround myself with firsthand witnesses of the Holocaust, an ever-shrinking population that was diminishing before my eyes. But that privilege came at a cost. The job forced me to come to terms with the cruelty of life.

I grappled daily with the harsh reality that lives are not valued equally. And I learned that when power is left unchecked, there are those who will sacrifice the autonomy of others to satisfy their own lust for wealth and control. Viktor Frankl's *Man's Search for Meaning* became a guide for me, and it still is. Frankl, a psychiatrist who survived the Holocaust, says that while some of us find meaning in pain and suffering, transcending to a higher level of self-actualization, for others, pain is a continual reminder of all they have lost.

At Selfhelp, I sat at deathbeds with clients who never found spiritual or therapeutic relief. They died brokenhearted, having spent their entire lives grieving for everything that had been taken from them. The perspective I gained on human suffering, and the rage I banked during those years informs everything I do for my clients today.

The people I worked with at Selfhelp were either "Holocaust survivors" or "Nazi victims." The distinction is that "survivors" had been in concentration camps or in hiding during the war, while "victims" had fled Europe before the war. My job entailed making home visits to my clients, most of whom lived in Washington Heights, Inwood, and Riverdale. I had a caseload of fifty people, and saw about three clients each day. I'd walk miles and miles in four-inch heels up and down streets in the hilliest parts of New York. I don't remember why I started wearing heels, but it became my signature. And boy, I got hell from my clients if I wasn't wearing them. Many of my clients were homebound. Their connection to the outside world was daytime talk shows, Meals on Wheels, and me. I felt it my duty to dress to impress.

I was the youngest caseworker at Selfhelp. Most of my colleagues were middle-aged; my clients were in their late seventies and eighties. Their spouses and friends were dead or dying. Their bodies were failing them. For people who'd survived the Holocaust, especially those who'd been in the camps, aging is different than it is for the general population. In captivity, physical health meant survival. The awareness that their bodies were slowing down felt like a betrayal to many of my clients, and came with a sense of impending doom. When survivors' memories started to go, many would imagine they were back in the camps, and revert to speaking only their native tongue, living in a constant loop of dementia-fueled PTSD.

One client had her tattered concentration camp uniform hanging in the closet. She confided to me that she would sometimes wear it to bed. Another, Ms. W., who emigrated in the '30s from Germany, would hallucinate about her father coming back from World War I. For reasons no one knew, every day she'd get out of bed and move all her furniture to build a blockade against her bedroom door. Eventually, her home-care workers emptied the drawers of Ms. W.'s bureau so that it was light enough for her to move without hurting herself. Ms. W. was blind and didn't remember me from one visit to the next. When I stopped by to check in on her, I'd speak with the home aide, then sit and pat Ms. W.'s hand. She had no family. When she finally died, I was called to identify her body. The owner of the cemetery and I were the only people at her funeral. Ms. W. was 109 years old.

Sometimes, the only thing my clients wanted when I visited was for me to listen to their stories. Other times, I'd accompany them to their doctors' appointments, or to the bank, or to see their lawyers. I'd find them referrals for home health aides and cleaning ladies. I'd visit them in the hospital, or nursing home, if they got sick. I'd help them with their medical benefits and negotiate with their insurance companies if a procedure or pill wasn't covered. I did whatever needed to get done.

One very religious woman whose entire family lived in Israel asked me to pluck her chin hairs. Another woman wanted me to remove the stitches doctors had put in her head after she'd injured herself in a fall. If I took them out, she insisted, I'd save her from having to go back to the doctor. I accepted clients' invitations for Passover and went with them on Saturdays to visit the Museum of Modern Art. I admit, I did not know anything about maintaining professional boundaries. I grew to prefer the company of my clients to hanging out with my peers. I bought my clients presents for their birthdays and introduced them to little joys of life, like massages and this crazy new thing, the internet. I found a translation program online that helped me read the government letters my clients received from Germany and Austria.

My clients shared bits and pieces of their lives with me—often the saddest parts were what stuck with them. Mrs. C., who'd survived the Holocaust in Shanghai, told me that her husband made her get an abortion every time she got pregnant because he wanted to wait until they had the money to support a baby. She died many years after him, childless. Mr. H., whom I adored, lived in the same building as Dr. Ruth. He and I would go on long walks around Fort Tryon Park, looking at the flowers. Mr. H. told me he'd survived the war by taking his boat out to sea but got shipwrecked off the coast of Italy. No country would claim him. It was a harrowing story that ultimately became a book. Mr. H. was addicted to infomercials. His apartment was full—like, hoarder full—of plastic baby dolls, ThighMasters, and souvenir plates. Every surface was covered with stuff. When he died, he died alone.

There was always something: I'd get calls informing me that a home aide hadn't shown up; a home aide was stealing underwear; a client's daughter was in town and wanted to meet me. I'd get calls that somebody fell out of their wheelchair, had a stroke, a cancer diagnosis, wouldn't get out of bed, couldn't get out of bed, died in bed.

One of my most painful memories from that time involves what happened with Mrs. P. She was a widow and childless. She had survived the camps and was fiercely private. Unlike most of my other clients, Mrs. P. didn't bother masking her anger. She lived in a prewar building near our offices, and she'd go out all day, almost every day. I never knew where to. Maybe she was at the synagogue or visiting her husband's grave. Mrs. P. and I kept in touch mostly by phone. As private as she was, she still let me bring her food packages for Yom Kippur and Rosh Hashanah. And she would usually come to the "Kaffehauses" we'd have once a month on Saturdays. We'd serve cookies and coffee and invite the hokiest performers, including a guy who wore cartoonish giant foam hands and acted out the disco classic "Y.M.C.A." I took Mrs. P.'s willingness to attend our modest social events as a sign of trust.

One week, I was trying to get in touch with Mrs. P., but she wasn't answering my calls or returning my messages. I left her a note on her door asking her to contact me. Nothing. I asked her neighbors if they'd seen her. They hadn't. I had this horrible feeling that she'd died inside her apartment. She had no friends, no family, no home-care attendant, no relationship with any of her neighbors. She was the most isolated person I'd ever known. So I called the police. When they arrived, we climbed onto the neighbor's fire escape and tried to peer into Mrs. P.'s apartment, but we couldn't see a thing. The police broke the locks. I expected the worst—but her body wasn't there. It was just a really sad and dark apartment, sparsely furnished, with plastic bags containing more plastic bags littering every surface. I left a note on her door asking her to phone so I could explain what had happened.

The next day, Mrs. P. called me. She was furious that I'd broken in. She accused me of trespassing and complained that she'd had to fix the locks. When I replied that I was worried about her and didn't know where she'd been, she said she didn't need to report her comings and goings to me. "It's none of your business," she said. And she was right. She'd been fine for years without me, she added. "Just leave me alone." She never spoke to me again.

At Selfhelp, I'd grown proud of my ability to stay calm and problem-solve. No matter what my clients needed, I'd figure out a way to deliver. But helping without being intrusive is a delicate balance. With Mrs. P., I had inadvertently crossed a line. It's one of the biggest regrets of my life. It was also a wake-up call: Was my fear about her safety reasonable? Or had I fabricated an emergency to respond to?

In retrospect, it's crazy that, at twenty-two, I was serving the complex needs of people who'd survived such unimaginable brutality. It's also crazy that I stayed working there for so long. For five years I convinced myself my clients needed me; I'd become addicted to managing their crises, and their pain.

———

Working at Selfhelp was a really hard job. Not before or since have I had a job as emotionally challenging. The whole time I worked there, I never stopped thinking about my clients. And I became obsessed with the Holocaust. I'd read about the atrocities committed at the camps and watch documentaries about survivors. I'd spend my days off visiting Holocaust museums in New York and DC. One year for vacation, I went to Auschwitz. Sometimes at night I would dream I was on a cattle car with all my worldly possessions.

When I wasn't at work, I tried to escape my thoughts. During the week, if I wasn't at the gym, I was sleeping. On the weekends, I got high. It was the only way I could bear being around people my own age—my friends with their cool New York jobs at Condé Nast or doing reception work at art galleries and feminist nonprofits. Back then I didn't possess the maturity to know how important it is for me to create some distance between myself and my clients' suffering for my own mental health.

These days, whenever I give a talk, invariably somebody asks what I do for "self-care." They always sound concerned. After a momentary cringe (I HATE that question so much—maybe because it's a question none of my male colleagues ever get asked), I usually respond with, "My self-care is real simple: 450 milligrams of Wellbutrin a day, running marathons, and sex." The sex thing always startles them. As though somebody who rails against nonconsensual sex can't also celebrate consensual sex. But I digress.

In 2003, after I'd been at Selfhelp for several years, I decided to enroll in law school. I had a dream that maybe with a law degree I could do the same type of work I was doing with my clients at Selfhelp—advocating for survivors of genocide—but on a larger scale. I imagined myself one day working at an advocacy organization like Human Rights Watch. Or maybe doing something with international truth and reconciliation tribunals. The only problem was I felt guilty every time I thought of "abandoning" my clients at Selfhelp. (I know better now—if a person survives a genocide, she can survive her twenty-five-year-old buddy going off to school. But I didn't have that perspective then.) So instead of leaving Selfhelp entirely, I enrolled in Brooklyn Law School, where I could pursue my degree at night.

The days were long. I'd leave for work at eight a.m., ride the subway forty-five minutes, work until five p.m., and cram on the hour-long subway ride back to Brooklyn. Then I'd run to class, which lasted until nine at night. Law school was hit-and-miss. I made some good friends, but I also met a lot of jerks—the type who love debating random legal concepts but don't have a clue about real life.

One night I got into a debate in my first-year torts class over the idea of bystander liability. I argued that if a person witnesses another person getting hurt and is able to help, it's immoral for that person to do nothing. I said, "You know, the train tracks to Treblinka went through a lot of private property." The next thing I knew I was in the midst of a heated argument with two other students and a teacher who accused me of "going there." I wanted to tell them all to fuck off. "Going there" was what I did every single day, from nine to five, before lugging twenty pounds of legal textbooks into class to debate ideas with these privileged assholes who were competing mercilessly against one another for the few "good" jobs doing mergers and acquisitions at some midtown law offices.

I had a crap attitude about law school. I didn't study except during my commute, and the esoteric legal concepts just didn't click. Not surprisingly, I got a lot of shitty grades.

But in some classes, I excelled. I loved the hands-on legal work we did in clinics. I was best in show at my mediation clinic and worked on three successful asylum cases at the Safe Harbor Clinic. One of the most interesting classes I took was about the ethics of medical experimentation. At Selfhelp, I'd had several clients who'd been experimented on by Nazis in the camps. Mrs. G. had been part of Josef Mengele's twins experiments. Mengele, known as the Angel of Death, would cut out prisoners' eyes, remove their teeth, amputate limbs, and inject deadly viruses and lethal chemicals into their bodies, just to see what would happen. He performed many of his experiments on children; he once sewed a pair of toddler siblings together to create conjoined twins (they died of gangrene a few days later).

Mrs. G. wasn't a twin herself but had twin brothers, which made her of interest to Mengele. One day, shortly after 9/11, I was at her home in the Bronx. Mrs. G. was comparing the ashes at Ground Zero to the ashes of prisoners killed in Hitler's gas chambers that had been dumped in the Vistula River. Suddenly, she pulled up her housecoat and showed me a huge hole in her buttock from where she'd been injected while imprisoned at Auschwitz.

She'd shown it to me before. Anytime we talked about the financial restitution Holocaust survivors were paid after the war, Mrs. G. would raise her housedress to emphasize how much more she'd suffered than some of the Nazi victims who'd immigrated to the United States before the war. Some victims who'd fled Germany early received hundreds of thousands of dollars over the years in German social security payments. By comparison, Mrs. G. had been freed from Auschwitz by the Russians and spent most of her life behind the Iron Curtain before immigrating to the United States in the mid-1990s. Consequently, she was not entitled to this benefit issued by the German government. In fact, Mrs. G., who'd lost her twin brothers, parents, and all her friends in the camps, qualified for almost nothing in financial restitution.

In her living room that day, I told Mrs. G. about a new compensation fund we could apply for that had been created especially for victims of medical experiments. But I felt horrible explaining that the one-time lump sum payment was only a paltry $2,500—an insult. Many of my clients were ambivalent about restitution payments. Some considered accepting "blood money" a betrayal of the family they'd lost in the camps. Others felt that taking the payments was akin to accepting an apology. They didn't want the money, but when they saw their friends take it, few could resist. I filled out Mrs. G.'s paperwork; she used the money to pay the arrears she owed her landlord.

———

In law school, during my first-year torts class, I learned about distributive and corrective justice and immediately recognized how my work with Holocaust reparations fell into a legal framework. I believe in economic justice: if somebody is injured, the person or entity responsible must pay. This concept drives a lot of the work I do with my clients today. The criminal justice system is all about meting out punishment to people who break the law. Meanwhile, the victim of that crime walks away with nothing. It's the civil justice system that enables us to sue and actually get tangible compensation for the injured person from the wrongdoer. I know it's crude to put a price tag on suffering, but sometimes it's the only way to make things right. The idea is that the dollar amount should be enough to make a victim "whole." Money won't take away pain. But it will make your life more comfortable. Justice for my clients includes a more comfortable life.

During the years I worked at Selfhelp, major developments were happening with funds available for victims of Nazi persecution. Suddenly, there was money available for people who'd put their life savings in Swiss banks and for Hungarians who did forced labor in Austria. Non-Czech citizens could get partial compensation for real estate they'd fled and seek the return of art that had been confiscated by the Nazis. Hungarians, who'd previously been eligible for only a measly $200 for each parent or sibling killed in the Shoah, in 2003 could apply for a second payment of $1,800.

I spent a lot of time on one particular restitution program: Germany had announced that it would credit forced labor toward social security. I had three Polish clients, all of whom had been forced to work at the same Nazi-held airfield in Poland. I applied for all three. Germany gave one client a lump sum of more than $20,000 and ongoing payments of several hundred dollars a month for the rest of his life. Another client's application was rejected. The third client received something in between. I started focusing more and more attention on the seemingly arbitrary application of financial restitution. My anger over the issue is one of the factors that prompted me to study law.

At Selfhelp, I became known as the queen of reparations. I once added up all the money I'd secured for my clients. It was close to $2 million. But I actually saved them many times that amount because I discovered that if we deposited the money they'd received in reparations into specifically designated accounts, those funds were tax-free and exempt when calculating their eligibility for US benefits. This meant that when they got sick, they'd qualify for Medicaid sooner, which would pay for nursing homes and home health attendants, and they would still have money left over for life's little luxuries and maybe something to leave their grandkids.

———

I graduated from law school in 2007 with big plans to do important work in human rights. But I couldn't get my foot in the door. I didn't have a foreign-language background. I didn't have a degree from a pedigreed school. I didn't even have the grades needed to answer phones at Human Rights Watch. Nobody cared about my experience.

I applied for job after job at nonprofits until I was finally hired by the nonprofit agency Housing Conservation Coordinators to do tenant litigation for low-income people facing eviction in Hell's Kitchen. It was not the policy job at Human Rights Watch I'd envisioned for myself, but it was the best thing that could have happened to me. I was immediately thrown into the courtroom by my take-no-prisoners boss, Aurore DeCarlo.

The litigation skills and done-is-better-than-perfect industrious work ethic I learned from Aurore have been invaluable since. Two years later, in 2009, I got a job at the Vera Institute of Justice in the Guardianship Project. The people in my care were elderly or mentally incapacitated. Just as I had been at Selfhelp, at the Vera Institute I was a lot of things to a lot of people. Some were facing life-and-death decisions and had no family to advocate on their behalf.

One elderly man was at the end of his life, dying from stomach cancer. The doctors proposed invasive tests, radiation, and chemo. My client had no family and no friends. His dementia was too advanced for him to express his medical wishes, and he never shared an end-of-life plan with anybody we could find. At the time, the legal default for hospitals was to treat patients aggressively unless the hospital had an instruction not to. That instruction needed to come from the patient or a proxy the person had legally appointed. The Vera Institute was court-appointed to make medical decisions but not end-of-life ones. I petitioned the court to let my client die with dignity. The doctors testified that the interventions might lengthen his life but also his suffering. The judge granted in my favor, and we opted out of the painful treatment. The ruling was a case of "first impression," meaning the law I used was being applied for the first time. There was even a little write-up about my handling of the case in the *New York Law Journal*. After that, petitioning for the peaceful passing of our dying wards became a regular part of my job.

The work I did at Vera was exhausting but also exhilarating. I got to use the law in all sorts of new and creative ways. I filed a lawsuit and won back the deed to a delusional client's $7 million brownstone after she'd been tricked into transferring the title to some crooks. For another client, I sued a hospital to stop it from getting Child Protective Services involved preemptively in a case involving an eight-months-pregnant woman who'd suffered a traumatic brain injury. I successfully petitioned the court to allow my client's aunt to adopt my client's healthy baby boy. My work gave me a sense of purpose and accomplishment, and the same adrenaline high I'd felt when I got restitution for my Holocaust survivors. My professional life couldn't have been going any better. My personal life, however, was a different story.

During those years, I'd gotten married and amicably divorced. Newly single, I discovered I was really terrible at dating. Then, in 2012, I met the man I thought was going to be the love of my life. He seemed like Mr. Perfect and swept me off my feet. Months later, *my* life was the one spinning out of control.

CHAPTER 6

PROFITEERS OF PAIN

I was working at the Vera Institute in the winter of 2012 when I first started dating my psycho ex. He found me on the dating app Ok-Cupid. Before we met in person, he said he'd already fallen in love with my profile, which, I admit, was a compendium of quirkiness. In the "self-summary" section, I'd written that the best moment of my life was in a mosh pit at a Nirvana concert, that I'd gone to law school "to distract myself from the Holocaust," and that "I love the look of diamond rings and blingy bracelets while butchering chicken." There were a lot of Brooklyn hipster chicks on the site; I was trying to stand out. I also mentioned that I could high-kick like a Rockette.

Right away my ex and I fell into easy and constant communication, spending hours on our phones texting late into the night. He sent me links to his fashion label and told me he'd gone to Wharton business school. He casually bragged that he'd also completed "80 percent" of a law degree at UPenn while he was there. But mostly, he wanted to know about me. "Where you from?" he messaged. "What do you listen to? Fav movies? Food? Afraid of? What are three things you want/need that you don't have?" I told him about my phobia of worms and confessed that I yearned for my dead grandfather's revolver from World War II. I told him about the childhood blankie I slept with every night until I was twenty-five then left at a hotel in DC when visiting the Holocaust Memorial Museum. I told him I hate the feeling of a gentle breeze, the sound of bagpipes, and being cold. He seemed enthralled by every detail I shared. I'd spent my entire adult life devoting myself totally to the needs of my clients. His attention felt like the perfect antidote.

I remember our first date. We planned to meet at Montero Bar a few blocks from the Kings County courthouse in Brooklyn, where the Vera Institute had its offices. That afternoon, I was attending a guardianship hearing for an elderly client who had recently had her social security cut off. The hearing room was stuffy, with flickering fluorescent lights and stained ceiling panels, and filled with exhausted adults and crying babies. As I waited for my case to be heard, all I could think about was finally meeting the man I'd spent hours messaging with online. Anticipation is a great aphrodisiac.

I glanced around the room to make sure no one was looking, then slid my phone from my purse and quickly snapped a pic. It was a leggy shot of my fitted black pencil skirt, crossed legs, and black patent leather Narciso Rodriguez crocodile-embossed stilettos. I hit "send" and slid my phone back in my purse. I felt sexy, flirty, and in control.

We sent each other a lot of snapshots in those early days. Well, *I* sent them and he replied enthusiastically. On a trip to Washington State to visit my family, much to my brother's and sisters' consternation, my ex and I texted nonstop. At night I sent him graphic pics, illuminated by the mirrored lamp in my childhood room. "Beautiful!!!" he texted back. "Send more." I did.

A few weeks into our relationship, on Valentine's Day, he gave me a present: an iPad mini with a green rubber cover. He liked to film me when we were in bed. He wouldn't always ask. I'd just open my eyes and catch him leaning over me with a grin. We broke up four months later, after I realized that what I had mistaken for "intensity" and "devotion" were actually the warning signs of a possessive, volatile freak. My psycho ex went off the rails as soon as I told him we were done.

In less than a week, he bombarded me with 277 texts, seventy emails, and twenty-five minutes of voicemails. Peppered between declarations that he still loved me were accusations that I was a whore. He forwarded to me every single email that I'd written him in our early days, a reminder that he knew my secrets. One day, the super at the building where I lived told me that my ex had tried to trick him into giving him keys to my apartment when I wasn't there.

Terrified, I went to stay with my best friend. In the middle of the night, after she and her family had gone to sleep, I opened my laptop and found an avalanche of emails from my ex. One by one, I clicked them open with shaking hands. They contained dozens of pictures of me, some clothed, many not. Attached to one email was a sexually graphic video of me he'd filmed without my knowledge. He said he'd blind-copied my boss and judges I worked with on the email. I slammed shut my laptop and had one of those out-of-body experiences where you feel like you're suddenly free-falling through space. I took deep breaths until I felt steady enough to stand. I quickly dressed and went to the police precinct to report the crime. The officers shrugged and told me there was nothing they could do.

The following Monday morning, I went to Kings County Family Court to petition for a temporary order of protection. Judges routinely issue orders of protection, also known as restraining orders, to limit the type of contact one person can have with another in cases where there is an alleged, or proven, history of stalking, threats, or violence. For instance, a judge might order an abusive man to stay one hundred yards away from his ex and not contact her family or friends.

I wanted a court order instructing my ex to stay away from me. But I also requested that the judge add language to the order specifically forbidding my ex from distributing my intimate images or videos online.

Working at the Vera Institute, I'd spent a lot of time at the courthouse—a dreary high-rise in downtown Brooklyn—representing my guardianship clients. But this was the first time I was there seeking assistance for myself. I dug into my purse for the Secure Pass that attorneys use to skip the snaking line of people waiting to get through the metal detectors on the first floor. Then I remembered that in the tumult of the previous week, I'd lost my wallet. I had no choice but to join the procession of weary men holding manila folders, and exhausted-looking women balancing fidgeting toddlers on their hips.

I sat for what felt like hours on a wooden bench in the waiting area before the clerk finally called my name. But the minute I stepped inside the courtroom, I froze. I recognized the judge immediately as a former court attorney whom I'd encountered multiple times while working guardianship cases in Manhattan. When the judge glanced up from his bench I could see a flicker of surprise flash across his face. *Just act normal*, I told myself, straightening my back. I tried not to think about what my former colleague was imagining as he read my petition, which, of course, mentioned sexually explicit photos and my desperate plea to keep them off the internet. I held my breath and waited for his response.

Finally, he looked up. "Miss Goldberg," he said. "I know you're a lawyer, but I suggest you find someone to represent you. This is family court. What you have here is a First Amendment problem." The judge explained he couldn't order my psycho ex to not post my pictures online because it would violate his right to free speech.

I felt like I'd been punched. I'd asked this judge to protect me from having my privacy violated. He'd responded by letting me know that my ex had a constitutional right to express himself by exposing my naked body to the world. I tried to argue, but the judge cut me off. He issued a temporary no-contact order and scheduled a hearing for a month later for a permanent order of protection. He said he was recusing himself from the case due to our prior work relationship, but I could take up my concerns about privacy with the new judge.

I felt totally defeated leaving the courthouse that day. Actually, it was worse than that: I was terrified. All I could think of were the photos my ex had in his possession and the public humiliation and professional ruin he could cause me with just a few clicks of his mouse. "A tsunami is coming," he'd warned me. "There is no hole deep enough for you to hide."

My ex did many shitty things to me after our relationship ended: he threatened me with violence, harassed my friends and family, contacted my exes, spread vicious lies about me through social media, and filed a fake police report that got me thrown behind bars. But of all the terror he wrought, his threats to distribute my naked photos shook me the most.

In the few days before I was able to get a temporary order of protection preventing him from contacting me, my ex texted me constant reminders that he still had the iPad mini with the green rubber cover, filled with intimate, sexual, and embarrassing photographs of me.

One night he threatened to fax the images to my niece's preschool. In 2013, New York State, like many jurisdictions at the time, did not have a law on the books that made it illegal to distribute someone else's naked pictures without their consent. The state wouldn't pass such a law until 2019.

For years, I lived with the sickening reality that my ex could do whatever he wanted with my naked photos. I felt, like so many of my clients, as though I'd lost all control. Sexual privacy is one of those things you don't really appreciate until it's taken from you. Still, to be robbed of this basic right is commonplace. Roughly one in twenty-five Americans—or ten million people—has faced the threat or reality of having their intimate pictures exposed without their consent, according to a 2016 study by the Center for Innovative Public Health Research. And more than 90 percent of victims of this type of abuse experience mental health consequences; almost 50 percent report contemplating suicide. That's how hopeless this type of violation can make victims feel.

———

In my practice, we receive at least half a dozen phone calls and emails every day from desperate and inconsolable victims whose nude pictures have been delivered to the internet on a silver platter. And once an image is released on the web, it can go anywhere. I have dozens of clients whose intimate images were circulated on *hundreds* of different porn websites. If you google their names, you'll find page upon page of results featuring close-ups and videos of my clients' breasts and genitalia along with vile commentary posted by trolls or, as they sometimes call themselves, "fans." These violations are commonly known as revenge porn, but that moniker misses the point. It isn't always about revenge.

The real issue is the violation of victims' rights to privacy and ability to control who gets to see them naked. This is about consent. A more accurate term to describe the offense is "nonconsensual pornography" or "nonconsensual distribution of intimate images." Either of these terms is certainly more reflective of the range of circumstances that lead people to my door.

I have clients whose private photos have been uploaded to the web by angry exes, jealous friends, horny frat boys, teenage trolls, malicious hackers, vicious pimps, and even their rapists. Sometimes these explicit images and videos are made public to humiliate or "punish" a target. Other times they are used as a means of extorting sex or money.

Frequently, my clients only learn of the violation after their images turn up on dedicated porn websites with their contact information attached, and some pervy guy contacts them. Or the images land on social media. In January 2017 alone, Facebook reported receiving fifty-one thousand complaints about revenge porn. Multiply that number by twelve months and factor in all the other social media platforms that people use, and you begin to grasp the extent of the problem. The distribution of revenge porn is widespread precisely *because* the motives of perpetrators extend far beyond revenge. Sometimes there is no discernable motive other than the perverse thrill some offenders get from viewing, sharing, and commenting on private images that the subject did not give them permission to see.

––––––

In 2010, well before the term "revenge porn" became a thing, eighteen-year-old Rutgers University freshman Tyler Clementi, a talented and soft-spoken violinist, asked his roommate if he could have the room for a few hours because he had a date. Unbeknownst to Clementi, his roommate, Dharun Ravi, had turned on his computer's webcam and trained it on Clementi's bed. From the dorm room of a female friend, Ravi and the girl spied on Clementi as he embraced and kissed another man. Ravi posted about the incident on social media, and his friends responded with amusement and disgust (by all accounts, none of them called out Ravi for his shitty behavior). Ravi then announced his plans to spy on Clementi the following day, inviting others to log on and watch the feed.

Clementi soon discovered he'd been spied on and read the nasty comments Ravi's friends had posted on Facebook. On September 22, three days after Ravi first violated his privacy, Clementi killed himself by jumping off the George Washington Bridge. Ravi would later tell Chris Cuomo on *20/20* that he meant his roommate no harm. "Even though I wasn't the one who caused him to jump off the bridge," Ravi said, "I did do things wrong and I was stupid about a lot of stuff."

Whether perpetrators claim fun, revenge, or stupidity as their motive for sharing nonconsensual porn is irrelevant. The victims suffer deeply. For some, the pain and humiliation of exposure is so unbearable that they socially isolate, harm themselves, or stop eating and sleeping. In some cases—such as Tyler Clementi's, Amanda Todd's, Jessica Logan's, and Hope Witsell's, to name but a few—victims end their own lives.

I've worked with hundreds of victims of revenge porn. Each and every one of them will tell you that the violation—by a dickhead ex, frenemy, or frat boy—was only the initial blow. What catapulted their pain into the stratosphere was what happened next, when these images fell into the hands of offenders I call a$$holes. Just like school-administrator assholes, a$$hole scumbags also specialize in blaming, shaming, and punishing victims. But while many administrator assholes' bad behavior is the result of a toxic mix of ignorance, negligence, and arrogance, a$$holes are motivated primarily by greed. When a$$holes encounter a person in distress, they look for an opportunity to turn that pain into profit. Drug dealers who prey on addicts are a$$holes, for example. So, too, are pharmaceutical companies that jack up prices on lifesaving drugs. The guys who invented subprime mortgages, also a$$holes. I could go on and on. But the a$$holes I'm determined to take down are the ones who make their money from the distribution of nonconsensual porn.

I encountered my first a$$holes not long after I started my firm in 2014, when a woman I'll call Jennifer called me for advice. Jennifer's ex was trying to extort her by threatening to expose naked pics she'd shared with him when they were dating. Working in cahoots with his uncle, Jennifer's ex had created a website using Jennifer's first and last name, filled the site with her private images, then told Jennifer he was going to send her friends and family a link. Jennifer frantically begged her ex and his uncle to take down the webpage. Instead, they offered to sell her the domain for the bargain price of $75,000. Their extortion plan was despicable, but Jennifer refused to give in. Instead, she sued her ex and his uncle for intentional infliction of emotional distress, and the case was settled out of court. This degenerate duo's privacy-violation-for-profit scheme was poorly executed and hardly original. They were amateur-hour a$$holes. But the internet is filled with thousands of sites created by countless pricks, like Jennifer's ex, trying to make a dollar from revenge porn. Many of these slimy operators were inspired by the success of Hunter Moore, one of the most loathsome a$$holes in the game.

In 2012, Moore, a tattooed wannabe-rockstar PoS out of Sacramento, California, became internet infamous as the mastermind behind IsAnyoneUp.com, one of the first, and most notorious, revenge porn sites. The timing was uncanny. While Moore was living it up, earning tens of thousands of dollars a month posting intimate images without subjects' consent, I was working at the Vera Institute, paralyzed with fear that my own pictures would wind up on his site.

————

Hunter Moore was twenty-four years old when he first stumbled upon the idea, in 2010, that he could make money ruining innocent lives. At the time, Moore—a high school dropout who'd done stints as a party promoter and an occasional hairdresser on fetish-porn shoots—was sleeping with the fiancée of some guy in a semifamous emo band. One night, Moore's lady friend sent him a couple of nude photos. Moore's first impulse—a harbinger of things to come—was to share the pics with his friends. He tried to group-text them, but his phone was glitching. So he logged on to a dormant website he'd originally created for party promotions called Is Anyone Up, and uploaded the pictures there.

Over the next few weeks, Moore and his friends continued to upload images of naked women. The site was steadily gaining traffic, but it didn't blow up until a few months later when someone sent Moore naked pics of Zack Merrick, the bassist for Baltimore's pop-punk band All Time Low. Moore threw the images up on his site. Almost immediately, Merrick's dickpics became a trending topic on Twitter.

"That pretty much sealed the deal for me as far as nudes," Moore told Camille Dodero of the *Village Voice* in 2012. Moore began aggressively soliciting submissions for nudes via social media. Although some of the photos were self-submits shared voluntarily by men and women seeking a particular type of fame, overwhelmingly the pics were sent without the subjects' knowledge or consent.

What made the enterprise particularly loathsome was Moore's insistence on posting, along with the explicit images, victims' identifying information, including their full names, cities of residence, and links to their Facebook, Twitter, and LinkedIn accounts. This meant if anyone—a prospective employer, a romantic partner, a grandmother—searched a victim's name on Google, the images Moore posted on his site would pop up in their results.

To add insult, literally, to injury, each image was also accompanied by ridiculing commentary and GIFs courtesy of Moore and the degenerate trolls who visited his site. Women were derided as "ugly," "whore," "slut," and "white trash" and compared to all manner of farm animals and bulbous sea creatures. Is Anyone Up quickly became the go-to destination for vindictive exes, malicious hackers, and bitter ex-friends. At its peak, Moore claimed, users were submitting up to 350 images a day.

Moore's victims included the daughter of a GOP campaign donor, a semifinalist on *American Idol*, a cast member from the *Real Housewives* franchise, and multiple musicians. Overwhelmingly, though, the images were of regular people: housewives, students, young mothers, and elementary school teachers. Many of the pictures were sexy selfies, presumably intended for partners and private enjoyment. But some naked images were clearly not meant to be sexual at all. These images, it would later be revealed, were obtained by a hacker Moore hired to procure images for the site. One woman appeared to be documenting her weight loss, and another was pictured with her breasts bandaged and bruised, both nipples exposed. The picture had been taken in a doctor's office, post-surgery.

Moore quickly became known as "the most hated man on the internet," a label he seemed to relish. He famously advertised himself as "a professional life-ruiner," and told *Village Voice* reporter Dodero, "People want to point the finger at me, but I didn't fucking raid your house and steal your phone . . . I don't see how I'm supposed to be sorry."

Moore defended himself on ABC's *Nightline* in 2012, explaining he'd created the site for "public humiliation," and he was just "taking advantage of other people's mistakes." Moore claimed that his site was getting three hundred thousand unique visitors a day. Not surprisingly, he also had plenty of enemies. He received death threats; was banned from music festivals; and was targeted by the hacktivist group Anonymous, which doxed Hunter, publishing his private information, including his social security number and phone number, online. One woman confronted Moore in person and stabbed him in the shoulder with a ballpoint pen.

Legally, though, there was little victims could do to get their pictures removed from Moore's site. Plenty tried, including at least one multimillion-dollar record label representing an artist whose naked photo was featured on Is Anyone Up. When individual victims contacted Moore, begging and pleading for him to take down their pictures or threatening to sue, he ignored them. Like most bad actors on the internet, Moore was resting easy knowing he was legally protected by Section 230 of the Communications Decency Act.

Moore told the *Village Voice* that when he first started his site he didn't understand the law and would get nervous when he received notices from angry victims intending to sue. "Then I got fucking wise," he said. "I found out the laws and I was like 'fuck you.'" When the star of A&E's reality show *Storage Wars* sued Moore for defamation after Moore posted her explicit images on his site, Moore sent her lawyer a dickpic.

By 2012, Moore was reportedly taking in up to $30,000 a month from advertisers and merchandise he sold his fans. He spent his money on sexcapades and debauchery, details of which he chronicled on the site as part of his "brand" and shared eagerly with the press. The *Village Voice* feature opens with a scene of Moore in the back of a limousine, sloppily making out with two women at once. A profile in *Rolling Stone* includes a description of a woman snorting coke off Moore's erect penis while Moore snaps her picture to post on Tumblr. A Daily Beast feature showed Moore celebrating his twenty-sixth birthday at New York's Webster Hall. "I've fucked most of the girls here," Moore told the reporter.

For Moore, life was a nonstop party. Meanwhile, his victims were in hell. Many were treated like perverts or fools for taking the pictures in the first place. It's the same victim-blaming mentality that prompts people to ask rape survivors what they were wearing that might have "invited" the attack. It's maddening. Nobody asks homeowners, "Why'd you buy all that nice furniture?" after they've been robbed.

———

The devastating impact of nonconsensual porn on victims has only recently become the focus of serious research. Much of the most important work has come from the Cyber Civil Rights Initiative, a nonprofit organization aimed at increasing public awareness about nonconsensual porn, supporting victims, and advising lawmakers and internet companies about effective policies to combat the crisis. The organization was started by my friend and colleague Holly Jacobs after she, too, was victimized by an ex who sexually exposed and exploited her online in 2011.

Within days of her ex posting her private photos, images of Holly's naked body were circulating on three hundred separate porn sites, along with her name and contact information. Pervy men were nonstop harassing her, emailing crude comments and pictures of themselves masturbating to her pics. Holly went to the police and contacted the FBI, who told her there was nothing they could do. The images appeared in Google searches of Holly's name and quickly led to questions from the human resources department where she worked, and the dean at the university where she was pursuing her PhD. In a desperate attempt to stem the damage to her career, Holly legally changed her name and switched jobs. Then she decided to fight back.

Holly organized a coalition of survivors, activists, and legal experts, including my brilliant friends, legal scholars Mary Anne Franks and Danielle Citron. The Cyber Civil Rights Initiative was incorporated in 2013. When I opened my practice the following year, I Twitter-worshipped this crew. They warmly invited me to join the board of directors, where I served for four years. During that time, we led the conversation about the internet being the next big theater for a civil rights revolution.

In 2017, the research team at CCRI conducted the first national survey on the prevalence of nonconsensual porn. Significantly, the study included not only people who had experienced revenge porn but also those who'd only been threatened with exposure. Researchers found that more than 10 percent of social media users had been victimized, and women were twice as likely as men to be targets. Earlier research by CCRI detailed the impact of this abuse. More than 90 percent of victims reported suffering significant emotional distress. Almost as many—82 percent—described experiencing "significant impairment" in their work or social lives. More than a third of victims said their relationships with friends and family had been jeopardized.

In the first peer-reviewed study focusing exclusively on the impact of revenge porn on victims, published in 2016 in *Feminist Criminology*, researcher Samantha Bates noted "striking similarities between the mental health effects of sexual assault and revenge porn for survivors," including anxiety, depression, and PTSD. Adding to victims' distress, and compounding their feelings of isolation, hopelessness, and terror, is the relentless harassment they endure from trolls and pervs who consume these images. CCRI researchers found that almost 50 percent of victims were stalked or harassed online by people who'd seen their private images; 40 percent were stalked offline as well, including in person or by phone.

This data is critical in helping the public, policy makers, and legislators better understand the crushing impact of revenge porn. But statistics only show so much. They don't capture the terror of sitting at your computer, clicking open an email from your ex, and being assaulted with vivid close-ups of your naked body, taken without your knowledge. Statistics don't describe what it's like to live with the constant threat that your psycho ex might share your private pictures with the world, or that your new boss might see a video of you having sex that was posted online without your consent. Statistics don't convey what's it's like to have that fear and anxiety haunt you for years.

––––––

At first, Hunter Moore's site was the only game in town. But as the market for revenge porn exploded, other a$$holes jumped into the fray, eager for a piece of the action. By 2014, experts estimated there were more than three thousand internet sites, worldwide, featuring nonconsensual porn. Inspired by Moore's success, some enterprising a$$holes devised even more ruthless tactics to capitalize on victims' pain.

Colorado-based a$$hole Craig Brittain ran the revenge porn site IsAnybodyDown.com (an uninspired rip-off of Moore's Is Anyone Up), and the inexplicably named ObamaNudes.com, with similar business models to Moore's. Both sites featured nonconsensual nudes, nasty comments, and identifying contact information. But Brittain took his abuse a step further. Is Anybody Down also promoted a link to another site, TakedownHammer.com, a content-removal service purportedly run by an attorney who, for a fee between $200 and $500, would get the sensitive images taken down. A federal investigation later determined that Takedown Hammer was actually run by Brittain himself. He was impersonating the lawyer as part of a malicious extortion scheme to extract money from the very women he was already exploiting.

A$$hole Kevin Bollaert ran a similar hustle via his revenge porn site, UGotPosted.com, and his takedown service, ChangeMyReputa tion.com, which was linked to a PayPal account. One of Bollaert's victims, a middle-aged, married mother of two teenagers, ran a daycare center out of her home. Her picture appeared on the site along with her home address and the caption "For a good time, she can be found at this address." "This was not porn," the victim told a reporter from the *San Diego Union-Tribune*. "These posts were like hate crimes."

These revenge porn a$$holes would do just about anything to milk a dollar from the misery of their victims. Moore heavily promoted nonconsensual explicit images of elementary school teachers because they increased traffic to his site. At least one teacher lost her job as a result. Craig Brittain instituted a "bounty system," offering to pay $100 for photos or identifying information.

By 2013, attaining nonconsensual porn by any means necessary had become a competitive sport. One a$$hole referred to these ill-gotten images as "wins," and named his revenge porn site WinByState.com.

For the tens of thousands of (mostly female) victims whose intimate pictures were on the internet without their consent, there were few options available for having the images removed. One strategy that emerged was to use copyright law. Under the Digital Millennium Copyright Act of 1998 (DMCA), a person automatically owns the copyright to any image he or she takes, including selfies. If a copyright holder sends a website a takedown notification warning them to remove an image from their site, the website is legally obligated to comply. But the DMCA is not a cure-all. If a woman's naked image was captured by someone else—say, a boyfriend who snapped a pic during sex or while she was sleeping—she has no grounds to claim copyright infringement. Technically she doesn't own the image; her boyfriend does. If he's a shithead and decides to distribute the picture online without her permission, well, tough luck. Even if a victim took the picture herself, each and every copyright infringement requires a separate takedown notification. Since a single image can land on a dozen different websites overnight, for some victims, filing DMCA notifications became a full-time job.

Even more infuriating, while some website operators comply with takedown requests, other a$$holes, like Hunter Moore, ignore them. In fact, Moore was notorious for posting takedown notifications on his site to further humiliate his victims. Sometimes guys like Moore would submit DMCA notices to Chilling Effects (now called Lumen), an online archive created in 2001 by a bunch of internet activists at Harvard and the Electronic Frontier Foundation who worried that DMCA notices were having a "chilling effect" on free speech. Chilling Effects would publish victims' DMCA notices, which, by law, contained victims' real names, descriptions of the offending material, and the URLs where the images appeared.

By 2014, the revenge porn crisis was spiraling out of control. As desperate victims searched for protection, their images spread. Non-consensual porn was displayed on dedicated revenge porn sites and on platforms devoted exclusively to hard-core porn. Alarmingly, revenge porn was also spreading across social media—on Facebook, Tumblr, Reddit, Twitter, Snapchat, Instagram, YouTube, Pinterest, and Kik. Offenders had caught on that they could amplify the injury to targets by creating fake social media profiles and posting sensitive images to platforms where victims' friends and families were sure to see. Back then, most internet companies had no real policy about posting other people's naked pictures without consent. And why would they? Thanks to Section 230 of the Communications Decency Act, tech companies were under no obligation to keep this content off their platforms. Instead, they profited from the traffic revenge porn brought to their sites.

Reddit, which bills itself as the "front page of the internet," is one of the most-trafficked sites on the internet. The platform's "anything goes" ethos has allowed for some spectacularly offensive displays, such as the now infamous /r/creepshot subreddit, which featured sexualized voyeur photos of women taken in public without their knowledge or consent (think up-skirting, or close-up pics of women bending over in yoga pants).

In 2011, Reddit was blasted for its /r/jailbait subreddit, which displayed images of adolescent girls with highly sexualized commentary. Some of the images were family vacation photographs, copied from Facebook, of girls dressed in bathing suits innocently playing on the beach. Anderson Cooper did a segment on CNN criticizing Reddit for hosting the forum. The following day /r/jailbait received 130,000 more visitors than usual, millions of page views, and more than a thousand new subscribers. Reddit's general manager at the time, Erik Martin, defended /r/jailbait as "the price of free speech on a site like this." This is the kind of fucked-up thinking we were up against. But it's not surprising.

Women were the most frequent targets of revenge porn. But leadership at virtually every major social media platform was then, as it is today, almost exclusively male. The gender gap isn't confined to the upper echelons of tech companies, either. In 2014, only 10 percent of Twitter technical jobs were filled by women. Men run and rule the internet, which might explain why, for so long, so little attention was paid to the crisis of sexual exploitation, harassment, and abuse on their sites. It wasn't a priority because these attacks weren't happening to the people in charge.

Instead of instituting policies prior to 2015 to protect users, internet companies like Twitter and Reddit focused more on congratulating themselves for being bastions of free speech. Social media managers expressed little interest—and zero sense of urgency—in addressing the growing problem of nonconsensual porn.

Then came "the Fappening."

———

Ask any activist on the front lines of the war against revenge porn and she can probably tell you exactly where she was on August 31, 2014. I was on a plane headed home from Los Angeles. As the flight attendant told passengers to fasten our seat belts for takeoff, I took one last glance at my phone. My Twitter feed was alight with the news: hackers had breached the password protection of dozens of celebrities' iCloud accounts—among them, accounts belonging to Kirsten Dunst, Kate Upton, and Jennifer Lawrence—and stolen hundreds of private photographs, including a trove of nude and seminude selfies. The photos were published on anonymous image-sharing sites 4chan and Anon-IB, and quickly made their way to Reddit.

A subreddit devoted to the leak gained one hundred thousand followers in a single day and made the site more than $150,000 in additional revenue in less than a week. The hack, known as the

Fappening—a portmanteau of "the happening" and a crude slang term for masturbation—immediately made international headlines, which only drove more eyeballs to the sites.

Jennifer Lawrence was the first to call the attack what it was. In the November 2014 issue of *Vanity Fair*, she spoke about the emotional trauma she suffered, and famously referred to the gross invasion of privacy as "a sex crime."

"It's my body," said the then twenty-four-year-old actor. "And it should be my choice, and the fact that it is not my choice is absolutely disgusting. I can't believe that we even live in that kind of world." Lawrence added to anyone who had viewed the images: "You're perpetuating a sexual offense. You should cower with shame."

Less than twenty-four hours after the *Vanity Fair* interview was released online, asshole hackers infiltrated Lawrence's Wikipedia page and posted her naked pictures there. You could almost hear the trolls cackling with delight at their cruel, sick joke. What these snakes didn't know was that their time was running out.

———

I like to think of the year 2015 as the Great Revenge Porn Reckoning, although, looking back, for me, the year had a less than auspicious beginning.

Here's a snapshot from the first day of March: It's an unseasonably cold and blustery Sunday afternoon. I'm dressed in a bright red skirt suit and matching heels, standing outside a police station in small-town New Jersey, fighting back tears of anger in the middle of a fucking snowstorm.

I was representing my newest client, Norma, a nineteen-year-old fashion student whose mother had reached out to me after Norma's evil ex, C.M., had posted pictures of Norma on Pornhub, which is basically the Disneyland of online porn. The site has been in operation since 2007 and a decade later was entertaining eighty-one million visitors per day. Like YouTube, the content on Pornhub is free and the scope of its offerings encyclopedic. The platform is organized into porn-specific genres with an internal search engine that allows users to find anything from "anal" and "blowjob" to "teen" and "stepmom." A lot of the videos are low-budget or homemade. These days, anybody with a smartphone can make porn and put it on the web. But most of this amateur porn is created and distributed consensually. By comparison, Norma's ex had not only uploaded her private images without her consent, he had also posted comments suggesting she was available for oral sex. She only discovered her pictures and contact information were on the site after a stranger who'd seen her there texted her. Norma went directly to her local police. They told her there was nothing they could do. That's when her mother contacted me.

"Of course I can help you," I reassured Norma's mother over the phone.

Compared to other victims of nonconsensual porn, I thought Norma was in luck. In 2004, New Jersey had become the first state in the country to enact what is now commonly referred to as an anti-revenge-porn law. In fact, the invasion of privacy statute that prohibits people from sharing sexually explicit images without consent is the same law that Rutgers University student Dharun Ravi was convicted of violating when he used his webcam to spy on his roommate Tyler Clementi in 2010. Norma's ex was breaking New Jersey law.

The day after I spoke with Norma's mother, I printed out a copy of Section 2C: 14-9 of New Jersey's Code of Criminal Justice, slid it carefully into a manila envelope, and splurged on a car service to Jersey. Norma's family couldn't pay me, but I didn't care. I was sure this was going to be my first slam-dunk arrest of a perpetrator, and I felt confident I was going to get this sweet girl some justice and relief. I marched into the precinct with Norma and her parents convinced that once I spoke to the officers they would immediately go arrest Norma's ex. I was there to save the day.

I cleared my throat and rapped on the plexiglass window to get the attention of the on-duty cop at the front desk. "We're here to report a crime," I announced.

The officer gave me a bored look. "Oh yeah?" Then he noticed Norma standing beside me. "She's been here already," he said. "We told her she doesn't have enough proof. Besides," he continued, "how do you know her boyfriend isn't the one who was hacked?"

I pulled out my folder and started reading aloud from the invasion of privacy statute. The officer, who barely bothered to contain his eye rolling, waited until I was done with my impassioned explanation before telling me that he'd been given specific instruction from the local prosecutor to not enforce this particular law. When I asked why, he just shrugged. "There's nothing I can do," he said flatly. Then he waved to the exit and threw us out into the snow.

I was embarrassed. But more than that, I was furious. "This isn't over," I told Norma. "I am not stopping until we get your ex arrested."

The next day in my Brooklyn office, I tracked down Jason Boudwin, a prosecutor from another New Jersey county who had successfully litigated the revenge porn case of Anisha Vora, a volunteer at the Cyber Civil Rights Initiative. The case had been one of the few in the country in which a perpetrator was sentenced to time behind bars. I asked Jason if he could recommend a prosecutor in the county where Norma lived who might understand the seriousness of this case. That's how I found Seth Yockel. To my great relief, as soon as I explained Norma's situation, Seth immediately got it. He not only had experience with domestic violence cases; he was also tech-savvy. He issued subpoenas to a variety of internet providers to track the IP address from which Norma's pictures had been uploaded. The IP address led him right to Norma's ex.

C.M. was charged with invasion of privacy and cyberharassment.

He struck a plea deal, and was sentenced, in 2015, to five years' probation. It wasn't the jail time we'd hoped for, but sitting in court listening to Norma read her powerful victim impact statement is a moment I'll never forget. The best part of this story is that a few years after her case was resolved, Norma graduated college and joined my firm as the client relations coordinator. Now we get to see each other every day.

C.M. was a single cog in the giant Industrial Revenge Porn Complex, but to me, getting the prosecutor to take such swift action was a sign that change was on its way.

For years, my colleagues and I at the Cyber Civil Rights Initiative had been working with heads of tech companies, explaining to their safety and privacy teams that having naked pictures online without consent can be as life-ruining as having all your financials out there for the world to see. They'd nod, say something about free speech, and do nothing. But a combination of negative press over internet companies' complicity in the Fappening, murmurs about regulation, and the rising clamor from the "shrill harpies" of CCRI, as we were once called by an adversary, were finally getting through.

In February 2015, Reddit, the site that only a year earlier had been the go-to destination to view stolen celebrity nudes, announced it was banning nonconsensual porn from the site. "We missed a chance to be a leader in social media when it comes to protecting your privacy," Reddit moderators explained in a site-wide announcement. "No matter who you are, if a photograph, video, or digital image of you in a state of nudity, sexual excitement, or engaged in any act of sexual conduct is posted or linked to on Reddit without your permission, it is prohibited on Reddit." In March, Twitter, a company that for years had been criticized for not responding to users' complaints about nonconsensual porn, announced that it, too, was banning revenge porn from the platform. Soon after, search engines Google, Yahoo, and Bing instituted new policies allowing users to request that revenge porn images be de-indexed from their search engines to prevent the images from popping up when you search a person's name. Finally, nonconsensual porn was getting treated with the same protections search engines had in place to keep other sensitive material—like bank account information and social security numbers—private.

In October 2015, even Pornhub got on board. The greatest disseminator of naked images on the web instituted protections to make it easier for victims to have revenge porn removed from the site. I tweeted about it at the time, calling Pornhub my Twitter-crush of the day. Apparently, once internet companies finally admitted they were part of the problem, they felt obliged to be part of the solution. Or maybe it was all the bad press. Either way, it was a titanic industry-wide shift and a giant step in the right direction.

———

The year 2015 was full of victories but none were won without a fight. Battling on the front lines was the Cyber Civil Rights Initiative. Since its inception, the organization has been working tirelessly on their campaign to end the nonconsensual distribution of pornography, lobbying states' legislatures to consider bills that would make revenge porn a crime. When I opened my firm, I was determined to join the charge. One of the first things I did was recruit my niece, who was in middle school at the time, to help me create a spreadsheet of the mailing addresses for every single New York State assembly member and senator so I could send them a letter I'd written detailing why the state needed a revenge porn law.

I had a compelling argument: I'd logged onto one of the most notorious revenge porn websites at the time, the now-defunct MyEx .com, and searched for all the New York victims published there. I calculated that together these victims had received more views than the capacity of Yankee Stadium fifty times over. Years later, I was invited to speak at an event organized by the Mayor's Office to Combat Domestic Violence. One of the other guests, an elected official, stepped to the dais and read my letter word for word as his own. That, I laughed to myself, was a victory.

By 2015, we were beginning to get some traction. Seventeen states had implemented revenge porn laws, and we'd gained some fierce allies, like Kamala Harris, who at the time was California's attorney general. Harris established her state's Cyber Exploitation Task Force, which I was part of, and launched an effort to educate and train local law enforcement. Harris's office was also aggressively prosecuting offenders like Kevin Bollaert, the a$$hole behind the revenge-porn-extortion scheme UGotPosted/ChangeMyReputation.

In February 2015, Bollaert was convicted of twenty-one counts of identity theft and six counts of extortion, all felony crimes. Federal investigators found more than ten thousand images of nonconsensual porn on Bollaert's site. The felony arrest warrant, issued in San Diego, noted the thousands of desperate emails that had been sent to the site, many of them pleas from women begging to have their photos taken down. At Bollaert's sentencing, several brave women stepped forward to offer impact statements. One victim shared that her parents kicked her out of the house when they learned of the photos. "My life has just gone through a down spiral," she said. "I'm homeless because of this. I lost my family."

Before handing down his sentence, the judge read aloud a portion of an interview transcript in which Bollaert was asked by an investigator why he'd started the site. Bollaert had responded with: "I don't know, dude. Like, it was just fun . . . but now it's kind of ruining my life."

Alarmingly, at the time of his arrest, Bollaert was already on probation for an unrelated federal crime. The year before he'd admitted to listing a post office box number instead of a home address on an application while acquiring thirty-one firearms from various gun dealers in San Diego. I shudder to think what he was planning to do with all those weapons. Bollaert, then twenty-eight, was sentenced to eighteen years behind bars.

In 2015, Craig Brittain, the a$$hole who impersonated a lawyer to scam victims in his revenge-porn-extortion operation, also went down. Brittain, the a$$hole behind Is Anybody Down, was investigated by the Federal Trade Commission, the governmental body charged with protecting consumers from unfair and fraudulent business, after it was deluged by reports from women whose private pictures had appeared on the site. The FTC's complaint noted that in addition to impersonating a lawyer, Brittain had also pretended to be a woman on Craigslist to con unsuspecting females into sending him naked pictures, which he then put on his site without their knowledge. On behalf of CCRI and our best-friend nonprofit Without My Consent—another advocacy organization for victims of privacy violations, founded by two of the finest lawyers in the country, Erica Johnstone and Colette Vogele—I drafted an official public comment about the need for the FTC to treat this matter seriously.

In 2015, the FTC charged Brittain with engaging in deceptive business practices and banned him from publishing images without consent, effectively shutting down his operation. It was the first time the commission had gotten involved in the fight against nonconsensual porn.

You're probably wondering what happened to Hunter Moore, the sleazebag who started it all. In December 2015, he went down, too. The warrior responsible for Moore's demise is the fearless Charlotte Laws, a badass mom from California whose daughter's topless photo ended up on Moore's site even though she'd never sent the picture to anyone. Her computer had been hacked.

After repeatedly contacting Moore with DMCA takedown notices, which he ignored, Laws took matters into her own hands. She reached out to dozens of other victims using the contact information Moore had posted on his site. She spent hours piecing together their stories and discovered that, like her daughter, many of the women had been hacked. That's how Moore was procuring fresh images for his site.

Laws contacted the FBI and presented agents with a foot-high stack of evidence, including the hacker's alias and details of his modus operandi. Following her leads, the FBI launched its own investigation. Moore and his hacker, Charles Evens, were arrested and indicted on fifteen federal charges, including conspiracy, identity theft, and hacking. Evens pleaded guilty and was sentenced to two years behind bars; Moore, who also pleaded guilty, was sentenced to two and a half.

The only thing more satisfying than watching these a$$holes topple like a row of dominoes is knowing they were felled by the very people they'd tried to destroy: women who refused to be quiet and would not back down.

———

In 2010, when dickhead Hunter Moore first got the idea to sexually exploit people for profit, there was only one state—New Jersey—with a law making nonconsensual porn illegal. By 2016, we began to see real change on a national level. Thanks to coordinated efforts of the Cyber Civil Rights Initiative, media attention, and the brave victims who stepped forward and said, "It happened to me," thirty-four states and the District of Columbia had laws in place. I'd worked on about a dozen of them, helping draft legislation and testifying before lawmakers.

Despite our hard work, as of 2019, there were still five states that refused to pass legislation making revenge porn a crime.

Part of the problem is that a lot of people still don't get it. Occasionally, say, at a dinner party, I'll hear someone wonder aloud about why we even need revenge porn laws. "If people were just comfortable with their bodies," they'll muse, "nobody would care!" But being "comfortable" with your body does not protect you from public ridicule, or losing your job, or getting kicked out of your parents' home. You can be "comfortable" with—even proud of—your body and still not want everybody to look. People have a right to keep their naked images safe from public scrutiny. Sexual privacy is a right that should be protected by law.

What we really need—and what the Cyber Civil Rights Initiative has been advocating for since its inception—is a federal law criminalizing the distribution of nonconsensual porn. This would cover victims in states where no revenge porn laws exists, and allow law enforcement to harness the full power of the FBI and the Department of Justice, arguably the agencies best equipped, staffed, and trained to investigate these crimes. We have federal laws that protect our personal, financial, and medical information from being shared without our consent. There is even a piracy law that makes it illegal for you go to a Beyoncé concert—or any concert—tape the show on your phone, and post it online. These protections must extend to include sexual privacy.

In 2016, California representative Jackie Speier introduced to Congress the Intimate Privacy Protection Act, the first federal bill aimed at protecting victims of revenge porn. The bill—the brainchild of Mary Anne Franks—was a fucking work of art. It recognized the devastating impact of cyberexploitation on victims, regardless of the intent of the perpetrators, and made the nonconsensual distribution of explicit images a federal crime. On the day the bill went to Congress we held a press conference in the Cannon House Office Building, and I spoke about the suffering I'd seen. I described how my clients' naked images had been served up for strangers to devour without their consent; how they'd been harassed and blackmailed by a never-ending parade of pervs and creeps. I told of clients who'd been forced to move, quit school, change jobs, and change their names after their sexual privacy was violated online. The bill did not pass that year. But we didn't back down. In 2017, the bill was reintroduced by Senator Kamala Harris as the Ending Nonconsensual Online User Graphic Harassment (ENOUGH) Act. The bill was referred to the Committee on the Judiciary and was still pending as of early 2019. Meanwhile, the fight goes on.

I have a client in Chicago I'll call Sarah. She's in her late twenties, a teacher, and engaged to be married. As a teenager, Sarah, like countless other young women, shared a few intimate images with her long-term boyfriend. Now, years later, her day begins with her getting out of bed, sliding into her slippers, putting in her contacts, pouring herself a bowl of cereal, and switching on her laptop. She then spends forty minutes combing the internet, scouring for all the new URLs where her naked image is posted, and sending DMCA takedown notices to those sites. Another client, a nineteen-year-old student I'll call Arianne, has never taken a naked photo herself. Some asshole stole a picture of Arianne at the beach from her friend's Facebook page, photoshopped off Arianne's bikini, replaced it with images of someone else's breasts and genitalia, and posted the image on a revenge porn site. "All these people think they've seen me naked," she says. "It's not my body. But they don't know that."

In our first five years, my firm has helped countless victims like Sarah and Arianne. We've removed tens of thousands of nonconsensual images and videos from the internet. It sounds like a lot. But we've only just begun.

CHAPTER 7

WHEN TROLL ARMIES ATTACK

Imagine one day you open your computer and log onto Twitter, Facebook, or your blog and compose a post. Maybe you have something to say about politics, that great accomplishment you had at work, or a fascinating thing you learned at school. Or maybe it's something personal, a thought about your body, race, or sexual identity. When you're done typing, you close your computer and go to sleep.

The next morning, as you're making coffee, you glance out your front window and gasp. Standing in your yard is an angry mob. You notice some people in the crowd wearing T-shirts declaring their affiliation: "Nazi," "men's rights activist," "misogynist," "racist," "fat shamer," "pussy grabber," and "homophobe." You don't recognize any of these people, but they are calling you names, ridiculing your opinion, insulting everything about you. Someone shouts graphic details of the sexual assault he has planned for you. You notice the mob is growing larger. It feels as though every protester invited all his friends. You try to keep from panicking. But you're terrified. These people want to hurt you and they know where you live. The scene reads like an overwrought passage from a dystopian novel. But for some of my clients, getting attacked by mobs of raging trolls is a reality they face every time they go online.

At my firm, I represent a range of individuals—including students, journalists, sexual assault survivors, celebrities, professional women, and abortion providers—all of whom have been viciously targeted by angry trolls. If you've never experienced a troll attack firsthand, it might be hard to imagine how ruthless it can be. In 2013, web game developer Zoë Quinn became the target in a highly public online mob assault known as Gamergate after her ex-boyfriend wrote a ten-thousand-word blog post accusing Zoë of sleeping with a journalist in a quid pro quo arrangement for a favorable review for her latest game. The review in question didn't even exist, yet Zoë became a lightning rod—a symbol in the minds of misogynist bro-trolls of what the gaming industry might become if women had their way. Or something. Who knows what got these mouth-breathers all worked up. None of them offered a reason for attacking Zoë. Their rage seemed to be fueled by nothing but bitterness and hate.

"If I ever see you are doing a panel at an event I am going to, I will literally kill you," read one of the thousands of messages Zoë received at the time. "You are lower than shit and deserve to be hurt, maimed, killed, and finally, graced with my piss on your rotting corpse a thousand times over."

When fellow game developer and Massachusetts politician Brianna Wu spoke out against the trolls attacking Zoë, they turned on Wu, too. One Twitter user with the handle Death to Brianna wrote, "I've got a K-Bar and I'm coming to your house so I can shove it up your ugly feminist cunt." Another chimed in, "I'm going to rape your filthy ass until you bleed and then choke you to death with your husband's tiny Asian penis." Moments later, the same troll sent another message: "Guess what bitch, I know where you live," and included Wu's home address. Wu and her husband fled their home in terror.

Brilliant writer Jessica Valenti, founder of the blog *Feministing*, was forced to make her social media accounts private after she received rape threats aimed at her five-year-old daughter. Another writer, my friend and inspiration Anita Sarkeesian, who is featured with me in the 2018 documentary *Netizens*, was targeted after launching a Kickstarter campaign to fund her project *Tropes vs. Women*, in which she explores the portrayal of women in video games. Not only did Anita receive an avalanche of death and rape threats; one enterprising troll scum created *Beat Up Anita Sarkeesian*, a video game in which players can administer blows to Anita's face and watch her avatar become bloody and bruised.

Almost 50 percent of Americans have experienced some form of online abuse, everything from getting called offensive names to being sexually harassed or threatened with physical violence, according to a 2016 joint study by the Data & Society Research Institute and the Center for Innovative Public Health Research. Women, members of the LGBTQ community—especially trans people—and people of color are often singled out for especially vile and graphic attacks. "You could be sitting at home in your living room, outside of working hours, and suddenly someone is able to send you an incredibly graphic rape threat right into the palm of your hand," Laura Bates, founder of the Everyday Sexism Project, shared with Amnesty International for the organization's 2017 report "Toxic Twitter," about online abuse of women. "The psychological impact of reading through someone's really graphic thoughts about raping and murdering you is not necessarily acknowledged," said Bates.

In fact, the force of a targeted mob troll attack can be devastating, psychologically, socially, and professionally. It can effectively silence victims by pushing them offline. More than 80 percent of women harassed on Twitter, for instance, changed the way they used the platform, from self-censoring to leaving the site altogether, according to the Amnesty International report. The organization considers online harassment and abuse of women a matter of human rights.

———

When she was first targeted with death and rape threats, Jessica Valenti called the FBI. She was advised to move out of her home until the threats subsided, never walk outside alone, and be vigilant of any cars or men who seemed to be following her. "It was totally impossible advice," Valenti told Amanda Hess, who wrote the defining work on gender-based online harassment for the Pacific Standard in 2014. "You have to be paranoid about everything," added Valenti. "You can't just not be in a public place." Hess, who had her own harrowing experience with trolls, noted in her piece that Valenti eventually had to hire private security for her public speaking events. She signed up for a cybersecurity service to scrub the web of her personal information, and rented a private post office box. These precautions, which many public women are forced to take in response to targeted troll attacks, cost time and money. As Hess puts it: "Every time we call the police, head to court to file a civil protection order, or get sucked into a mental hole by the threats that have been made against us, zeroes drop from our annual incomes."

But how did we get here? It feels as if it was not that long ago that trolls were regarded as little more than an annoyance. Back when the internet was in its infancy, trolls were known as online pranksters who'd get their jollies doing things like posting absurd or sarcastic comments on Usenet's discussion board to disrupt the conversation.

In 1993, a Usenet poster asked for advice about how to deal with a pair of cats in heat. This earnest request was met with "an explosion of maniacal solutions, each more ludicrous than the last: do-it-yourself spaying, execution by handgun, incineration and, perhaps inevitably, sex with the cats." Early trolls were the computer-nerd version of a young Adam Sandler. Funny, if you like that kind of thing.

By the early aughts, however, troll humor took a sharp turn for the mean and nasty. Using avatars to disguise their identities, trolls would lurk in the comments sections of sites like CNN and shit on other posters' comments with extravagant insults and invectives, just to piss people off. Apparently, this was wildly amusing to fellow trolls and their fans. As one troll described it to the *New York Times* in 2008 "[The enjoyment] is watching someone lose their mind at their computer two thousand miles away while you chat with friends and laugh."

Sometimes trolls pushed the bounds of trash-talking. In 2008, a group of hacker trolls attacked the Epilepsy Foundation website with flashing images in an attempt to cause seizures among sufferers with photosensitivity. At least one person reported experiencing a seizure after being triggered by the images. The trolls did it for the lulz, that is, laughter generated at someone else's expense. In other words, the dickhead version of LOL. The more frustrated, angry, or upset the targets become, the greater the lulz.

In *The Dark Net: Inside the Digital Underworld*, author Jamie Bartlett notes that the problem with lulz-seeking is that lulz "are a bit like a drug: you need a bigger and bigger hit to keep the feeling going. Trolling can quickly spiral out of control."

In 2006, Mitchell Henderson, a sweet-faced seventh-grade boy with braces from Rochester, Minnesota, shot himself in the head with his parents' rifle. A troll stumbled upon the MySpace memorial page created by Mitchell's classmates and found a grammatical error. One of Mitchell's friends had called him "an hero." The troll posted about Mitchell on 4chan, mocking the memorial and turning "an hero" into a meme. A legion of lulz-seeking trolls quickly joined in (child suicide being hilarious and all).

Trolls superimposed Mitchell's face over scenes from hard-core porn and posted photographs of the boy's grave site marked up with snide comments. Some of them called Mitchell's house, leaving messages for his grieving parents, like "I'm Mitchell's ghost. I'm at the front door, can you come down and let me in?" The attacks on Mitchell's memorial page are gleefully documented on Encyclopedia Dramatica, the Wikipedia of internet trolling. Like many entries on the site, the description of Mitchell's suicide is rife with homophobic and racist commentary, and peppered with crude and nonsensical references to incest and bestiality.

Mitchell's suicide wasn't the only death mocked by trolls. In fact, while the rest of us were using Facebook to look up our high school crushes, "RIP trolling" was becoming an actual thing. Trolls would find Facebook memorials, particularly those dedicated to children or teens, and go crazy defacing the pages with sick comments and stupid memes like "LOL YOUR DEAD."

In 2011, British RIP troll Sean Duffy was arrested and jailed for four months after mocking the deaths of several teenagers, including a child who'd been hit by a train. Duffy wrote on the tribute Facebook page created by the victim's brother, "I fell asleep on the track lolz." He was prosecuted under Britain's Malicious Communications Act, which, among other things, criminalizes trolling meant to deliberately cause "distress and anxiety." To date, the United States does not have any comparable law. But maybe we should.

———

It goes without saying that much of this bad behavior is the direct result of the cloak of anonymity trolls can hide behind on the web. Common sense dictates that people are more inclined to be assholes when their identity is concealed than if they have to take ownership of their shitty behavior. But this phenomenon actually has a name: the online disinhibition effect.

In 2004, psychologist John Suler published some of the earliest research on the effects of online anonymity. Suler maintains that masking one's identity causes "disassociation," an effect that can lead people to engage in behaviors they wouldn't normally. Suler explains:

> In a process of dissociation, [anonymous posters] don't have to own their behavior by acknowledging it within the full context of an integrated online/offline identity. The online self becomes a compartmentalized self. In the case of expressed hostilities or other deviant actions, the person can avert responsibility for those behaviors, almost as if superego restrictions and moral cognitive processes have been temporarily suspended from the online psyche. In fact, people might even convince themselves that those online behaviors "aren't me at all."

In other words, according to Suler, people who engage in bad behavior online under masked identities have slipped into a sort of alternate reality. They rest easy knowing that their "public" self will never be held accountable for any shenanigans their anonymous self gets into online. Face-to-face, people take care to keep their extreme views and sadistic tendencies in check for fear of losing friends, alienating family members, or even getting fired. But anonymous on the internet, people feel free to engage in unbridled assholery with zero repercussions. This has led to some spectacular instances of people leading double lives.

In 2012, journalist Adrian Chen, reporting for *Gawker*, a now-defunct celebrity gossip and news site, uncovered the true identity of Violentacrez, one of the most notorious trolls on Reddit. Violentacrez was responsible for creating and moderating four hundred subreddits, many of them staggeringly offensive, including /r/chokeabitch, /r/niggerjail bait, /r/picsofdeadkids, and /r/jewmerica. He was also the mastermind behind /r/jailbait, which was basically a photo-share for pedophiles. For a time, "jailbait" was the second most frequently used search term, after "Reddit," bringing traffic to the site. In addition to his moderating duties, Violentacrez was also notorious for posting racist, violent, and dehumanizing images, as he did when he posted a photograph of a woman who'd been brutally beaten on the subreddit /r/beatingwomen. Offline, Chen discovered, Violentacrez led a very different existence.

Violentacrez's real name is Michael Brutsch. He's a husband, father, and cat lover from Arlington, Texas. When Chen contacted Brutsch, who at the time worked as a programmer for a financial firm, Brutsch defended his actions with little more than a shrug: "I do my job, go home, watch TV, and go on the internet. I just like riling people up in my spare time." But when Chen told Brutsch he intended to reveal his identity on Gawker, Brutsch pleaded with the reporter to reconsider. "My wife is disabled," he implored. "I got a home and a mortgage, and if this hits the fan, I believe this will affect negatively on my employment." Brutsch was right. Less than twenty-four hours after the story went live, he was fired. Offline, being a world-class dick has consequences.

There are plenty of experts who, like Suler, point to anonymity as the main driver of toxic behavior online. But there is another school of thought worth considering. Some experts claim trolls are more than merely a product of their environments. They are, in fact, evil, tending toward cruelty even when not online, the thinking goes. One of the earliest studies of troll psychology, led by Erin Buckels in 2014 out of the University of Manitoba, looked at a possible connection between trolling behavior and a quartet of personality traits known as the "dark tetrad." This ominous-sounding constellation of behaviors is a stew of Machiavellianism, narcissism, psychopathy, and sadism. Put another way, someone who exhibits dark tetrad traits is self-obsessed, with a propensity for manipulating others, lacks empathy, and enjoys inflicting pain.

Researchers found that dark tetrad scores were highest among survey respondents who listed trolling as one of their favorite online activities. More specifically, the study noted that the greatest correlation was between trolling and sadism in particular. "In fact," wrote the researchers in the journal *Personality and Individual Differences*, "it might be said that online trolls are prototypical everyday sadists . . . Both trolls and sadists feel sadistic glee at the distress of others."

Former FBI profiler and technology expert Lisa Strohman also notes distinct similarities between troll behavior and patterns she's observed in serial killers. "Once they get first blood, they tend to push the limits more and more," Strohman explained in a 2016 *Conversations* podcast interview about troll psychology. "It's kind of the same mentality—that it's exciting to be able to manipulate other people and hurt them."

———

In late 2013, a tenth grader in Canada who went by the online name Obnoxious embarked on what would become one of the most notorious trolling cases of all time. Obnoxious, who reportedly had been raised in a troubled home by an abusive father and mentally ill mother, targeted female gamers on Twitch, a streaming service that allows gamers to post live feeds of themselves playing so their fans can tune in and watch. The platform is wildly popular; in 2018, Twitch averaged almost a million users logged on at any given time. At first, Obnoxious would contact young women on the platform, just wanting to talk, according to journalist Jason Fagone, who wrote about Obnoxious in 2015 for the *New York Times Magazine*. He'd eventually ask for "fan signs"—selfies of the gamers holding signs that said "Obnoxious." Then he'd start demanding the women send him nudes. When they refused, he'd hack into their accounts to find their real names and addresses. Then he'd prank them by sending to their homes pizzas they hadn't ordered—and no one would ever eat—like no cheese and all anchovies.

Within a year, Obnoxious's attacks had escalated. He began threatening his victims with violence and swatting them repeatedly. He was good at it, too. He'd call in fake police reports of hostage situations, bombings, and murders, triggering heavily armed SWAT teams to descend on unsuspecting targets' homes.

One victim, Allison Henderson, had her Costa Mesa, California, home surrounded by police after Obnoxious called in a phony report. When Henderson opened the door, she was met by a phalanx of officers with rifles aimed right at her. "It was the most terrifying experience of my life," Henderson told reporter Fagone. Henderson added that when she tried explaining the attack to the officers who later questioned her, they didn't understand the concept of swatting. "They were completely lost on the idea of a stranger harassing us over the internet. It's a feeling like you're drowning, and the person doesn't understand what water is."

For the better part of 2014, Obnoxious continued his assaults. He swatted a girl's high school in Fort Meade, Florida, telling the police he would "shoot everyone with an AK-47." The school went into lockdown for hours. He called police in Ontario, California, claiming to be a local man who'd just shot his father with an AR-15 and was thinking about killing his mother. The police department dispatched thirty-two units to the address Obnoxious had given, including multiple squad cars, a heavy-duty armored military van, a helicopter, and a canine unit—90 percent of the police department's available resources, according to the *New York Times*—only to find a woman, her boyfriend, and her son at home and not in any danger. The son was a gamer who'd pissed off Obnoxious by defending one of his victims online.

From his home in a suburb of Vancouver, Obnoxious used his computer to attack female gamers across the United States and Canada—in Arizona, North Carolina, Florida, Montana, and Toronto. Some of them were so freaked out they stopped gaming altogether, even when it was their primary source of income. Obnoxious timed his swatting so the episodes would be captured on the gamers' live feeds, which added the sting of public humiliation to the assault. One of his victims was so shaken she dropped out of school.

In an epic final act of his months-long crime spree, on December 1, 2014, seventeen-year-old Obnoxious logged on to multiple gaming sites and broadcast live, for more than eight hours, as he called in fake emergencies and swatted victims across the country. In the background of his live stream, male fans watching the chaos on their own computers could be heard egging him on. Obnoxious was eventually arrested and charged with forty-six counts, including criminal harassment and extortion. He pleaded guilty to twenty-three charges and was sentenced to a year and four months in juvenile detention.

Sixteen months seems like a stunningly short sentence for an offender who caused so much chaos and harm. But not every troll who orchestrates these brazen attacks gets off so easily.

In 2018, Ryan Lin, a psycho hacker stalker troll who'd targeted one of my clients and terrorized dozens of other victims was put away with one of the longest prison sentences ever handed down to a criminal who used the internet to attack.

Two years earlier, then twenty-three-year-old Lin answered a Craigslist ad posted by my client, whom I'll call Stacey. Stacey was looking for a housemate. Lin moved in, and within days Stacey became the target of some of the most vicious psycho trolling I've ever seen. Lin hacked into Stacey's computer and stole her diary, which contained private entries about her sexual and mental health, and distributed the information to hundreds of people. Stacey moved out of the shared house and went to stay with her mother, but Lin kept up his attacks. He created spoof accounts in Stacey's name and used those accounts to invite strangers to her home with the promise of "gang bangs." Lin also sent child pornography to Stacey's mother and various other people.

Stacey ran a pet-sitting business and used an app called Rover to communicate with her clients. Ryan infiltrated that, too. He hacked into her account and sent pornographic pictures to her past clients, used her linked credit card to make hundreds of dollars in purchases, and sent a message to one client saying Stacey had murdered her cat and put the corpse in the freezer: "Hey I'm so sorry to tell you this but Wink is dead," he wrote. "I had a panic attack suddenly and smothered Wink to death. I'll pack her remains into a Ziploc bag and you can come pick her up. Sorry!"

Lin terrorized not only my client and her family and friends, but also the entire community of Waltham, Massachusetts, where Stacey lived, and surrounding towns. He called in more than 120 hoax bomb threats, including to schools and daycare centers.

At his sentencing in October 2018, half the town showed up: cops, teachers, lawyers, waiters, cooks, FBI agents, and hotel workers. I've never seen a courtroom so packed. As people stepped up to give their victim impact statements, it felt like an open mic at a wedding. Stacey spoke and so did her mother. A school resource officer shared, through tears, the terror young children experienced during the multiple bomb threats Lin had called in to their schools. The Waltham chief of police said that in his entire career, he'd never seen anybody cause such fear and wreak such havoc in the community. He said he dispatched fire and police units more than 150 times in a three-month span to deal with Lin's fake bomb threats.

Lin, dressed in a brown prison jumpsuit and shackles, was also given a chance to speak. "When I get out of jail, I hope to use my computer skills to improve and innovate society," he said. The entire courtroom gasped. Lin pleaded guilty to seven counts of distributing child pornography, nine counts of making fake bomb threats, three counts of computer fraud, and one count of identity theft. He was sentenced to seventeen and a half years, the longest sentence an offender against one of my clients has ever received.

———

Psycho trolls Ryan Lin and Obnoxious worked solo. They were one-man wrecking crews. But that's not how trolls typically inflict maximum damage. What I see most often in my practice are attacks by troll armies: battalions of anonymous foot soldiers who've coalesced over a shared grievance to launch an assault on a single target. These online mobs are a relatively new phenomenon, a possible manifestation of the us-against-them-ism that has gripped the nation. They find one another on forums like Reddit and 4chan, or on discussion boards that exist in the dark recesses of the web, lather themselves into a rage over this or that issue, then lash out at whomever they've identified as the enemy of the day. And there is almost no telling what might set them off.

Journalist Amy Guth found herself on the receiving end of a barrage of online rape threats and calls for her beheading after she suggested during a radio interview that people wish one another "happy holidays" as an alternative to "merry Christmas." Professional athletes and referees have been attacked by angry trolls, some of whom have threatened to rape their young children. YouTube makeup artist Em Ford was trolled by men accusing her of "trickery" because she wore makeup.

When comedian Leslie Jones starred alongside Kristen Wiig, Melissa McCarthy, and Kate McKinnon in a 2016 remake of the 1984 hit *Ghostbusters*, the women were attacked online by misogynist trolls who objected to the all-female cast. Undoubtedly, Jones, who is African American, received the worst of it. She was bombarded on Twitter with all manner of racist and misogynist tweets, including photos of gorillas—invoking a grotesque racist trope that has existed since slavery. One troll sent an image of a defaced photo of Jones that he claimed to have covered with semen.

It's not uncommon for people of color to be targeted with particularly denigrating attacks, noted African American actress Pia Glenn. "When a white woman gets terrible harassment about being raped, attacked or killed, that's very serious," Glenn complained to AlterNet. "[But] there's a whole other section of ugly, hideous things people feel they can say to us . . . It takes fewer back-and-forth vollies to get to 'nigger bitch,' 'nigger cunt.'"

Women who've come forward to share their experiences of rape, abuse, and abortion are also frequent troll targets. I represent several sexual assault survivors who've had their privacy violated by men's rights activists who've exposed my clients' identities online, accusing them of lying. I also represent an abortion storyteller who was attacked by a gang of Nazi trolls who posted my client's parents' home address online. Their house was plastered with Pepe the Frog stickers.

In another case, my firm filed a federal suit on behalf of the National Network of Abortion Funds (NNAF) in response to a troll cyberattack that interfered with the organization's fund-raising efforts, costing NNAF hundreds of thousands of dollars in lost donations. The troll made fake online donations adding up to trillions of dollars. The flood of traffic shut down the entire site. This tactic, called a distributed denial-of-service (DDoS) attack, is a favorite of hacker trolls who target large organizations. Many of the fraudulent donations to the NNAF were made in the name of "Adolph Hitler" and were visible to anybody who logged on to donate. Supporters of the organization were sent emails from "Adolph" saying, "I believe the Aryan race is the Master Race . . . it tickles me to fund abortions for the lower races, such as Negros and the Jews."

In the wake of particularly vicious troll attacks, I've advised clients to move out of their homes, hire private security, and take special precautions to safeguard their kids. But it's rarely a single troll that causes panic. It's the sudden pile-on of thousands that brings victims to their knees. A troll mob is a dangerous force.

———

Mob behavior has been studied for generations. In the late nineteenth century, French psychologist Gustave Le Bon, a pioneer in the field, first posited the theory that when people find themselves immersed in groups, their individual impulses are overwhelmed by the will of the collective—and not in a good way. According to Le Bon, crowds display more "primitive" behaviors than individuals. They are more violent, ferocious, and spontaneous. Le Bon wrote: "By the mere fact that he forms part of an organized crowd, a man descends several rungs in the ladder of civilization. Isolated, he may be a cultivated individual; in a crowd, he is a barbarian."

Le Bon also argued that mob behavior is contagious. So, let's say you're walking down the street and you see a high-end jewelry store with a broken front window and a full display case of shiny trinkets, just sitting there. By Le Bon's reckoning, you'd be more inclined to grab yourself a bracelet and make a run for it if you saw fifteen other people already looting than if you walked by the broken window alone.

A study on trolling behavior conducted in 2017 by researchers at Cornell and Stanford Universities suggests that social contagion happens online as well. According to the study, only about 50 percent of trolling behavior is carried out by habitual trolls (that is, people who act like shitheads online as a regular thing). Other trolling, the researchers maintain, is the result of people witnessing negative behavior—bullying, name-calling, general troll assholery—and jumping into the fray. All it takes, explained Jure Leskovec, senior author of the study, is one person behaving badly to set off a "spiral of negativity."

Let's assume all these theories are true: (A) one person can set in motion a cascade of bad behavior, (B) bad behavior can spread easily from one person to the next, and (C) negative behavior becomes worse as a mob swells in size. The only thing that would make this scenario more frightening would be the existence of an evil leader who keenly understands the mechanics of mob mentality; one with an army of followers and a list of innocent victims to attack. Of course, we don't need to imagine the firestorm monsters like this could ignite. It's already happening all around us.

———

By all accounts, American Nazi Andrew Anglin had a pretty normal childhood. He grew up in a comfortable home in an upper-middle-class neighborhood in Columbus, Ohio. As a boy, Anglin collected comic books and loved to read. In high school, he hung out with the hippie vegan crowd. He styled his hair in dreadlocks and wore a hoodie with a "Fuck Racism" patch on the back, according to Luke O'Brien, who penned an exhaustive and illuminating profile of Anglin for *The Atlantic* magazine in 2017. But as he neared the end of high school, Anglin began behaving erratically, banging his head against walls and burning himself with lighters. He started listening to right-wing conspiracy theorist Alex Jones's radio show and became obsessed with Jones's claim that the terrorist attacks of 9/11 were a hoax.

On July 4, 2013, Anglin launched a Nazi propaganda website he called the Daily Stormer, after *Der Stürmer*, Hitler's favorite white supremacist rag. (Anglin briefly ran another site called Total Fascism.) With Daily Stormer, Anglin strove to appeal to millennial Nazis, and focused on clickbaity headlines and pithy racist hashtags like #Hitler WasRight and #GasTheKikes. Nothing was too extreme.

In 2017, a day after activist Heather Heyer was killed while protesting a white supremacist rally in Charlottesville, Virginia, Anglin published an article titled "Woman Killed in Road Rage Incident Was a Fat, Childless 32-Year-Old Slut."

Anglin is one of the most prominent and powerful alt-right voices in the country and also a "prolific troll and serial harasser," according to the Southern Poverty Law Center. Indeed, several white supremacist murderers have claimed allegiance to the views propagated by Anglin on his site. Dylann Roof, who, in 2015, entered an African American church in Charleston, South Carolina, and gunned down nine congregants as they met for Bible study, is a Daily Stormer fan. So, too, is James Harris Jackson. In 2017, twenty-eight-year-old Jackson boarded a bus from Washington, DC, to New York with a plan, as he later told police, to hunt black people. On St. Patrick's Day, Jackson attacked sixty-six-year-old Timothy Caughman, an antipoverty worker from Queens, New York, stabbing Caughman to death with a twenty-six-inch sword.

On Daily Stormer, Anglin is careful to warn his followers "not to threaten targets with violence," explains *The Atlantic*'s O'Brien, "a disclaimer meant to shield him from law enforcement." Instead, Anglin rallies his troops to launch attacks online. He calls his followers the Stormer Troll Army, or Stormers for short, and shares with his troops best practices for inflicting maximum damage to targets online. Anglin taught his followers how to "register anonymous email accounts, set up virtual private networks, mask their IP addresses, and forge Twitter and text-message conversations," according to O'Brien. "He created images and slogans for them to use."

In December 2016, Anglin sicced his troll army on Tanya Gersh, a Jewish real estate broker in Whitefish, Montana. Gersh had allegedly gotten into a dispute over the sale of some property with the mother of white nationalist Richard Spencer. You may recall Spencer from his appearance in a viral video taken days after Donald Trump was elected president. In the video, Spencer is shown speaking at the National Policy Institute, a white supremacist group, celebrating Trump's victory. He raises his arm in a Nazi salute and gives a hearty "Heil Trump!" He's *that* guy. Incidentally, Spencer is also the guy who famously got punched on camera by a protestor, an encounter that turned into a meme. Anglin reportedly admired Spencer and immediately sprang into action upon hearing that Spencer's mother was arguing with a Jewish woman.

Anglin rallied his troops: "Are y'all ready for an old-fashioned Troll Storm?" he wrote. "Because AYO—it's that time, fam." Anglin published at least thirty articles about Gersh on the Daily Stormer website, urging his followers to "TAKE ACTION!" Anglin shared Gersh's contact information and personal details, including the Twitter handle of her twelve-year-old son. "Tell them you are sickened by their Jew agenda . . ." he urged his army. "This is very important." For weeks, Gersh and her family were terrorized with a barrage of anti-Semitic harassment and threats. One troll played the sound of gunfire into Gersh's phone. Daily Stormer webmaster and infamous white nationalist troll Andrew "Weev" Auernheimer left a voicemail for Gersh: "You fucking wicked kike whore . . . This is Trump's America now." Anglin posted a picture of Gersh's young son superimposed against the gates of Auschwitz. Gersh was so terrified she kept a packed bag on her bedroom floor in case her family had to suddenly flee their home. She developed a shoulder injury from holding her body curled in a constant state of fear. She needed therapy to help her deal with the trauma.

Gersh wasn't Anglin's only victim. In 2017, the Nazi also directed his troops to terrorize twenty-one-year-old college student Taylor Dumpson, the first African American woman elected student government president at American University, in Washington, DC. Anglin's troll army terrorized Dumpson with racist abuse, including messages telling her to go back to Africa, and comparing her and other black people to monkeys and gorillas. When Anglin discovered that campus police were guarding Dumpson in the wake of his troll army attack, he posted an article on his site proclaiming, "Nigger Agitator Gets Police Bodyguards Because of Daily Stormer." Dumpson was diagnosed with PTSD as a result of the abuse.

———

The internet can be a nasty place. First Lady Melania Trump agrees. In March 2018, Melania met with tech company heads to launch her much-touted anti-cyberbullying initiative. Melania was short on specifics, but reading from prepared statements, she expressed her concern about making the internet a nicer place. The irony was lost on no one. Days before Melania's speech, the *New York Times* published a detailed list of hundreds of people and entities her husband had attacked online since announcing his run for the White House, including athletes, rival politicians, members of his own party, a retired marine general, and scores of working journalists, all of whom he identified by name.

In a *USA Today* opinion piece about Melania Trump's be-nice-on-the-internet initiative, political strategist and Trump critic Cheri Jacobus noted wryly that the president himself "had attacked and lied about people like me and then unleashed his army of Twitter trolls to depict me as raped, beheaded, dismembered, shot, stabbed, starved in a concentration camp, or grossly disfiguring my face because I am a Trump critic."

Troll armies are impossible to prosecute. Not only are the members anonymous; individually their actions don't necessarily meet the threshold of a crime. Cyberstalking, for instance, requires that the offender engage in a course of conduct, or series of acts, that would cause a person to feel as though they or their family were in danger.

An individual troll making a threat does not constitute a "course of conduct." But a *thousand* trolls making threats feels like a singular terror.

In an interview with *The Atlantic*, University of Maryland's School of Law professor Danielle Citron likened a troll attack to being assaulted by a swarm of angry bees. "You have a thousand bee stings," said Citron, author of *Hate Crimes in Cyberspace*. "Each sting is painful. But it's perceived as one awful, throbbing mass." Protected by anonymity, inspired by their leaders, and excited by the fervor of the mob, armies of trolls roam the internet, igniting one storm of terror after another.

———

In the fall of 2016, few people outside of the insular circle of right-wing conspiracy theorists had ever heard of Pizzagate. But for trolls congregating on Reddit and 4chan and in alt-right chat groups, the Pizzagate conspiracy was all anybody was talking about. The chaos started in late October when a bot Twitter account using the handle @DavidGoldbergNY posted a series of tweets containing links to a bizarre Facebook post that claimed presidential candidate Hillary Clinton was running a child sex trafficking ring out of the basement of Comet Ping Pong, a popular DC pizza place. The outrageous story quickly spread across social media, on Facebook, Reddit, 4chan, YouTube, and Twitter. The assertions became more lurid by the day. Fake news sites filled with stories claiming there were "kill rooms" in the basement of the restaurant and an elaborate system of underground tunnels. (In fact, the restaurant does not have a basement.) There was chatter about "satanic rituals" and phony reports that Comet Ping Pong had pornographic pictures in the restrooms and secret pro-pedophilia symbols featured on their menus. Michael Flynn Jr., son of now-disgraced former national security advisor General Michael

Flynn, tweeted about Pizzagate. Billionaire Erik Prince—the brother of Trump's secretary of education, Betsy DeVos—discussed Pizzagate on Breitbart Radio, insisting it was true. But the loudest voice to propagate the Pizzagate conspiracy was alt-right radio host and Donald Trump hype man, Alex Jones.

At the time, Jones ran a YouTube channel and several fake news websites, including the wildly popular InfoWars, which in 2016 received as many as ten million unique page views per month. Jones's media empire was built on bizarre conspiracies, bald-faced lies, and frothy paranoia. Jones insisted 9/11 was an inside job and maintained that the Obama administration manipulated the weather and summoned hurricanes at will. Jones also promoted the horrific lie that the 2012 Sandy Hook Elementary School massacre was a hoax orchestrated by a cabal of left-wing operatives. "I mean it's fake!" Jones proclaimed, repeatedly. "You've got parents acting . . . it's just the fakest thing since the three-dollar bill."

It's unclear whether Jones believes these assertions himself, or if he's only in it for the money. In 2013, Jones was reportedly making as much as $10 million a year from his subscription-based TV network and radio advertising. But Jones's position on the veracity of his claims hardly matters. His fans are true believers.

For years after Sandy Hook, Jones's followers mercilessly trolled grieving parents, accusing them of faking their own children's deaths and demanding "proof" the children had ever existed. Leonard Pozner, the father of slain six-year-old Noah, received an avalanche of death threats from Jones's supporters, including from Lucy Richards, a fifty-seven-year-old InfoWars superfan from Florida. "Did you hide your imaginary son in the attic?" Richards wrote in one of her many missives. "Are you still fucking him? You fucking Jew bastard. Look behind you. Death is coming to you real soon." Richards was sentenced to five months in prison for threatening Noah's family. As a condition of her parole, a judge ordered that Richards cease consuming Info-Wars. But that didn't stop other trolls from continuing to harass the family. The threats were so menacing, Noah's parents were forced to move seven times in five years for their own safety.

When presenting his insane theories to his fans, Jones yells, screams, and sputters. He's all fury, no facts—the very definition of a raving lunatic. In a now-deleted video Jones uploaded to YouTube on November 4, 2016, Jones raged about Clinton and Pizzagate: "When I think about all the children Hillary Clinton has personally murdered and chopped up and raped, I have zero fear about standing up to her . . . yeah, you heard me right. Hillary Clinton has personally murdered children. I just can't hold back the truth anymore."

Jones continued to cover the conspiracy for weeks. In another now-deleted YouTube post from November 27, he ranted about Pizzagate for more than thirty minutes, referencing bizarre satanic "feasts of blood" and semen. "I don't know what the hell's going on with these people," he told his acolytes. "But I know devil worship when I see it!" Jones implored his followers: "It's up to you to research it for yourself."

Less than two weeks later, Edgar Maddison Welch, a twenty-eight-year-old InfoWars fan from Salisbury, North Carolina, heeded Jones's call. According to court records, Welch spent December 1 binge-watching YouTube videos about Pizzagate. The father of two texted his friends his intention: "Raiding a pedo ring . . . Standing up against a corrupt system that kidnaps, tortures and rapes babies and children in our own back yard."

A few days later, Welch loaded up his car with a folding knife, a .38 revolver, and an AR-15 semiautomatic and drove five hours north, to Washington, DC. He entered Comet Ping Pong wielding his semiautomatic and made his way into the kitchen. When he came upon a door that had been secured shut, he lifted his weapon and shot off the lock. Instead of the entrance to a basement torture chamber, Welch found a closet with cooking supplies. He later told police that he'd gone to "self investigate" the child sex ring, as Jones had suggested. Thankfully, nobody was injured. In June 2017, Welch was sentenced to four years in prison for his trouble.

Activated by misinformation and hate he'd found online, Edgar Welch had taken his anger, and his weapons, into the physical realm, putting dozens of people in danger. I remember wondering at the time of his arrest if Welch's behavior was an aberration or a sign of things to come.

———

Less than a year a half after Welch set off to investigate Pizzagate, five hundred miles away in a suburb of Toronto, Canada, twenty-three-year-old Alek Minassian was struggling with his own inner demons. Socially awkward, Minassian did not have an easy time with women. Online, he discovered a community of like-minded men. Incels (the word stands for "involuntarily celibate") rail against women, whom they hold responsible for their sexual frustration. They speak of an "incel rebellion" in which men will overthrow the feminist state, and they revere Elliot Rodger who, in 2014, went on a shooting rampage in Isla Vista, California, killing six people and then himself. He left behind a collection of misogynist rants blaming women for his virginity and promising to punish them for his pain.

On April 23, 2018, Alek Minassian got behind the wheel of a white rental van and headed to a busy street in northern Toronto. He drove up onto a crowded sidewalk and deliberately plowed down dozens of pedestrians, killing ten people and wounding fourteen more. Moments before the rampage, Minassian had logged on to his Facebook page. "All Hail The Supreme Gentleman Elliott Rodger," he wrote. "The Incel Rebellion has already begun!" There was a time before

Minassian and Welch, before InfoWars, Pizzagate, and troll army attacks, when people used to think that what happens online stays online. Now we know the truth.

———

For years, victims, advocates, and attorneys—myself included—have been trying to devise effective strategies to combat troll attacks. By the spring of 2017, an amazing battle plan was beginning to take shape. With the support of the Southern Poverty Law Center, Tanya Gersh, the Montana real-estate broker whose family was targeted by neo-Nazi Andrew Anglin and his Stormer Army, struck the first blow.

In a potentially groundbreaking legal move, Gersh sued Anglin for instigating the attacks, citing, among other crimes, invasion of privacy, intentional infliction of emotional distress, and violating a Montana anti-intimidation law. Gersh's federal suit is a potential watershed moment in the battle against trolls: one of the first legal actions initiated against a troll army commander. The case would decide if unleashing a troll army is protected by the First Amendment. The following month, Taylor Dumpson, the African American student government president who was also attacked by Anglin's troll army, sued Anglin, too, citing intentional infliction of emotional distress and conspiracy to commit stalking.

Neo-Nazi Anglin is not the only troll commander getting hauled into court. In April 2018, the parents of slain Sandy Hook first grader Noah Pozner sued Alex Jones for defamation in Travis County, Texas. A few months later, in August, six more Sandy Hook families filed another defamation suit against Jones in a Connecticut court. The cases were covered extensively in the news. The general public—people outside of Jones's circle of crazies and trolls—were outraged. In response to the widespread criticism, Facebook, YouTube, Google, iTunes, and Spotify all imposed sanctions on Jones, citing his violations of their platforms' guidelines concerning hate speech and other bad behaviors. His videos were taken down, his accounts put on suspension. In September 2018, Twitter permanently banned all accounts connected to Jones and InfoWars from the platform.

Predictably, Jones's supporters cried "censorship" and claimed the provocateur's right to free speech was being violated by the big bad boys of tech. But that's not how the First Amendment works. The Constitution only bans government-mandated restrictions on free expression. Private companies can set whatever rules they like. And they already do: Twitter limits the number of characters you can type in a post. Facebook has rules against nudity. Internet companies have the power to censor content and ban bad actors from their sites. They have the know-how to alter their algorithms to protect their users and minimize abuse. Given the horrors that happen on their platforms and search engines every day, it's a crime that they don't do more.

Since the earliest days of the internet, trolls have been pushing the boundaries of what's acceptable, possible, and legal online. For years they've been winning their war on human decency, targeting and terrorizing victims with abandon. But warriors like Tanya Gersh and Taylor Dumpson, the heartbroken Sandy Hook families, Zoë Quinn, Jessica Valenti, and countless other victims, survivors, and advocates are coalescing into our own unstoppable force. We are pushing case law, pressuring internet companies, and demanding comprehensive legislative reforms. If we can't slay the mob, we'll take down their commanders. If we can't fight them on the internet, we'll drag them into the court. They may have won some battles, but the war has just begun.

CHAPTER 8

PORN TROLL SEX POLICE

The Craigslist ad said, "Director looking for an adventurous, open minded actress." I've never asked Anna why those words caught her attention or what made her answer the ad. I've never asked her what ran through her mind when she went to the address the director had given her and it turned out to be a strip motel in a seedy part of Pasadena, where Anna had never been before. I've never asked her what she thought when the room door opened and she glanced inside to see three men, all of them old enough to be her father, and, in the corner, a video camera set up on a tripod. I've never asked Anna, who was eighteen at the time, any of these questions because I don't care what act of teen rebellion led Anna to the motel room that day. All I care about is the damage that was done when she closed the door behind her.

What happened to Anna set in motion an avalanche of abuse that devastated not only her but also her entire family. It started with the men in that room, but quickly snowballed to include tens of thousands of trolls who joined in, piled on, and made Anna's life unbearable. By the time she finally came to see me in 2017, Anna and her family had been trying to undo the damage for almost a decade.

The men inside that Pasadena motel room told Anna they were making a video for a client in Asia. "For his personal, exclusive viewing," they said. One of the men handed Anna a Solo cup filled with vodka and 7UP. Another gave her a paper and a pen and pointed to a place where she should sign her name. "For the collector," he said. "It's nothing, just sign."

Anna wasn't used to drinking. She remembers feeling buzzed. She isn't exactly sure when the camera turned on, but she remembers someone saying that the guy in Asia had special requests; he liked it rough. Then everything started moving fast. Anna remembers getting slapped, then choked. She remembers two men taking turns with her. There was laughter, she recalls, and one of the men growling, "Take it, you dumb bitch." She remembers starting to cry.

The men insisted the video was for a private collection, but as soon as Anna left the motel, the producers put the tape online. Almost immediately it became a sensation, posted and reposted on dozens of porn sites and viewed tens of thousands of times. Anna looked young for her age, with fine features and enormous blue eyes. And there was something about the image of Anna, looking terrified, with a man's hands around her neck, which garnered a special kind of attention. "This looks really rape-y!" one commenter posted. He meant it as a compliment.

It wasn't long before someone from Anna's high school came across the tape. The boy recognized Anna. And then, of course—because *HolyFuckingShitDuuuude!!!!!*—he put Anna on blast, texting links to the video to all his friends. Someone went into the comments section of one of the most popular porn sites and added Anna's real name and the name of her school. Quickly, more information appeared in the thread: her parents' names, the places where they worked, the family's home address.

Porn trolls sent Anna pervy and harassing text messages about what they'd seen and what they wanted to do to her. They posted filthy comments on her fifteen-year-old sister's Facebook page. They sent rape threats to her parents' house. Someone emailed a link to Anna's father, a TV executive. He was at work when he clicked open the message and was assailed with images of his teenage daughter getting a penis rammed into her mouth, choking and gagging, with tears running down her face.

Soon, the video was the first and only thing that came up when you googled Anna's name. Pages and pages of search results linked Anna to the video that had migrated across the internet and landed on hundreds of porn sites, along with all her identifying information. Anna closed her email account, got a new phone and changed her number, but somehow the trolls got that number, too. The constant harassment was so bad Anna had her name legally changed. Her parents did, too. They thought new identities might give them cover, make them less easy to find. They even moved, buying a house in a gated community the next town over. None of it helped. The trolls figured out the family's aliases and their new address and doubled down, harassing Anna's family even more.

Anna was afraid to go to college, convinced the porn trolls would track her down. She was terrified to get a job. What if someone sent her boss a link? She was even afraid of moving out because roommates have computers. When I met her, Anna was in her late twenties and still living with her parents. She felt like a prisoner held hostage by the pervs. Shockingly, her story is not uncommon.

Anna is one of more than a dozen young women I represent who've appeared in porn videos and, for years after, been stalked, harassed, and threatened as a result. I know this is not the story of all women who work in the adult industry. I recognize there are plenty of emotionally gratified and well-compensated adult actresses, exotic dancers, cam girls, dominatrices, and escorts. But these are not the women who hire me. My clients were exploited and deceived. Some of the videos featured on porn websites are actually scenes of my clients getting raped on film. The women I represent were violated first by unscrupulous porn producers. Then, as they tried to put the experience behind them, they found themselves targeted by hundreds of thousands of trolls.

Plenty of porn trolls call themselves "fans," but nothing could be further from the truth. Real fans respect and adore their favorite entertainers. Porn trolls go out of their way to make performers' lives hell. And they are relentless. Once a porn troll identifies a target, he'll spend hours scouring the internet looking for information to reveal her identity. When he finds it, he'll gleefully post it online so other porn trolls can join in the all-out campaign of public shaming.

These tech-savvy degenerates consider themselves porn aficionados. But I think they are best understood as part of the "manosphere," a rapidly growing online brotherhood of loosely affiliated misogyny forums and male supremacist hate groups. The manosphere encompasses a sprawling array of women haters, from incels and Men Going Their Own Way (male separatists who eschew relationships with women, who they think can't be trusted) to red pillers (who believe women want to be physically and mentally dominated, even raped) and pickup artists (who shun the idea of consent and share tips for manipulating women into sex by degrading them).

Ask any porn troll why he's targeting an adult actress for abuse and he'll likely tell you she "deserves it." Like the most twisted misogynists, porn trolls get off on punishing women for being sexual. That's what turns them on.

———

Despite legislators' fervent attempts to keep "smut" off the internet in the mid-1990s with the introduction of the Communications Decency Act, today the internet is home to a staggering amount of porn. Consider Pornhub, one of the most trafficked porn sites on the web. Pornhub operates like YouTube for sex. Fans upload their favorite porn clips, many of them pirated, and anyone can watch for free. In 2017 alone, users uploaded more than four million videos to Pornhub. That's enough content to fill 595,482 viewing hours, or sixty-seven years. The amount of data transferred through Pornhub in a year would fill the memory of every single iPhone in the world. And that's just one site out of the many thousands of places you can find porn online.

There is more pornography on the internet than any one person would be able to consume in their lifetime. And yet, inexplicably, consumers' hunger for new material is insatiable. No matter how much is out there, porn fans always want more, especially if it involves a performer they've never seen before. There is a huge market for new faces and young bodies. To meet this demand, pornographers place enticing, and sometimes deceptive or misleading, ads on the internet to solicit a steady stream of young women from across the country to replenish their supply.

Netflix's 2015 documentary *Hot Girls Wanted* offered a rare glimpse into the lives of these newbie adult stars. In one scene, we see a nineteen-year-old performer who goes by the stage name Stella May sitting on a bed holding a giant dildo, which is—no exaggeration—the size of a baseball bat. Stella speaks directly to the camera, explaining that a producer gave her the dildo to practice with and offered her

$1,000 if she could insert half of it into her vagina. We learn that Stella had been in the industry three months and was finding that offers for more conventional work were starting to dry up. As the film points out, unless a girl is a breakout star, porn producers will typically book an actress only two or three times before they are on to the next. Like the other young women featured in the documentary, Stella recognized that if she wanted to keep earning money, she was going to have to do something more extreme, like masturbate with a grotesquely huge dildo or perform anal sex. Anal used to be something an actress would not be expected to do until she'd been in the industry for a few years. Now, it's six months. Onscreen, Stella held the dildo in both hands and sighed.

Of course, porn has never had a great reputation for treating women performers well. But the advent and availability of free porn has totally transformed the industry, creating even more avenues for exploitation and abuse, and putting young women like my clients especially at risk. What makes this reality even more tragic is that before the explosion of internet porn, the industry seemed headed in a very different direction.

For decades, starting in the early 1970s, most American porn was produced in the same place. California's San Fernando Valley (aka San Pornando) was home to a booming, multibillion-dollar porn industry, much of it made by Wicked Pictures and Vivid Entertainment, two of the largest porn production houses at the time. The companies ran like old-school Hollywood studios, boasting large rosters of behind-the-scenes talent—including set designers, hair and makeup crews, lighting guys, scriptwriters, and film editors—and bevies of "contract girls," adult performers the studios groomed for stardom and catapulted to fame. For more than a decade, the industry flourished, driven in large part by the availability of VCR, and later DVD, players, which allowed people to easily watch porn in the privacy of their own homes. These studios, and others like them, churned out some impressive productions, including historically accurate period pieces, high-concept futuristic porn set against sleekly designed minimalist backdrops, and gauzy romantic "erotica." There were fan clubs, conventions, branded merchandise, and an official trade magazine. *Adult Video News* hosted a glitzy awards show every year, which was considered the Oscars of adult entertainment. Most important, contract girls were getting paid. In 1995, twenty-year-old newcomer Jenna Jameson signed on as a Wicked girl. Jameson's contract paid her $6,000 a month to perform in eight to ten adult feature films per year. Jameson notably took home significantly more money in the mid-'90s than many young women entering the industry two decades later. And she was expected to do far less. For instance, Jameson famously never did an anal scene.

In 2000, Jameson launched Club Jenna, her own subscription website and adult film production company. She hired her own stable of performers, reportedly paying annual salaries of between $50,000 and $150,000, plus a percentage of sales if a performer's DVDs sold more than ten thousand copies, according to a *Forbes* magazine profile, which noted her business acumen. Club Jenna was a phenomenal hit. The company posted revenues of $30 million in 2005, per *Forbes*.

Jameson wasn't the only female performer turned producer at the time. Vivid girl and former *Playboy* magazine cover model Tera Patrick operated her own porn empire, TeraVision. Adult actress Stormy Daniels, who signed an exclusive contract with Wicked in 2002, began writing and directing adult films a few years later. She quickly rose to prominence, specializing in "romantic" porn that focused more on relationships than on hard-core sex. Daniels was soon directing ten feature-length films a year.

Who knows what might have happened if this trend had continued. What would the industry be like today if more women were in positions to determine not only what porn looks like, but also how it gets produced and distributed? Would performers be treated and compensated differently if more women were in charge? Of course, there's no point in imagining this alternate reality. We know what really happened.

In 2007, the porn industry underwent a cataclysmic disruption that sent it on a completely different path. That's when a group of college-bro tech-nerds in Montreal, Canada, figured out they could make a shit ton of money from porn if they started giving it away for free. The dudes launched Pornhub the same year the first generation of iPhones hit the market and immediately began developing their platform for use on mobile devices. Porn consumption changed almost overnight. Suddenly, all a horny porn fan needed to access hours of delight was a smartphone and an internet connection.

Of the many industries impacted by the advent of the internet, porn has arguably undergone one of the greatest transformations. The studio system that made Jenna Jameson a millionaire is long gone. These days, online distribution puts billions of dollars into the hands of website operators who generate revenue from advertisements while keeping money away from the people who produce and star in these films. Critics compare the way the industry works now to a sweatshop. All the money is concentrated at corporate headquarters; meanwhile, the women on the factory floor are doing all the hard work.

By 2018, Pornhub had become one of the most trafficked websites on the internet, with ninety-two million visitors per day. For obvious reasons, this new business model was a sweet deal for porn fans (it's free and in my phone!), but a catastrophe for the industry as a whole, and performers in particular. Production companies that had previously specialized in high-quality feature-length adult DVDs began to go out of business. In their wake, a generation of independent pornographers emerged. These guys aren't interested in investing in contract performers and making careers. Their specialty is amateur porn, which means low-budget, unscripted, frequently hard-core videos featuring novice, and often very young, performers. The girls come from small towns and large cities. Some are seeking a certain type of celebrity (this is a generation who grew up knowing a sex tape launched Kim Kardashian's career, after all); others are desperate for cash. These days, a performer might be paid anywhere from a few hundred dollars to a few thousand if they are willing to do something more specialized, like hard-core double penetration. But the financial rewards are fleeting. During the '80s and '90s, adult performers enjoyed careers that spanned years, sometimes even a decade or more. In the free-porn economy, a typical career is over within a year.

———

One of Pornhub's most ingenious innovations is the platform's search functionality, which allows users to browse porn by category: from the obvious ("blowjobs," "babysitter," and "teens") to the less so ("closed caption," "cosplay," and "smoking"). It's also worth noting that since Pornhub is a crowd-sourced website, whoever posts the material gets to choose the caption and the tail for the URL. So, let's say a video gets posted to Pornhub called "Emily Dickinson Chokes on a Big Cock." The URL would be something like www.pornhub.com/emilydickinsonchokesonabigcock. You could search her name on Pornhub and find the video. But Pornhub also has great search engine optimization, which means if you googled Emily Dickinson, a link to the video would come up in the results. Even if I got the video removed from Pornhub, the link would still exist, directing you to Pornhub's home page.

On Pornhub, each video caption is carefully crafted for maximum market appeal, like "The new girl at work blows her bosses for a raise" (more than sixty thousand views); or "Exxtra small teen gets punished after she cheated on her boyfriend" (sixteen million views). Although a category called "romantic" exists, much of the porn offered on the site is rooted in images of male aggression, including millions of videos depicting men choking and slapping women, and ejaculating on their faces (also known as "facials"). An entire subgenre of porn features women performing "forced blow jobs" (also known as "facial abuse," "extreme face fucks," "gagging and choking"). These scenes typically show a close-up of a woman's face while a man aggressively rams his penis into her mouth and simultaneously slaps, punches, chokes, and berates her in the most vulgar language imaginable. Also popular is white supremacist porn in which a white man will "facially abuse" a woman of color while hurling racial epithets. Sometimes the women are bound in chains, like slaves. Researchers estimate that 90 percent of the most popular porn contains depictions of violence against women.

In the 1970s and '80s, feminist writer Andrea Dworkin tried to explain to anyone who'd listen that porn isn't just another form of entertainment. By offering visions of women who appear to be enjoying aggressive, violent, and degrading sex, porn promotes and normalizes violence against women, Dworkin argued. She famously described pornography as a "celebration of rape and injury to women." Not many agreed. Dworkin was dismissed, even by other feminists, as too "radical." She was accused of espousing a man-hating agenda and derided for having hairy legs. But in 2016—almost four decades after Dworkin wrote her groundbreaking and definitive work on the matter, *Pornography: Men Possessing Women*—a meta-analysis of twenty-two different studies of pornography published in the peer-reviewed *Journal of Communication* found an overwhelming correlation between regular porn consumption and people who hold a "favorable attitude" toward, or engage in, acts of sexual aggression. Of course, this is not true of all porn consumers. For many people, porn is a positive part of their sex lives. Still, there is a body of research that links porn consumption with various negative behaviors, including a higher likelihood of using verbal manipulation, drugs, and alcohol to coerce people into sex. In other words, a case could be made that the power dynamics we see acted out in front of the camera are not only a reflection of how the product gets made; they may also influence viewers to adopt these same attitudes about control and dominance. It's all connected.

Notably, some of the porn Dworkin was railing against decades ago seems almost quaint by today's standards. Back then, some of the most popular pornography was story-driven, feature-length films like *Deep Throat* and *The Devil in Miss Jones*. These flicks played in movie theaters (this was before VCRs and DVDs, back when people had to watch porn in public), were reviewed by mainstream film critics, and became huge box office hits. Plot-driven porn dominated the market until the mid-2000s. A slickly produced porn about, say, the antics that ensue when a bevy of cheerleaders get together for a slumber party might run forty-five minutes. By comparison, in 2017 the typical amount of time people spent on Pornhub for each, ahem, session was nine minutes and fifty-nine seconds. These viewers aren't looking for a plotline. It's all about the sex, which is exactly what amateur porn producers deliver.

Most porn production companies today are low-budget, shoestring operations, like the type Anna encountered in that hotel room—think two guys and a camera. These pornographers have abandoned the pretense of plot altogether and replaced it with single-concept shoots, often depicting a scenario in which a woman gets coerced, tricked, threatened, or physically forced into sex. From "casting couch" to "forced blow job," lack of consent *is* the story.

Some of the most popular adult entertainment available online features young women who've never before appeared in porn. Adult sites are filled with videos of fresh-faced, "barely legal" teens perched on beds in random hotel rooms. Often, the voice of an off-screen male director can be heard interviewing the girls about how excited they are to be doing porn for the very first time. Sometimes, the warm-up questions are meant to humiliate: "You're not too bright, are you?"

After the interview comes the sex. Often discomfort, even fear, is clearly visible on the young woman's face.

First-timer porn is so in demand that there now exist many websites dedicated solely to this market, including one subscription site I've come to know well, GirlsDoPorn.com. For $29.99 a month, subscribers are offered a new forty-five-minute video every week of a girl getting initiated into the world of porn. "You will not find these girls on any other website," promises the banner on the site's home page. "All girls are 100 percent exclusive—this is the one and only time they do porn." Beneath the banner are thumbnail images of hundreds of girls posed fully clothed and smiling demurely on neatly made hotel beds. Below each thumbnail is a video clip of the same girl naked, on her knees, having aggressive sex with a male actor whose face is never shown. Presumably, the conceit of the website is that innocent girls actually love rough sex with complete strangers. But some young women who appear on these porn videos were coerced into it, or worse. I represent almost a dozen women between the ages of eighteen and twenty-two who are suing Girls Do Porn for multiple horrific and criminal acts.

———

Almost every woman I represent in the suit against Girls Do Porn tells the same story: she responded to a Craigslist ad calling for models. But the ads were deceptive, with links leading to innocuous-looking websites with benign-sounding domain names like BeginModeling.com, ModellingGigs.com, or BubbleGumCasting.com, all of which were actually run by the owners of Girls Do Porn. None of the ads mentioned anything about porn. Instead, aspiring models were told to send photos of themselves, along with their height, weight, and contact information.

Each of my clients was contacted by a man who said he was interested in hiring her. Eventually, he disclosed that the job would involve nudity and sex. When my clients balked, as many of them did, he reassured the women they had nothing to worry about. The video was for a private client, he explained, some rich guy who lived in Australia or New Zealand. It will never appear on the internet, he promised. Your name won't be used. *No one will ever see it.*

The producers even put some of my clients in touch with a girl named Kailyn who had supposedly filmed for the company before. In text messages Kailyn was warm and reassuring. "I am a very easily sketched out person when it comes to stuff like this," she texted one of my clients. "I felt like a complete idiot because I realized I had nothing to worry about haha. . . . There is no way anyone will find out. . . . It goes out to wealthier countries: yea DVDs and stuff like that, but nothing is online!"

My clients were offered up to $6,000 for less than an hour of work. For young women looking to make some extra money, the offer was too good to pass up. Each of my clients was flown to San Diego and driven to a nice hotel, often a Marriott or Radisson, for their shoot. At the hotel, the men behind Girls Do Porn had their scheme down like clockwork. First, they'd persuade the girl to consume alcohol and marijuana to help her "relax"; then they'd present her with a release form filled with indecipherable legalese, which they'd rush her into signing. "Here," the men would say, shoving the contract in a girl's face. "It's nothing. It's a tax form. Just sign your name."

For their on-camera interviews, the girls were coached to act bubbly and enthusiastic. If they didn't act happy or flirtatious enough—like when they were presented with the question "Is this your first time doing porn?"—the producers would stop filming and make the girls re-answer the question until they appeared sufficiently enthused. When one of my clients got cold feet and told the producers she wanted to leave, the men threated to sue her for the price of the airline ticket and insisted they'd cancel her return flight home. She had no choice but to do what they wanted.

The shoots would last many hours, sometimes days. They were frequently painful for my clients and involved multiple sex acts—many of which had not been agreed upon in advance. My clients were rarely paid the amount they'd been promised. As she was leaving her shoot, one young woman was handed, as her payment, a roll of money with a hundred-dollar bill on top. She later discovered the producer had wrapped the hundred-dollar bill to disguise what was actually a roll of singles. Another client was promised a $7,000 fee. But when the shoot was over the producer said he'd only pay her $2,000 because she looked too "old." Other clients, who were paid less than the agreed-upon amount, were told it was because they had bruises, cellulite, or visible scars.

The girls were powerless to negotiate. They were thousands of miles from home and the men held their plane tickets. Realizing they'd been manipulated, the women tried to put the episodes behind them and get on with their lives after they returned home. They'd been promised over and over that no one would ever see the sexually graphic videos. But every client I represent says that within weeks of their filming, the videos were posted online.

The full-length videos were featured on the Girls Do Porn subscription website. Shorter teaser clips got posted on the company's other site, Girls-Do-Porn.com, which gives viewers free access while promoting links to the subscription service. Clips were also posted on Pornhub, where they were given captions like "Dumb 18 Year Old

Blond Throated Hard at Facial Abuse." Some of my clients' videos were viewed more than a million times.

This is no surprise. The innocent-girl-next-door-goes-wild-for-sex trope has been a favorite in commercial porn for decades. There is an entire babysitter subgenre based on exactly this premise. In the past, though, these vignettes were often acted out by seasoned adult stars dressed in pigtails and cheerleader outfits. Consumers knew the cheerleader/babysitter/schoolgirl they were jerking off to was all a big act. But the young women featured on Girls Do Porn are different. They aren't facsimiles of innocence and inexperience; they're often the real deal. Fans became obsessed with learning the young women's true identities. In the comment sections on the site, fans ask one another over and over, "What's her name?"

It was only a matter of time before my clients got doxed. Trolls uncovered, then posted, the girls' full names and identifying information, the names of the high schools they attended, the places they worked, and links to the social media accounts of their family members. Sometimes, this is how my clients learned that their explicit videos had been posted online: their mother or brother or boyfriend or boss would get sent a link by a porn troll trying to ruin the young woman's life. One of my clients was a high school physics teacher. A porn troll emailed the principal at her school links to a porn video that my client had made years earlier. Within days, my client was fired. Another client had once posted on YouTube a video of herself performing in a ballet recital as a child. A porn troll created a mash-up of my client's recital with clips of her having anal sex. He then posted it online under her real name. Her family no longer speaks to her. On behalf of almost two dozen plaintiffs, my firm is one of several jointly suing Girls Do Porn for committing multiple crimes, including fraud, negligent misrepresentation, and intentional infliction of emotional distress. I only wish we could also sue the trolls.

———

Since the earliest days of Usenet groups, tech-savvy trolls have made a sport of finding individuals' private information—everything from home addresses to high school transcripts—and revealing it online. "Dox" is a neologism of "docs," as in "dropping docs," which is what some folks called it back in the day. Hackers especially love doxing. In 2008, the hacker collective Anonymous doxed the senior leadership of the Church of Scientology and sent them death threats as part of a coordinated attack that spanned several countries and disrupted service on the official website for days.

In many cases, doxing leads to offline attacks. In fact, sometimes that's the point. In 2015, Walter Palmer, a dentist from Minneapolis, Minnesota, was doxed after it was reported that he had tracked and killed Cecil the lion, a beloved resident of a protected wildlife reserve in Zimbabwe. Palmer's home and work addresses were tweeted and retweeted. He received death threats, his office was picketed, and his vacation home in Florida was spray-painted with the words "Lion Killer."

Most social media sites, like Twitter and Facebook, forbid users from posting other people's personal information. But these guidelines are routinely ignored, especially by political activists and extremists. Increasingly, these groups are using doxing as a weapon in their ideological wars. In the days following an August 2017 white supremacist rally in Charlottesville, Virginia, several left-leaning activists launched crowdsourcing campaigns on Twitter to dox the torch-wielding Nazis who'd been caught on video chanting racist slogans. One white nationalist was fired from his job after his identity was revealed; another was disowned by his family.

That same month, Nazi trolls launched a doxing counterattack, which was reported by The Intercept after the publication obtained chat logs from a white supremacist private discussion board. Nazis had collected the photographs, social media profiles, home addresses, phone numbers, email addresses, dates of birth, driver's license numbers, vehicle information, places of employment, and, in one instance, social security numbers of fifty individuals whom the white supremacists identified as opponents of their Nazi agenda. One of their targets, a twenty-two-year-old college student, found herself in the Nazis' crosshairs after she told one of them to "fuck off" on Twitter.

In June 2017, Massachusetts representative Katherine Clark, who had been a victim of a swatting attack herself, introduced the Online Safety Modernization Act, which would directly address internet-based crimes against individuals (as opposed to attacks on businesses or government entities, which have traditionally been the focus of cybercrime legislation). The bill would make doxing with the intention of causing harm, swatting, and sextortion federal crimes, and proposed that $20 million in federal grants be designated for training state and local law enforcement in how to identify and investigate these crimes. This is exactly the kind of comprehensive legislation we need to keep the most heinous troll behavior in check. The bill was referred to the Subcommittee on Crime, Terrorism, Homeland Security, and Investigation. As of this writing, the Online Safety Modernization Act is still collecting dust.

———

Doxing is a form of vigilantism meant to intimidate or terrorize a target. But for women who've appeared in adult videos—regardless of whether they participated voluntarily, through coercion, or against their will—getting doxed also violates a long-standing unwritten rule of the industry. In porn, performers use fake names. Aliases like "Bambi Woods," "Vanessa Del Rio," and "Stormy Daniels" are great for branding. But stage names also serve another purpose. They offer a measure of privacy and protection to adult performers and their families, especially their children. Until recently, respecting adult stars' right to keep their real names private was standard porn industry practice.

Porn trolls don't care. Instead, they expose and shame adult film stars with a focus and dedication I rarely see in other trolls. Sure, there are trolls who might harass their targets for a couple of days, maybe weeks. But porn trolls stay on task. Hiding behind a shield of anonymity—using masked accounts and untraceable avatars—they'll scour the internet tirelessly, using a staggering array of hacking skills and tricks, including facial-recognition software, to uncover the true identity of a target and details of her life, family, and friends. Doxing adult actresses has become so popular that, in 2010, some asshole created Porn Wikileaks, a website devoted entirely to exposing porn stars and fucking with their lives.

Within a year of its creation, Porn Wikileaks had exposed the identifying information of more than fifteen thousand adult performers. One actress complained to the Daily Beast, "They posted pictures of my dad, my mom, my sister . . . they put pictures of their residence, and their actual addresses and private phone numbers. They posted a photo of my apartment." She continued: "My mom is a school teacher and people have emailed and called the elementary school." The actress, who had been out of the adult industry for years, said she was driven nearly "psychotic" by the dox.

Doxing of adult stars and the harassment that follows can have profound effects on victims' personal and professional lives, and their mental health. These attacks are designed for maximum public humiliation; in some cases, they lead to rejection by family and friends. At least two of my clients who've been targeted by porn trolls have attempted to take their own lives. Worst of all, these attacks never seem to end. Once a woman's real name and identifying information get attached to a video, the harassment against her and her family can go on for years, just like it did with Anna.

Outing and harassing adult actresses is simply another iteration of slut-shaming, designed to sanction, humiliate, and silence women for their sexual behavior. Of course, slut-shaming is nothing new. In fact, it's an enduring American tradition, like racism. In seventeenth-century colonial America, women suspected of prostitution or other "bad" behaviors were strapped into wooden contraptions called ducking chairs and paraded through town to be ridiculed by their neighbors and friends. Historians note that some men of the day found the spectacle of a woman bound and deliberately humiliated sexually titillating. Some things never change.

———

By the time Anna first contacted me in early 2017, her life had been completely undone by the coerced porn and subsequent doxing and harassment she and her parents had endured. Anna had abandoned her plans for furthering her education, convinced porn trolls would find her on any campus. She had never applied for a job or lived with roommates. For years, Anna spent most of her days alone, holed up in her childhood bedroom in her parents' house. Still, she had dreams of something better. Anna is a gifted pianist. She'd been playing since she was a child and sometimes thought about performing in public. But as quickly as the notion came to her, she'd remember the video. By the time Anna was in her twenties, the video had been viewed millions of times. Anna was terrified the porn trolls would find out about her music and ruin that for her, too.

In 2017, Anna read about me in the *New Yorker* magazine. I'd been profiled by Margaret Talbot in a ten-page feature. Talbot described me as a "pioneer in the field of sexual privacy." The piece mentioned my work with one client who had been doxed after appearing in coerced porn, and with another, a cam girl, who had been the victim of sextortion. Anna called my office and set up an appointment.

She flew from Los Angeles to New York with her mother, who glanced uncomfortably around my conference room as Anna shared her story. Anna told me that, in the past, she'd contacted various websites and tried to have the video removed. She'd even offered to pay. Most site operators didn't respond to her inquiries, she said. But one who did explained to Anna that the producer who owned the copyright for the video was the only person with the power to have the video removed.

"He's right," I told Anna. Just like the women who'd been conned by Girls Do Porn, Anna had also been tricked into signing a release form that gave the producer ownership over the video. "Legally, the guy who filmed you can do whatever he wants," I said. "As long as he owns the copyright, you have no control."

"I don't understand why we can't sue the websites," said Anna's mother.

I gave Anna and her mother a quick primer on the evils of Section 230 of the Communications Decency Act. "As long as the material on the site is uploaded by users, the owners of the websites are protected from litigation," I added. "It's perfectly legal for those bastards to make money by exploiting you."

I did have an idea, though. I told Anna and her mother that I could try to track down the producer and offer to purchase the copyright from him. "He might want a lot of money," I cautioned.

Anna's mother looked up. "We'll pay whatever it takes."

It took weeks of working my contacts in the adult entertainment industry before my senior associate Lindsay Lieberman and I finally made some headway. I found not only the name of the producer, but also the producer's lawyer. I picked up the phone and gave him a call. He laughed in my face. "There's no way my client's gonna sell this," he said with a snort.

"My client wants to negotiate," I countered. After almost a month of offers and counteroffers, we finally had a deal. Anna is lucky to have wealthy parents. They paid the producer six figures for the copyright, more money than most people earn in a year.

Removing sexually explicit images from the web is an important part of the work we do at my firm. Most of the time, the photos or video have been captured or distributed without my clients' consent, as in cases of "revenge porn." But, as in Anna's case, some of the content is produced by pornographers. And some of these guys have lawyered up, hiring attorneys who specialize in protecting the "intellectual property" of pornographers and keeping adult content on the web.

I once had to negotiate with an attorney whose professional website includes XXXLaw in the URL. On his home page he's penned a patriotic-sounding message about liberty, freedom, and porn: "The battle we will wage—and win—is not a narrow struggle merely about what is permissible in adult entertainment," he declares, "but rather about the range of the human soul to freely dream, express, and receive." I was trying to buy the copyright to a brutally violent and exploitive film one of my clients had appeared in. The lawyer insisted the film was the "crown jewel" of his pornographer client's collection.

There are so many porn websites, and so many assholes who've downloaded images to their own computers and put them back up even after we've had them taken down, that handling our clients' porn-removal needs is practically its own job. My staff spends more than thirty hours a week scanning the internet looking for links to explicit images and videos of our clients and issuing DMCA takedown notices to the offending websites. According to the Digital Millennium Copyright Act of 1998, websites are legally bound to remove content if the copyright owner issues a takedown notice. But we need to send separate requests every time an image or video is reposted, and to each site on which the image or videos appear. It's tedious, time-intensive work, but worth it. By 2018, my firm had removed 30,000 videos and images from the web, including Anna's.

For months after the copyright was transferred from the pornographer to Anna, we spent several hours a week issuing hundreds of DMCA takedown notices to porn sites. We'd remove the video from a particular site, and a week later it would appear somewhere else. After we'd been working on Anna's case for almost half a year, we felt confident in our success. Her video was off Pornhub and hundreds of other sites. Explicit porn was no longer the first thing that came up when you googled her name. I could hear the change in Anna's voice when she called me one day to share some good news. She'd gotten her first job. Anna had been hired as a house pianist at a small supper club in West Hollywood, not far from where she still lived with her parents.

The day before the show, Anna forwarded me an email the club owner had sent to Anna earlier that morning. It was a screenshot of a message that had been emailed anonymously. It said, "I thought you might like to know about the other talent that whore is famous for." Underneath was a screen-grab of an eighteen-year-old Anna bound and gagged, with tears streaming down her face.

CHAPTER 9

POWER PERVS

I had been in business only six months when I received a call from a young woman I'll call Jonetta. When she told me about her terrifying predicament, the crime was so unfamiliar to me I didn't even know what to call it. There were elements of revenge porn—a man Jonetta had met online was threatening to expose explicit images of her without her consent—but none of the other details fit a typical revenge porn case. The man threatening Jonetta wasn't an angry or vindictive ex trying to "teach her a lesson," nor was he a psycho, like Juan Thompson, on a mission to destroy Jonetta's life. In fact, the two had never dated, or even met in person. The offender hadn't hacked into Jonetta's computer, either. He'd obtained the naked image of Jonetta one night while the two were talking via Skype. He'd coaxed her into disrobing for him, and then, without her knowledge, he'd screen-grabbed the image. The next day he messaged her, warning that he would share the image with all her contacts on Facebook if she didn't do as she was told. He demanded Jonetta masturbate in front of her webcam so he could watch, or else.

Jonetta was seventeen years old and a victim of a crime called "sextortion." Working Jonetta's case is when I first learned of the term. Two years later, in 2016, the Department of Justice would identify sextortion as one of the fastest-growing threats to children online.

Jonetta's ordeal began months before she'd contacted me, when she joined an online chat room for teens questioning their sexuality. There, she was immediately befriended by another teenage girl. The two messaged each other constantly, sharing their deepest fears and insecurities. Jonetta felt supported and understood. Eventually, Jonetta's friend offered to introduce Jonetta to a guy she might like. "He's a billionaire from Dubai," the friend said. Jonetta was intrigued.

Jonetta and "the billionaire" started messaging and video-chatting on Skype. He was friendly and solicitous. He asked Jonetta about school and her parents. He said he'd like to fly her to Dubai. He told her she was beautiful. One day, after months of communication, he told her he wanted to see her body. Jonetta was hesitant at first. But she trusted her new friend and the girl who'd made the introduction. Finally, she relented.

The next day, he told her he'd captured her image. "You can block me on Skype or delete your Facebook profile but it won't really help," he said. He threatened to send the pictures to everyone she knew if she didn't "behave." By the time Jonetta contacted me, she'd begun to wonder if maybe the girl who'd first befriended her in the teen chat room and the guy from Dubai—if he even really *was* from Dubai— were actually the same person. The entire operation, she suspected, had been an elaborate ruse, a setup. "I don't know what to do," she told me. "He's going to ruin my life."

I could hear the desperation in her voice, and it scared me. At the time, I knew of only one instance in which a predator attempted to blackmail a young girl into sending explicit images, and it had ended in horrible tragedy. In 2012, fifteen-year-old Amanda Todd uploaded to YouTube a haunting, nine-minute, black-and-white video that would soon go viral. Using flash cards, Amanda shared that when she was in seventh grade, two years earlier, she and her friends visited video chat rooms to meet new people. One afternoon, egged on by commenters who called her pretty and asked her to flash, she quickly bared her breasts in front of her webcam. A year later, a grown man who'd captured the image contacted her on Facebook, threatening to distribute the picture if Amanda didn't "put on a show." He knew Amanda's address and where she went to school. Eventually, the perpetrator sent the image to Amanda's friends and family. He created a Facebook account and used the image of Amanda's breasts as his profile picture. At school, Amanda was teased and ridiculed relentlessly. She suffered depression and anxiety and changed schools multiple times trying to escape the bullying.

"I can never get that photo back," Amanda wrote on a flash card for her video. "Everyday I think why am I still here." Less than two months after posting the video, Amanda took her own life at her home in Port Coquitlam, British Columbia. After her death, the video was shared millions of times, gaining international attention. Media reports at the time described Amanda's story as a tragic case of bullying. But before she was slut-shamed by her peers, Amanda had been targeted and sextorted by an adult male predator, just like Jonetta.

Jonetta's was my first sextortion case. But since 2014, I've represented dozens of clients who've been targets. The perpetrators are some of the most methodical, patient, and diabolical I see. Sextortionists will spend months, even years, hunting, grooming, and manipulating their targets, forcing them into sexual servitude that feels impossible to escape. The more victims beg and try to bargain with their captors, the more torture these criminals inflict.

Sextortion is a crime of escalating abuse. An offender armed with a single image will use that image to sextort a target into sending a video, then use the video to compel the victim to send something even more graphic. My sextortion clients have been forced to strip, masturbate, and engage in group sex. One child was forced to go into a school bathroom and eat her own excrement. Some offenders refer to their victims as slaves.

———

There was a time not that long ago when a sex predator had to have direct access to his target. If he preyed on children, he might maneuver his way into a position as a teacher, mentor, or coach. If he preferred adults, he'd choose a profession in which he'd have authority over young and impressionable, or financially vulnerable, subordinates. In the past, wealth, status, fame, and influence gave predators increased access to potential victims. But the internet has leveled the playing field. Now any tech-savvy criminal has the keys to a kingdom of potential victims, many of them children. Sextortionists—who studies show are overwhelmingly male—don't need to be anybody special in the offline world. Online, these predators are totally in control.

Consider, for example, the case of Luis Mijangos, whose story was captured in shocking detail by David Kushner in 2012 in *GQ* magazine. According to Kushner, thirty-two-year-old Mijangos lived in a single-story modest ranch house in Santa Ana, California, with his mother, two sisters, and half brother. As a teenager, Mijangos had been shot, caught in cross fire while riding in the back seat of a friend's car. A bullet had lodged in Mijangos's spine, rendering him paralyzed for life. Alone in his room, with nothing but a computer and days stretching out before him, Mijangos learned to code. He was naturally gifted and quickly became a skilled hacker. He taught himself how to infiltrate strangers' computers and infect them with malware so he could root through their hard drives, emails, and photos. He even discovered how to remotely control his targets' webcams. For hours on end, Mijangos would watch and listen to his victims. He kept elaborate files with their personal information. Armed with this ammunition, Mijangos began contacting victims through their computers, sending them naked images and videos he'd captured of them and describing their bedrooms so they'd know they were being watched. Eventually, he would threaten to expose his targets unless they produced, for his pleasure, sexually explicit videos of themselves.

When Mijangos was finally arrested in June 2010, federal investigators found more than fifteen thousand webcam videos and nine hundred audio recordings. He'd hacked into the computers of 230 people, forty-four of whom were minors. It was one of the first widespread sextortion cases handled by federal law enforcement. But as revealed in the Brookings Institution's groundbreaking report, *Sextortion: Cybersecurity, Teenagers, and Remote Sexual Assault,* Mijangos is hardly unique.

In 2016, the Washington-based think tank analyzed the fact patterns and outcomes of nearly eighty cases of sextortion involving an estimated three thousand victims, a number that Benjamin Wittes, lead author of the Brookings Institution report, calls the "tip of a very large iceberg." The study, which I was honored to contribute to, is considered the first comprehensive look at sextortion in the United States. The report focuses its attention on cases like Mijangos's that have been adjudicated in the courts or covered by the media. But most of the cases I've worked on exist in the shadows. Often my clients don't go to the police or speak to reporters. They are so devastated by their tormentors that their main objective, and my number one priority, is to get the offenders to leave them alone.

Several of my clients were sextorted by former partners who threatened to distribute their target's naked images or videos unless the women returned to the relationships or acquiesced to the offenders' demands for sex. In one case, a woman was coerced into marriage after her now-husband threatened to send photos of her scantily clad to her devoutly religious family. I've also represented clients who were violated three ways: first, when their images got posted on revenge porn sites by their asshole exes; second, when they were doxed by porn trolls who put their private information online; and third, when they were sextorted by offenders who used the information to blackmail my clients into sending more images, or engaging in video sex.

Sextortion is also a tactic employed by sex traffickers and other pimp-type assholes to enslave girls and get them to work for free. One of my clients was sextorted by a piece of shit who ran a cam girl website. He convinced my client to work for him temporarily. When she told him she was no longer interested, he threatened to distribute sex videos of her to her friends and family if she didn't continue working as a cam girl without any pay.

Disturbingly, I've also encountered several sextortionists who are minors themselves, some as young as thirteen. These underage offenders coerce and cajole girls from school into sending them images, the way Macie's high school boyfriend did with her. Then they use those images to force girls to send more—and more explicit—pics. Often this behavior is encouraged by peers who make a competition out of who can get the most sexually graphic images. And there is no reason to believe that adolescents fluent in sextortion techniques will not continue the behavior into adulthood. The growing threat of sextortion is yet another compelling argument for teaching young people consent and refusal skills in school.

My sextortion cases are varied, but the victims have one thing in common: they all feel trapped by the abuse. Isolation and despair can be especially acute in children targeted by adults. For many young victims, like Amanda Todd, suicide seems like the only option. In 2015, the FBI analyzed forty-three sextortion cases involving child victims: at least two children had killed themselves and at least ten others had tried to take their own lives. The desperation these children face is unimaginable.

According to a 2016 Department of Justice report to Congress about child sexual exploitation, sextortion is "by far the most significantly growing threat to children." According to the DOJ, sextortionists target more child victims per offender than all other child sex predators. And the offenders can be anywhere: down the street or across the globe. Amanda Todd's predator, Aydin Coban, lived in the Netherlands. In 2017, Coban, then thirty-eight, was sentenced to ten years and eight months behind bars for his sexual blackmail of almost forty young women, gay men, and children.

Sextortionists are skilled and ruthless manipulators, especially when targeting children. In 2015, a twenty-five-year-old Ohio man was sentenced to six years in prison after sexually exploiting a thirteen-year-old girl via Skype. The offender told the girl that if she didn't comply with his sexual demands, he'd blow up her computer, which she'd received as a Christmas gift. She believed him. Offenders have forced children to ingest their own ejaculate and perform sex acts with younger siblings and family pets. By demanding children produce explicit material, perpetrators thrust young victims into a psychic crisis: they feel responsible for their own torture and as though they've helped orchestrate their own abuse. Without the life experience to understand they are being manipulated, and with limited refusal skills for combating coercion, children are no match for these monsters.

The calls we get from young victims of sextortion are the most heartbreaking our firm receives. The children are in horrible crisis, and many are too afraid or embarrassed to tell their parents. I'll reassure them that it's not their fault, and offer to help them tell their parents. "We can talk to them together," I'll say. I'll even promise to take their cases for free. But, I'll explain, I can't represent them without their parents' consent. Before we end the call, I always give them the twenty-four-hour hotline number for the National Center for Missing and Exploited Children (NCMEC at 1-800-843-5678), where they can find excellent support for families and victims of sexual exploitation, including sextortion. Too often we don't hear from the kids after the first call. We'll follow up and follow up, but if they've ghosted, there's nothing we can do but hope that they reached out to the NCMEC.

———

When Jonetta contacted me in 2014, her family couldn't afford to pay any legal fees. But I wasn't going to turn her away. I offered her advice for free. I suggested she first report the crime to her local police. I wasn't surprised when she told me the police insisted they couldn't help her if the offender was anonymous. One of the officers suggested Jonetta come back to the precinct once she'd figured out her predator's identity. This is the catch-22 so many victims face. They need law enforcement to help them de-anonymize their offender, but law enforcement won't help them if they don't have a name.

Next, Jonetta and I reported the crime against her to the FBI. The agency has a dedicated website, the Internet Crime Complaint Center (IC3.gov), where victims can fill out online forms detailing offenses committed against them. The agency reviews the complaints, identifies trends, and forwards any recommendations for investigations to federal, state, local, or international law enforcement. But I wasn't confident the agency would investigate a report of sextortion. At the time, the FBI was more focused on sex predators who were targeting children online and luring the kids into meeting them in person.

I was hitting a brick wall when it came to getting law enforcement involved in Jonetta's case, but I had to do something. Sitting in my office one day, I had a hunch. Jonetta's perpetrator was threatening to share her naked pictures. If he made good on his threat, he'd be guilty of distributing child pornography. The penalties for such a crime are heavy. He could be looking at decades behind bars.

"What he's threatening to do could get him in a lot of trouble," I told Jonetta. "It might be helpful if you laid it all out for him. Tell him you aren't going to comply with his demands. Remind him you are underage. And let him know you are in contact with an attorney." I gave Jonetta the federal criminal codes and sentencing guidelines related to possessing and distributing child pornography. I was making a calculated guess that we could scare this offender away. I was right. After Jonetta messaged him with details of his possible jail time, the "billionaire from Dubai" backed off.

We were incredibly lucky. Battling sextortionists is usually not that simple. Since my first sextortion case, I've developed an arsenal of tactics for taking these fuckers out. If law enforcement won't assist, at my firm we do our own sleuthing to find the identity of an offender. We start with whatever information our clients are able to provide—a Twitter profile pic, a cell number, a website URL—and use open-source intelligence, digging and digging until we get a lead. One time, we figured out the name of an offender's fiancée. We checked out her Facebook page. The fiancée had helpfully announced that the couple had just purchased a home on a particular street in Louisiana. She posted a picture of the house. We blew it up and could see a number on the door. We sent the offender a scathing cease and desist letter as a housewarming gift.

Another time, we tracked an offender's IP address to an office building in Chicago. I was able to figure out the exact floor of the building the perpetrator was on. I called the employer and informed him that somebody on his staff was sextorting my client and provided the IP address. Then I messaged the offender, telling him, "You're attempting to extort my client. I've informed your boss." Sextortionists are banking on their anonymity to conduct these crimes. Invariably, once they see my firm is on to them—we know where they live, where they work, whom they live with—they stop harassing our clients.

Some of my most powerful tools are my cease and desist letters. They are also fun to write. I always open with, "I represent [my client]. I'll be taking over negotiations from here. Negotiations just ended."

The cease and desist letters I've sent sextortionists have been successful 100 percent of the time. But not enough victims have the benefit of a skilled lawyer by their side—they may not know that a person with this particular expertise exists, or they may think they can't afford it. To really combat the sextortion epidemic in a meaningful way that will protect the greatest number of potential victims, we also need law enforcement officers who understand how these offenders operate and comprehensive federal legislation that makes these behaviors a crime.

A few days after the Brookings Institution released their sextortion report, I was contacted by Massachusetts representative Katherine Clark, who was drafting a bill to help combat online sextortion. I was honored to help. To my delight, less than a month later, in June 2016, Clark cosponsored a bipartisan bill with Indiana Republican Susan Brooks. The Interstate Sextortion Prevention Act aimed to make sextortion a federal crime The bill was introduced but never voted upon. The following year is when Clark introduced the Online Safety Modernization Act to criminalize sextortion and other malicious internet crimes on a federal level. The bill also allocated $20 million for training law enforcement. This is the kind of initiative we need if we are going to help victims at the ground level, when they first report the crime. But as noted in the previous chapter, the Online Safety Modernization Act went nowhere.

I'd like to say I'm surprised by lawmakers' inaction. But I'm not. The American justice system creeps forward at a glacial pace, stymied in part by the efforts of the same powerful men who benefit from laws that protect their interests and forgive their sins.

———

Sextortion is a crime of domination and control. But make no mistake, as extreme and abhorrent as these offenders may seem, they are not monster outliers. Sextortionists are part of a vast league of sex predators who use intimidation, threats, and trickery to coerce victims into sex acts. I call these offenders "power pervs." At my firm, we deal with power pervs who've weaponized the internet, but we also combat those who operate offline. They are everywhere: in churches, in the military, on college campuses, and any place women choose to work. I've represented women who've been abused and assaulted by power pervs representing every industry, including partners at a law firm, civil rights activists, a Broadway producer, a parking lot magnate, multiple entertainment execs, a rap mogul, a politician, a comedian, a tech founder, and an inventor. My clients have been threatened with a myriad of punishments if they don't comply with their bosses' sexual demands, including being deported and losing their jobs. For generations, we've called these men sexual harassers. But this isn't about sex. Workplace sexual predators are driven by the same impulses as the most despicable sextortionists: they want to subjugate, humiliate, and bring a victim to her knees.

Like sextortion, there was a time when sexual harassment in the workplace was a problem that existed so far in the shadows it didn't even have a name. Then women started talking. In 1975, Carmita Wood, who worked in the nuclear science lab at Cornell University, was denied unemployment benefits after she decided to leave her job, where she'd been repeatedly harassed by a boss who would pin her against her desk and tell her how turned on he was. Wood subsequently joined with other activists, forming Working Women United. At a speakout event hosted by the organization, female clerical staff, factory workers, waitresses, and others shared war stories of the abuses they endured on the job. Women complained about being groped and propositioned, cornered and mauled. They spoke of bosses who demanded sexual favors in exchange for promotions, and humiliated their female employees with sexual comments every morning when they arrived at work. In 1975, the group's leaders coined the term "sexual harassment" as a way to describe the range of indignities, abuses, and assaults women were subjected to at work. That same year, the *New York Times* used the phrase in the headline of a widely reprinted article about the scourge. In the story, a twenty-seven-year-old nurse named Cathy Edmonson recounted an incident in which a surgeon exiting an operating room grabbed her from behind, with his hands clasped around her neck, and dragged her around the room. "Patients were there," Edmondson told the *Times*, "and doctors and nurses. It was his playful way of relaxing. I couldn't make a scene."

Another woman, Jan Crawford, then thirty-two, shared how she'd been fired from her job at a real estate firm after declining the invitation of a male supervisor who'd asked her on a date. "It was just devastating to me that everything could be pulled out from under me for no reason," Crawford recalled. "I had poured myself into the job . . . For several years after that, I had no ambition. I had the frightening feeling that it could all be taken away again."

Still, a decade after the term was introduced into the lexicon, the majority of Americans did not view workplace sexual harassment as a serious issue. In fact, in a 1986 *Time*/Yankelovich Clancy Shulman poll, only 17 percent classified it as a "big problem" for women at work. No one could have anticipated that only a few years later the rancorous Senate confirmation hearings of Supreme Court Justice Clarence Thomas would launch the issue of workplace sexual harassment into living rooms across America.

Thomas had been nominated by President George H. W. Bush to fill the seat left vacant after the death of Justice Thurgood Marshall. Both Marshall and Thomas were African American, but seemingly that's all they had in common. Marshall was the founder of the NAACP Legal Defense and Education Fund and a staunch advocate for civil rights. Thomas was an archconservative and, it was later reported, a porn aficionado and serial sexual harasser.

Multiple women had witnessed Thomas's bad behavior at work, including his initiating vulgar conversations about sex and female anatomy, and touching women staffers against their will. But only Anita Hill, an attorney who worked with Thomas at two federal agencies, including the Equal Employment Opportunity Commission, was asked to testify during the hearings. In front of the fourteen-member all-white, all-male judiciary committee, Hill recounted in vivid detail the way Thomas had propositioned her, made crude jokes about sex, and commented on her breasts and the size of his penis. Hill told the committee that Thomas had compared himself to porn star Long Dong Silver.

Twenty million people tuned in to watch Hill's testimony. Hill was poised, professional, and credible. But to many men, she represented a threat to their world order. She was ruthlessly attacked. In a coordinated smear campaign, conservative pundits dismissed her as delusional and unstable. A psychologist invited to testify before the committee claimed Hill possibly suffered from "erotomania," a mental illness that causes sufferers to fantasize sexual scenarios. In his bestselling book *The Real Anita Hill*, David Brock, who at the time was a right-wing operative, famously labeled Hill "a little bit slutty and a little bit nutty." Years later, Brock recanted his smears in spectacular fashion. In his memoir mea culpa, *Blinded by the Right: The Conscience of an Ex-Conservative*, Brock confessed that he'd deliberately published numerous blatant lies to support Thomas's reputation and admitted he did everything he could to "ruin" Hill's credibility, including threatening another woman who could corroborate Hill's claims, intimidating the woman into silence.

In the end, Thomas was confirmed to the Supreme Court. For decades, the justice has proven himself to be a stalwart supporter of the male power structure that put him there, voting against reproductive choice and to weaken protections for equal pay. Notably, Thomas has also voted in favor of tightening the definition of who counts as a "supervisor" in cases of sexual harassment brought before the courts, a ruling that "let a lot of people off the hook," noted Jill Abramson, coauthor of *Strange Justice: The Selling of Clarence Thomas*.

And so on it went. Men continued to sexually harass women at work: in offices, hospitals, hotels, fast-food restaurants, newsrooms, warehouses, department stores, doctors' offices; at military barracks; on factory floors; and at a paper mill on the edge of the Wishkah River in Grays Harbor, Washington, which is where it happened to me.

———

I don't know a woman who doesn't have a story of getting sexually harassed at work. Mine takes place the summer after my freshman year at Vassar. I'd envisioned spending my days writing poetry by the beach, but my father had other ideas. He'd helped reopen an abandoned paper mill and insisted I work there as my summer job. I wasn't excited about the work, but my father was paying for college; I didn't want to say no.

I worked in a warehouse the length of a football field, where the machine parts were kept. My job was to inventory stock, which included moving every item I logged from one shelf and placing it on the shelf below. While I stood on a step stool facing the shelves, with my hands filled with bits of machinery, the guys at the mill would pass by and slap my ass. Or grab it. It was as though I were one of those statues people pat for good luck. Only my eighteen-year-old ass was the totem. I hated it, but didn't say a thing, not even to my parents. My breaking point came when someone told me that a foreman had concocted an elaborate plan to "seduce" me as we hauled recycling in his truck. I begged my dad to let me quit, without ever giving him a full account of what was going on. Of course, he refused. At work I kept smiling, but at home I was miserable. I acted out my desperation in all kinds of ways. I had screaming fights with my parents. One afternoon while riding in the car with them, I threatened to open the door and jump out of the moving vehicle. I went on a hunger strike. By the end of the summer, my diet consisted primarily of Baskin-Robbins Rainbow Sherbet and these little white pills we called "mini-thins" that truckers used to stay awake.

In September, I returned to Vassar, but I still wouldn't eat. By November, I'd become so skeletal that the student health center called my mother to come get me. I was whisked off and spent a few weeks as an inpatient in a psych ward in Ballard, Washington, getting treated for an eating disorder. When I got out, it wasn't clear whether I'd be able to return to the fancy college that I'd worked so hard to get into.

I took a semester off, enrolled in a statistics class at the community college with my brother, and helped my blind aunt make a cookbook. At the time, my parents blamed my then boyfriend for making me crazy. But looking back, I know it was not having the coping skills to deal with men who felt entitled to touch my body that made me feel powerless. Like a lot of young people, I stopped eating because it was the only way to feel in control.

I worked in that factory almost two decades ago, in the mid-1990s. Since then, every boss I had until I opened my firm has been a woman. I've been fortunate to have a career in which fending off, or tolerating, unwanted advances, touches, and assault is not part of my job requirements. But for many women, and some men, intrusions into their physical space, threats to their safety, and humiliating sexual violations are a regular feature of working life.

Enduring repeated sexual harassment at work is not only demoralizing and exhausting; it can also knock women off their career paths, sometimes at great financial cost. The Stanford Center on Poverty and Inequality reported in 2018 that as many as eight in ten women who've been severely sexually harassed at work leave their jobs within two years. Even when they stay in their positions, victims of harassment, especially those who don't comply with their abusers' sexual demands, often face financial consequences: they are passed over for pay raises and promotions by spiteful bosses and denied opportunities to advance. Over the span of a career, women can lose tens, even hundreds, of thousands of dollars in wages; not to mention the emotional toll of stymied ambitions.

Workplace sexual abuse violates victims' physical safety, imperils their psychological well-being, and impedes their ability to control careers, finances, and professional destiny. Yet for generations, ever since women entered the workforce, sexual predation has been so ingrained in American workplaces it's as though our economy rested on pillars of harassment and abuse. To ensure the structure remained intact, women were routinely, and in myriad ways, intimidated, threatened, and shamed into not reporting their mistreatment. The Stanford study found that 30 percent of women who were sexually harassed or assaulted at work told nobody. As with other sex crimes, silence is built into the matrix of abuse.

But then, in the fall of 2017, the wall of silence came crashing down. The shocking story of movie producer Harvey Weinstein's decades-long pattern of gross sexual misconduct exploded into the mainstream, in October, when both the *New York Times* and the *New Yorker* magazine ran lengthy feature stories about Weinstein's abuse. Weinstein, the cofounder of Miramax and one of the most powerful figures in Hollywood, preyed upon young actresses, luring them to his hotel room under the pretense of meeting for business, only to expose himself, demand sex, forcibly grope, and even rape the women, his victims alleged. If his advances were rebuffed, the women were blacklisted. Peter Jackson, the director of the Lord of the Rings trilogy, admitted in the wake of the Weinstein scandal that he'd been directed by the mogul-predator to not hire actors Ashley Judd and Mira Sorvino because they were difficult. Both women had refused Weinstein's sexual advances. He retaliated by preventing them from getting work. That's the kind of power Weinstein wielded over the women he abused.

I represented five Weinstein accusers, including marketing executive Lucia Evans, who was instrumental in moving the New York District Attorney's Office to press charges against Weinstein. In May 2018, Weinstein was arrested and charged with first-degree rape, third-degree rape, and criminal sexual act in the first degree in connection with Lucia's accusations and those of another woman. (He'd eventually be charged with three more sex crimes relating to a third accuser.) At Weinstein's arraignment, lead prosecutor Joan Illuzzi explained the initial charges stemmed from months of investigation and that Weinstein had "used his money, power, and position to lure young women into situations where he was able to violate them sexually."

In the weeks leading up to the arrest, Illuzzi had been attentive and engaged, calling, emailing, and checking up on Lucia. As is expected of many victims involved in criminal sexual assault cases, Lucia sacrificed her privacy and time to assist the DA's office. She sat for days of questioning by investigators from both the prosecutor's office and the New York Police Department about the most intimate details of her life. She disclosed medical and professional records and was made to visit the crime scene. Many of her family members, friends, former work colleagues, college roommates, and ex-boyfriends were contacted or questioned.

While it appeared nothing was off-limits, prosecutors failed to reach out to the most critical witnesses—such as the woman she was with the night she met Weinstein—in a timely manner, if at all.

Lucia displayed phenomenal strength. Meanwhile, the prosecutors at the DA's office were buckling under the nonstop media scrutiny and clearly intimidated by the swagger of Weinstein's defense attorney.

Two days before the court date, in October 2018, Illuzzi called and said she wanted to meet with me at my office. The DA's office was dropping my client's charges, she said. "It's not that we don't believe her," Illuzzi told me, "because we do." Illuzzi blamed faulty detective work in gathering evidence. In one fell swoop, she threw the New

York Police Department under the bus and abandoned my client. When Weinstein's then lawyer, Benjamin Brafman, began a campaign to smear Lucia, claiming she'd perjured herself during her grand jury testimony, the prosecutor who'd asked so much of my client sat silent. Now if you type Lucia's name into Google, the first eight pages of results are populated by articles containing not only the lurid details of the most humiliating and traumatizing event of her life, but also claims by one of the most famous defense lawyers in the world that she is a false accuser and perjurer.

Hundreds, if not thousands, of news outlets all over the world published Brafman's false accusations about my client. Lucia's new, inaccurate, and damaging reputation as a criminal perjurer is now cemented on the internet. This is but one glaring example of the horrendous ways the criminal justice system fails victims of sexual predators. To date, Weinstein remains free on a million-dollar bail. Altogether, he spent about two hours behind bars. There are structures in place to ensure powerful men go free.

I am disgusted by the way the New York District Attorney's office handled Lucia's case. But still, I recognize the Weinstein moment as a watershed. The exposure of his crimes and misconduct changed everything. Suddenly, the conversation that for years I'd been having with my clients and friends exploded into the public space, galvanizing survivors and allies everywhere. I was invited to the palatial homes of prominent Hollywood actors for fruit and croissants. They wanted to know what they could do to help. Some of them raised and donated millions of dollars to the Time's Up Legal Defense Fund to assist less financially fortunate victims of sexual assault. But by far the most significant impact was made by the survivors themselves, the brave women and a few men who stepped forward and said #MeToo.

Within weeks of the first reports of his serial predation, dozens more women stepped forward to accuse Harvey Weinstein of acts ranging from masturbating in front of them to forcing them to engage in oral sex. Emboldened and inspired, other women reported to the press harrowing experiences they'd had with other high-profile men. Women, some of whom had kept their silence for years, told of getting groped by politicians, raped by music producers, and held captive in hotel rooms while their bosses masturbated in front of them. Within a year of Weinstein's first accusers speaking out, more than 250 powerful men—including politicians, celebrity chefs, movie directors, revered journalists, and titans of tech—had been publicly accused of sexual harassment and assault.

———

The flood of revelations in the weeks after the Weinstein story broke is widely regarded as the beginning of the Me Too movement. In fact, the movement had existed for more than a decade, the brainchild of Brooklyn-based activist Tarana Burke, who coined the phrase to help survivors of sexual assault, particularly women and girls of color, feel less alone. Then, in October 2017, after actress and activist Alyssa Milano tweeted a suggestion that women share their survivor stories on social media using the hashtag #MeToo, the movement became a worldwide phenomenon. The hashtag became a call-and-response among women who'd been targeted by the same serial predators: "He raped me"; "#MeToo." For months, it felt like every day there was a new story of another entertainer, mogul, or CEO who'd engaged in years, even decades, of rampant sexual misconduct, oftentimes with the assistance of a corporate or institutional power structure that helped cover up the abuse.

More shocking, even, than the numbers of accused were the details of their misbehavior.

Esteemed NBC newsman Matt Lauer was reported to have trapped female staffers in his office using a secret door-locking button hidden under his desk. In one stomach-turning incident, Lauer is alleged to have bent a frightened female employee over a chair and had sex with her until she passed out. Lauer was fired, and later issued a vague apology for the pain he'd caused others by his "words and actions." A few weeks later, in December 2017, sixty-seven-year-old federal judge Alex Kozinski was accused by six female clerks and other junior staff of sexual misconduct, including inappropriate touching and showing porn on his office computer, asking women if they were aroused. Kozinski resigned within weeks and issued an apology of his own for making anyone feel uncomfortable, citing his "broad sense of humor." After respected journalist Charlie Rose, who was seventy-five years old at the time, was accused of parading naked in front of female coworkers decades younger than himself, and groping their breasts and genitals, he also apologized. Rose insisted he thought he was "pursuing shared feelings, even though I now realize I was mistaken."

Of course, there are plenty of men who've risen to the top of their professions without exposing themselves to their female coworkers. Good guys *do* exist. And yet the seemingly never-ending parade of allegations levied at so many powerful men raises obvious questions about the pathology of it all: Do pervs seek power to enact their crimes? Or does power turn regular men into pervs?

———

Since the 1990s, University of California, Berkeley professor Dacher Keltner has researched the complex relationship between power and behavior. Keltner has come to some pretty interesting, though not all that surprising, conclusions. For instance, Keltner argues that the feeling of being powerful leads men to overestimate their sexual attractiveness (hello, Charlie Rose); reduces empathy and diminishes the capacity to recognize the impact of one's behavior on other people (here's looking at you, Matt Lauer); and prompts men to sexualize their work environments (ahem, you mean like watching porn in your judge's chambers in federal court, perchance?). Keltner, author of *The Power Paradox: How We Gain and Lose Influence*, says men in power are more likely to behave impulsively, flouting institutional rules and norms. Furthermore, as Keltner noted in a widely cited article he penned for *Harvard Business Review* in 2017, these abuses of power are "predictable and reoccurring."

Keltner is only one of many researchers looking at the impact of power on behavior. In 2016, Sukhvinder Obhi, a researcher at McMaster University in Ontario, Canada, discovered measurable differences when comparing the brains of powerful and less powerful individuals. Using a transcranial magnetic-stimulation machine, Obhi observed that a neural process known as "mirroring" functions differently in the two groups. Mirroring, which is considered instrumental in empathy, typically occurs when a person observes someone else doing an action; for instance, crying. The neural pathways associated with crying light up in the brain of the viewer, as though his or her brain is recognizing what crying feels like. It's the same mechanism that makes you wince when you see someone else stub their toe. To measure the mirroring response, Obhi and his team had subjects watch a video of a hand squeezing a rubber ball. Obhi found the brains of nonpowerful people lit up in response to the images. Powerful people, Obhi found, did not react as strongly. It's as though their sympathetic response was on mute.

Other researchers argue that the negative impact of power acquisition is so marked in certain individuals it qualifies as a personality disorder. Writing in the 2009 issue of *Brain: A Journal of Neurology*, neuroscientist David Owen and Duke University professor of behavioral science and psychology Jonathan Davidson offered diagnostic criteria, including fourteen symptoms, that defined a disorder they call "hubris syndrome."

The syndrome, which the researchers maintain is brought on by having years of substantial power and success, is marked by the presence of distinct behaviors, including a disproportionate concern for image and presentation, excessive self-confidence, contempt for others, recklessness, impulsivity, and "self-glorification through the use of power." While the study's authors do not specifically mention sexual acting out as a behavior associated with hubris syndrome, the description they give of those afflicted reads like the bio of at least one well-known power perv, the pussy grabber in chief. The authors warn that because those with hubris syndrome often wield tremendous power and influence, they can do "extensive damage" to the people around them. However, Davidson and Owen doubt hubristic individuals would be inclined to seek treatment, even if diagnosed. The best safeguard, they maintain, is for organizations to impose internal measures and external constraints—like independent oversight and penalties for bad behavior—to keep people in power in check.

Of course, the idea that power corrupts is as enduring as the Bible itself. Investigations into human psychology and neurobiology only confirm what we already know. Unchecked power, whether gained through money, fame, or excellent hacker skills, can be the gateway to entitlement, bad behavior, and abuse. Most important, these explanations don't excuse predators' misconduct and crimes. *Why* men behave this way hardly matters. The real question is, what are the rest of us going to do to hold these men accountable?

———

In the wake of #MeToo, the first wave of justice was poetic. Misbehaving men who'd benefited for years by silencing victims and covering up their crimes were dragged into the public square and humiliated for the world to see. These men were exposed and ridiculed on social media and in the press. They lost their jobs, future earnings, and professional reputations. In a seismic cultural shift, and perhaps one of the greatest victories of the Me Too movement, survivors spoke their truths, demanded to be heard, and changed the conversation. Finally, blame and shame were cast not on victims of sexual assault but on perpetrators, where they belong.

The second wave of justice happened when the outrage and indignation began to positively impact the lives of women who are too often ignored. The Me Too movement gained attention when relatively powerful women (actors Ashley Judd and Rose McGowan were the first Weinstein accusers to go public) stepped forward to expose even more powerful men. But there are millions of women who work in the service sector or retail jobs, in factories, on farms, and at hotels who don't have the financial freedom to speak out against their bosses. According to the Stanford Center on Poverty and Inequality's 2018 report on workplace sexual harassment, 32 percent of women who'd been severely sexually harassed on the job told no one. The force and fury of the #MeToo survivors' uprising ultimately meant gains for these workingwomen as well.

During the height of the movement, intrepid journalists, tipped off by courageous women willing to risk everything to expose the truth, reported on the serial sexual abuse of migrant farmworkers, hotel workers, restaurant staff, automotive assembly line workers, and more. Sharing and hearing long held secrets galvanized even more women, spurring them into action.

In September 2018, female employees at the country's largest fast-food chain, McDonald's, went on strike, walking out of restaurants from San Francisco to Chicago, demanding the chain take seriously and address their complaints of sexual harassment.

When Breauna Morrow, a fifteen-year-old cashier at a St. Louis Mc-Donald's, complained to her supervisor that an older male employee had made sexually graphic comments to her, she was allegedly told by the manager, "You will never win this battle." Morrow, along with nine other McDonald's employees from eight cities and seven different states, all women of color, took legal action against the multibillion-dollar company. They allege they experienced verbal and physical sexual harassment, and were ignored or retaliated against when they reported the abuse. Together they filed a complaint with the Equal Employment Opportunity Commission, the first step toward a federal civil rights suit. The complaint called on the federal agency to launch a nationwide investigation into McDonald's. The women also demanded McDonald's enforce a zero-tolerance policy regarding sexual harassment and implement mandatory training for management and staff. The chain is one of the country's largest employers, with almost 400,000 workers. This legal action has the potential to impact the lives of hundreds of thousands of women and girls working for minimum wage. The McDonald's employees' legal fees are being covered by the Time's Up Legal Defense Fund (the organization formed in the wake of the Harvey Weinstein revelations), and funded by some of the same actors who invited me to their homes to discuss what they could do to help. We are all connected in this fight.

It's no surprise that shocking and salacious stories about the degenerate behavior of multimillionaire predators make front-page news. But these high-profile power pervs are not the only enemy. Assholes, pervs, psychos, and trolls are all around us, at our jobs, in our schools, and sometimes in our own homes. They do their crimes out in the open, or after plotting and scheming in dark corners of the web. At any moment any of us can become a target. But we have extraordinary power to fight back. We can battle within the system or fight to change the system. Sometimes the best strategy is to fuck the system and work around it. We are just as ruthless and angry as the motherfuckers who are trying to take us down. We are an army of warriors. This fight has just begun.

~~CONCLUSION~~
WHERE WE BEGIN

A few years ago, I was invited to speak to a group of students at a prestigious liberal arts college about internet privacy. As I was leaving the venue, a young woman approached me to ask for advice. She introduced herself as an aspiring lawyer. "I want to do what you do," she said with a smile. She asked what classes I recommend she take, and if I had any suggestions for how she should focus her studies to prepare for a career in victims' rights. She looked at me expectantly, clutching her notebook and a pen. I took a deep breath and smiled politely.

I appreciated her energy and ambition, but the truth is I can't point to any deliberate decision or opportunity that brought me to where I am today. There was no course in law school, test I aced, book I read, clinic I interned at, professor who took a shine to me, job I worked, grades I got, or family member with connections who paved the way. In fact, I took such an unusual journey that I find it difficult to give a simple answer.

What I often tell people is that I opened my firm to become the lawyer I'd needed when I was fighting back against my psycho ex. I tell people that I taught myself about revenge porn, doxing, and swatting to help my clients navigate a legal system not designed to protect victims targeted by offenders who've weaponized the internet. I explain that I learned to become an advocate and got in the faces of lawmakers and internet company managers when I realized I needed to change policy and practices, not just punish individual offenders. While all these things are true, they don't tell the full story. In many ways, these explanations are a shorthand, a way to simplify the narrative. The truth is more complicated and not one I've wanted to share publicly, until now.

———

In early 2012, while I was working at the Vera Institute of Justice and before I met my ex, I did some online dating without great results. There was the cardiologist who pounded shots and slurred about how he'd show up at the next day's open-heart surgery like a mechanic reporting to the garage; and a metaphysicist who had to be chased away by the security guard at my office three days in a row after I told him "no thanks" to a second date. One time I went out with a guy who, over drinks, described a childhood surgery to remove part of his necrotic large intestine. Suddenly, he leaned across the bar table and grabbed my throat. He said he wanted to see how well his hands fit around my neck. There was no second date for him, either.

One afternoon I got a message on OkCupid from a guy who said he was a doctor. He seemed smart and charming. We sent flirty messages to each other for a couple of days before deciding to meet in person at an East Village bar. I felt anxious, as I often did when I met men for the first time. It was almost a relief when I saw him. He didn't look as good in person as he did in his profile pic. He had a slight frame and weak chin and was dressed in a hoodie, which made him look like he was trying too hard to be cool. Immediately, I knew I wouldn't have to worry about an awkward kiss or any "should I or shouldn't I" first-date indecision. Nothing sexual was going to happen between us; I didn't find him attractive. He kept telling me my maroon leather pants were "hot." His flattery came off as cloying and immature.

I ordered a whiskey, and we talked for a while about the Holocaust. His grandmother was a survivor, he told me. I shared stories about the clients I'd worked with at Selfhelp. As the night wore on, I excused myself to go to the bathroom. When I returned to the table, I found he'd ordered us another round. He smiled and slid a shot glass of liquor toward me. After that, things got mushy.

I remember the rest of the night as a series of hazy snapshots. He's leaning over to kiss me; I'm repulsed by the feel of his tongue darting in and out of my mouth. Then I'm standing up, announcing I want to go to a place on First Avenue for cheesy fries.

Next, we're in an apartment. My pants are around my ankles and I'm bent over on the bed. There's cat hair everywhere. The lights are bright. He is pouring rubbing alcohol on my ass and begins to suture me with surgical thread. He makes a joke about how sutures used to be made out of pig bristle. He laughs about them not being kosher.

I can feel the sharp sting of a needle going in and out of my ass cheek. I try to speak. I can hear my words slurring together. I ask what he's doing. He says not to worry, I'll like it. There's another sound: the familiar click of an iPhone shutter. It dawns on me that he is taking pictures. He finishes stitching, fucks me from behind, spits on me, hits me, and bites me so hard on the other ass cheek it feels like he is chewing off my flesh. But I don't care. I don't care about anything.

He came. Then I left.

I remember it was pouring rain. I bought a bagel at a twenty-four-hour deli. I tried to take the subway home but got off at the wrong stop. I hailed a cab and fumbled in my purse for money to pay the driver. I fell asleep curled up on my bed with my dog, still in my clothes. When I woke up the next morning, my eyes were crusted shut. I didn't feel hungover, exactly. This was different, as though nothing from the night before were real. I stripped off my clothes and looked in the mirror. There was a swastika sutured into my ass.

———

After you've been violated, there's an impulse to try to undo the damage by removing all traces that it happened at all. I see it with my clients all the time. When they come to me, they've already destroyed all their evidence. They've erased phone messages and texts, or thrown away the clothes they wore that night. They haven't reported the assault, or gone to the police, or had a rape kit done. It's a response to trauma no one talks about—this immediate need to wipe the slate clean. That was me.

After my assault, I went to see a plastic surgeon about the scar. She told me it would fade and warned me that I should be "more careful." But I didn't report my rapist to the police. I didn't get a rape kit done. I didn't want anything to do with him. All I wanted was to pretend the assault had never happened.

In my therapist's office, I deleted all the texts from the doctor and disabled my OkCupid profile. It didn't help. I could feel myself slipping into depression. For months, I spent nights and weekends in bed watching hours of mindless internet videos, eating individual-serving-sized containers of Lucky Charms for dinner and squirting low-fat whipped cream directly into my mouth, then feeding my Chihuahua the same way. I tried to numb myself with sugar and distract myself with bad TV. But fragments of memories from that night would suddenly burst through, filling me with shame. As I write this, I'm mortified by a recollection: During the rape, the doctor is behind me. I swivel my torso to try to kiss him. To kiss *him*. The man who'd drugged, beaten, and disfigured me.

In New York, the statute of limitations to file a civil case for rape in the first degree is five years. All that time, I thought of taking legal action against the doctor but didn't. I felt like a coward and a hypocrite. I worried I was endangering other women. Looking back, I know my inaction was the result of trauma. I get contacted all the time by individuals whose sexual assaults—by a boss, a boyfriend, a college acquaintance—happened ten, twenty years ago. They didn't report their crimes, either. The trauma never left them.

Sexual trauma lives in your body like a curse. It takes up residence in your stomach, your throat, or the back of your neck. It keeps you awake at night and makes you want to sleep all day. Carrying the pain is exhausting. The burden makes you feel weak. Predators are drawn to that vulnerability. They smell it like a pheromone; I'm sure of it.

I told my sister what happened to me. A couple of months later, she took me to Costa Rica to recuperate. The massage therapist at the hotel stuck his hands between my legs during a massage. Weeks later, when I was back in New York, I went on a date with somebody I'd met at a bar. We took a walk, and he insisted he had to show me something. He pulled me into a doorway, pushed me to my knees, and rammed his dick into my mouth.

I felt like I had a mark on me like a scarlet letter, only mine said "Victim." This was years before the Me Too movement emboldened an army of survivors to share their stories. It was years before I learned I didn't have to feel so alone. Back then, I felt powerless in the face of these attacks. The more they happened, the more inevitable they seemed. I secretly longed for a hero to protect me. I'm convinced that's what made me so vulnerable. My desire to feel safe made me an easy mark.

Not long after I returned from Costa Rica, I met my psycho ex. I'd restarted my OkCupid account in an attempt to have things "go back to normal." I tried to date as though nothing before had gone wrong. When my ex first reached out to me, his messages were funny and smart. He dazzled me with fancy dinner reservations and lavish gifts of clothing and jewelry. He courted me like no one ever had before. Most of all, he made me feel safe. He was a big guy, an ex–body builder and expert in jiu-jitsu. And he had a temper. He told me early in our relationship about a time he'd gotten so mad at some guy who'd insulted his girlfriend, he'd punched out the guy's car window in anger. At the time, his temper didn't frighten me. I thought as long as he was on my side, his passion would work in my favor. He seemed like the kind of man who'd protect me from harm.

On our first date, my ex asked me to tell him something no one else knew. I pulled out my phone and showed him the picture of my ass sutured with a swastika. The doctor had sent it to me after the rape. I'd kept it as a talisman, a reminder that what happened when I was barely conscious was real.

My psycho ex was horrified when he saw the image and flew into a rage. He made me promise not to tell him who had hurt me because he'd kill the guy. Then, a few weeks later, he demanded to know.

"Who the fuck did this to you?" he insisted, over and over. He wouldn't let it go. It was almost as though *he* was the one who'd been violated. He told me he was going to kill the doctor using liquid LSD. He had it all planned out. He claimed he "knew people." He was so focused on revenge, I became terrified that I was going to have to protect my rapist from my boyfriend. Sometimes I'd go to the Apple store and google on the demo laptops. I'd search the doctor's name to see if there was anything online about him being dead.

One day after my ex and I had been dating for a few months and were practically living together, he called me at work, furious. He said he'd hired an investigator. He had reports, he claimed, that indicated I'd seduced the doctor to engage in S&M sex play. He insisted he had proof that my encounter with the doctor had been consensual. I cried hysterically and tried to convince him that the rape had really happened. I *hadn't* wanted it. It *wasn't* consensual. For hours, I detailed for him every moment of that horrible night until, finally, he relented. My ex said he believed me after all. He was just testing me before proceeding with his plan to kill the doctor.

After we broke up, my ex sent Facebook messages to everyone in my family and told them about the doctor. He contacted my ex-boyfriends and told them, too. Nobody ever asked me about it. But I was haunted by the thought that everybody knew.

Within months of our breakup, I'd blown through tens of thousands of dollars fighting the phony assault charges my ex filed against me, and I'd lost the respect of my boss and coworkers, some of whom he'd contacted during his campaign of spreading lies. I felt like my life had spiraled completely out of my control. That's when my friend invited me to Ireland.

When I used to tell the story of how I started my own law firm, I'd say I had an epiphany standing on the edge of a cliff in a pounding rainstorm. But really, what happened to me that afternoon is I felt the urge to jump. I was so overwhelmed by the doctor's rape and the psycho's stalking, I felt hopeless. Like, end-it-all hopeless. The idea of hurling myself into the churning water of the Galway Bay didn't frighten me. Just the opposite. It felt comforting, like a permanent solution to my unbearable pain.

Suddenly aware I was teetering on the edge of danger, I panicked. I turned away from the edge and started running in the opposite direction, faster than I ever had before. Sprinting through the pelting rain, trying to outrun my most destructive impulse, I came up with a plan: I'd give myself a year to turn my life around. If it didn't work out, I could always come back to Ireland and end it all.

The true story is my firm is built on the wreckage of despair, desperation, and hopelessness. It's the product of a decision made by a suicidal person who gave herself one year to try something new.

But also true is the fact that my decision to step away from the edge set in motion my year of metamorphosis. It was a year of late-night strategizing, focusing, and going to battle, not only for my own safety but also for my clients. Nothing mattered but the fight. Somewhere along the way, I stopped inventorying the men who had fucked me over. I quit admonishing myself for making stupid choices and bad mistakes. I stopped seeing myself as a victim and reclaimed my control. That year I discovered the transformative power of fighting back.

———

Not that long ago, I spoke to another group of eager college students. Again, I was approached by an aspiring lawyer asking for advice about how she, too, could do this kind of work. "I want to make a change in the world," she said. This time I had an answer. "Identify your greatest problem," I told her. "Find your biggest obstacle, that thing that makes you feel most powerless, and ask yourself, 'How do I fix this?' *That's* the fight you should devote your life to." It's the message I want everyone to hear.

The world is filled with assholes, trolls, psychos, and pervs. These are the monsters who make us feel weak. But we don't have to be victims. And we don't need to fight alone. There are millions of us out here. Find your fellow warriors—the advocates, survivors, and students working at think tanks or nonprofits, as legal scholars or in schools—and arm yourselves with bullhorns, pussy hats, placards, and petitions.

Strategize at conferences, in coffee shops, or in your tiny apartment with documents spread across your living room floor. Study the organization or structure that gives your nemeses power. Figure out how the systems work and what it takes to dismantle them. Hold people, institutions, and companies accountable. If your enemies have the law on their side, find legal loopholes and charge through them. Be creative and relentless. And be good to yourself. This is hard work. We survivors, activists, and allies are just getting started untangling the harm wrought by eons of abuse, secrecy, shaming, and oppression. And we are already making a difference. All around us powerful men are running scared. They're accusing us of attacking them, crying "lynch mob" and "witch hunt." Listen closely; their protestations are nothing more than pathetic whimpers of defeat.

I know what it's like to feel desperate and alone. A lot of us do. But we are nobody's victims. To the Harvey Weinsteins, Larry Nassars, and R. Kellys of the world, consider yourselves on notice. To the victim-blaming, slut-shaming, chickenshit school administrators, cops, prosecutors, and judges, you've been officially warned. To all you dumbass tech titans and the venture capitalists who fund the idiot inventions that ruin our lives, you're in our line of fire, too.

It's a new day. We are going to take over and make things right. We will destroy Section 230 of the CDA and fuck with tech bros' algorithms. We will erect statues that depict us and write statutes that protect us. We will win elections, change the face of Congress, and move into the White House. Our heels are clicking down the warpath. To all you psychos, stalkers, trolls, and pervs, your time is up.

We may have been victimized once, but we're not victims.

We are an army of warriors and we won't back down.

A NOTE FROM THE AUTHOR

To my dear survivors, warriors, and friends,

What happened to you matters.

Even if you didn't tell anyone. Even if no one believed you.

What happened to you matters even if you thought you loved him or he told you he loved you. Even if he was a trusted friend or you didn't know his name. It matters even if it was years or decades ago.

What happened to you matters even if you didn't see the red flags or you ignored them. It matters even if you were drunk, or high, or too terrified to resist.

What happened to you matters because you matter, even if your school or the cops wouldn't help you, or a lawyer turned you away, or a judge or jury decided that the person who hurt you didn't deserve to be punished.

If the system failed you, your parents won't speak to you, your friends are sick of hearing about it, what happened to you still matters.

Even if you don't know what to call it, it matters.

You matter and you are entitled to support, advice, camaraderie, and love. You are entitled to talk about what happened or to change the subject if you want. You are entitled to all of your complicated feelings.

There's help if you need it and an army of warriors ready to stand by your side. You matter and you don't have to fight this battle alone.

You are nobody's victim.

Join us in proclaiming yourself Nobody's Victim.
Visit us at nobodys-victim.com.

CARRIE'S ESSENTIALS

If you are in crisis or know someone who is, or if you just need some information, here are my top recommendations for advice, support, and the facts you need to stay safe and fight back.

These links, phone numbers, and addresses are current as of April 2, 2019.

To contact my firm, or for updates on cases and helpful tips for dealing with sextortion, privacy violations, and other crimes discussed in this book, visit my website at CAGoldbergLaw.com or call us at (646) 666-8908.

If You Are in Crisis Right Now:

- You aren't alone. Please call the **National Suicide Prevention Lifeline at 1-800-273-8255** for free and confidential support twenty-four hours a day. You can also chat with a trained counselor online at suicidepreventionlifeline.org.
- For LGBTQ youth, **The Trevor Project** has trained counselors available around the clock for support and suicide prevention. Call

the Trevor Lifeline at 1-866-488-7386 or visit the Help Center at thetrevorproject.org.

For Victims of Revenge Porn, Sextortion, and Other Online Privacy Violations:

- Check out the **Cyber Civil Rights Initiative**'s "Online Removal Guide," cybercivilrights.org/online-removal, for tips on getting private images removed from the web. The CCRI also runs an end-revenge-porn crisis helpline where someone is available to help twenty-four hours a day. Call 1-844-878-CCRI (2274).

- **Without My Consent** offers great resources for victims of digital privacy violations, including detailed information on copyright registering, filing a takedown notice, and preserving evidence. Visit their website at withoutmyconsent.org.

- Formed in 2017, **The Badass Army** (BADASS is an acronym for Battling Against Demeaning and Abusive Selfie Sharing) is a survivor-led advocacy group offering victims badass strategies and guerrilla tactics (like how to flood an offending website with pictures of cartoons). Visit them on Facebook or via their website at badassarmy.org.

For Students and Parents:

- You can find tips, quizzes, and solid info about healthy relationships, dating abuse, consent, and coercion, online and off, at www.loveisrepect.org. **Love Is Respect** also has trained peer counselors for young adults and concerned family and/or friends available via online chats, by phone at 1-866-331-9474, or by texting "loveis" to 22522.

- Founded by survivors of campus sexual assault, **Safebae** has a great collection of educational videos about healthy relationships, consent, and Title IX available at safebae.org.

- For high school or college students battling sexual harassment or sexual violence on campus, **Know Your IX** offers solid information on Title IX protections, including for LGBTQ and gender nonconforming students. The website also has great tips for allies and survivors, including "Dealing with Unsupportive Parents and Peers" and "Activist Burnout and Self-Care." Visit know yourIX.org.
- Check out **Callisto** and **Reach Out**, two great mobile apps aimed at assisting victims of campus sexual harassment and assaults.

If Your Current or Former Partner Is a Psycho, Stalker, or Abusive Piece of Shit:

- Contact **The National Domestic Violence Hotline** at 1-800-799-SAFE (7233) or online at thehotline.org for information, support, and resources to help you stay safe.
- The **Stalking Resource Center**, operated by the National Center for Victims of Crime, offers information on stalking laws in each state and a wide variety of resources for victims, including safety plans, tips for relocating, and a downloadable stalking log template. Visit the Stalking Resource Center at victimsofcrime.org.

For Survivors of Sexual Assault and Abuse:

- If you've experienced a sexual assault, contact **RAINN** (Rape, Abuse & Incest National Network) at rainn.org or by phone at their Sexual Assault Hotline at 1-800-656-HOPE (4673). RAINN will connect you with sexual trauma and legal support services in your area.

For Children at Risk:

- If you have concerns about sexual exploitation, sex trafficking, or sextortion of a minor, contact the **National Center for Missing**

and Exploited Children at missingkids.com, or call their hotline at 1-800-THE-LOST (843-5678).

If Trolls Are Coming for You:

- Founded by two tech-savvy Gamergate survivors, **Crash Override Network** supports victims of online attacks with cutting-edge pro tips to combat doxing, hacking, swatting, and other digitally induced bad behavior. Visit the Resource Center at crashoverridenetwork.com.
- For a deep dive into the effects of trolling and an up-close look at how it impacted Anita Sarkeesian, check out Cynthia Lowen's fantastic 2018 documentary *Netizens*. For information about where to watch, visit netizensfilm.com.

For Sex Workers and Victims of Sex Trafficking:

- The **Sex Workers Project** at the Urban Justice Center is one of the country's oldest organizations providing legal assistance and counseling services to sex workers and survivors of human trafficking. Visit their website at sexworkersproject.org or call their "warm line" at 1-646-602-5617.
- **Polaris** (polarisproject.org) and **Thorn** (thorn.org) have partnered to offer the BeFree text line, which provides twenty-four-hour support to victims of human trafficking. Text "HELP" to BeFree (233733), or call the National Human Trafficking Hotline at 1-888-373-7888.

For My LGBTQI Friends:

- The **LGBT National Help Center** offers free and confidential support through their LGBT National Hotline at 1-888-843-4564 and their dedicated LGBT National Youth Talkline at 1-800-246-7743. The Help Center also provides moderated online chat groups for transgender teens and young adults. Visit glnh.org.

- Also check out the **National Center for Transgender Equality** at transequality.org; the **Tyler Clementi Foundation** at tylercle menti.org; and, for great resources for family members, check out **PFLAG** at pflag.org.

For Activists, Allies, and Agitators:

- The **Gay, Lesbian and Straight Education Network (GLSEN)** provides students and educators with research and resources to organize anti-bullying campaigns at their schools. Visit glsen.org.
- The **National Network to End Domestic Violence (NNEDV)** is dedicated to ending domestic violence and offers tech safety trainings via their Safety Net program. Visit nnedv.org.
- **Human Rights Campaign** is the leading watchdog organization fighting for LGBTQ civil rights, safety, and political action. Check out their online Action Center for ways to get involved. Visit hrc.org.
- The **Southern Poverty Law Center** offers detailed information about hate groups and extremist organizations that drive some of the most heinous troll armies active on the web today. See the Extremist Files at splcenter.org.
- The **American Foundation for Suicide Prevention** is the national leader in research and advocacy for suicide prevention. Visit afsp.org.
- The **National Organization for Women** is on the forefront of advocating for women's issues, including reproductive rights and ending the criminalization of trauma. Visit now.org to get involved.

Carrie's Twitter Picks (accounts I follow that you should, too)

- Lindsey Barrett: @LAM_Barrett—For whip-smart quips from a privacy scholar.

- Frank Pasquale: @FrankPasquale—Insights about privacy from perhaps the only person more cynical about big tech than me
- Professor Mary Anne Franks: @ma_franks—A peek into the inner brain workings of the most influential and change-making feminist professor of our time.
- Soraya Chemaly: @Schemaly—Author of *Rage Becomes Her*. As a woman, if you aren't pissed, you aren't paying attention. For a fast track to getting pissed, read Soraya's Twitter.
- The BADASS Army: @TheBADASS_army—If there is any mention of nonconsensual porn in the Twitterverse you can be sure to see it tweeted about here.
- Cyber Civil Rights Initiative: @CCRInitiative—Up-to-date news about tech and privacy and daily quotes that are well curated to be inspiring without being cheesy.

Recommended Reading:

- Gavin de Becker's *The Gift of Fear* was recommended to me when I first opened my firm. We all possess the ability to sense when we're in danger. Becker teaches us how to listen to our instincts and act on them. This advice can save your life.
- I first read psychiatrist Viktor E. Frankl's memoir *Man's Search for Meaning* when I was working at Selfhelp. Frankl, who survived Nazi death camps, argues that in the wake of great pain and loss we can find meaning and purpose.
- I give a copy of Don Miguel Ruiz's *The Four Agreements* to many of my new clients. Ruiz's message—that the stuff other people say and do is more about them than about you—has been a game changer for me. Whenever I feel like my life is spinning out of control, I listen to *The Four Agreements* to center myself and remember not to give a shit about what other people think.

- I read *Why Does He Do That? Inside the Minds of Angry and Controlling Men* by Lundy Bancroft when I was going through the worst days of my chaotic breakup with my psycho ex. It saved my sanity and reminded me that I wasn't alone.
- *Rage Becomes Her: The Power of Women's Anger* by Soraya Chemaly was one of my favorite books of 2018. Chemaly writes, "If ever there was a time not to silence yourself, to channel your anger into healthy places and choices, this is it." To me, these are words to live by.
- *Hate Crimes in Cyberspace*, by renowned law professor and my dear friend Danielle Keats Citron, is one of the first books to offer an in-depth look at the way tech can be weaponized to violate privacy and destroy lives. It's a must-read for anyone who wants to understand how we got here.

Links to all the resources mentioned in this book are available at nobodys-victim.com.

NOTES

CHAPTER 1: SLEEPING WITH THE ENEMY

9 **"I feared for my life every day":** Francesca's impact statement was published in *New York* magazine. See: Katie Van Syckle, "Cyberstalking Victim Calls Out NYPD for Failing to Protect Her in Powerful Court Statement," The Cut, December 20, 2017, https://www.thecut.com/2017/12/juan -thompson-cyberstalking-victim-francesca-rossi-statement.html.

12 **The editor-in-chief of The Intercept:** Betsy Reed, "A Note to Readers," The Intercept, February 2, 2016, https://theintercept.com/2016/02/02/a-note-to -readers/.

12 **Most notably, in his coverage of the 2015 massacre:** Doyle Murphy, "Disgraced Reporter Juan Thompson Hired, Fired from New Writing Job," *Riverfront Times*, September 19, 2016, https://www.riverfronttimes.com /newsblog/2016/09/19/disgraced-reporter-juan-thompson-hired-fired-from -new-writing-job.

12 **The story was picked up by multiple news outlets:** Erik Wemple, "How the Media Dealt with The Intercept's Retracted Story on Dylan Roof's 'Cousin,'" *The Washington Post*, February 3, 2016, https://www.washingtonpost.com /blogs/erik-wemple/wp/2016/02/03/how-the-media-dealt-with-the-inter cepts-retracted-story-on-dylann-roofs-cousin.

13 **a video of a guy named Juan Thompson:** Haym Salomon Center, "Juan Thompson Unconfirmed Vassar College Promo," YouTube video, 3:28, March 5, 2017, https://youtu.be/NoCd4KdvYoc.

15 **he'd recently covered the protests:** Juan Thompson, "'No Justice, No Respect': Why the Ferguson Riots Were Justified," The Intercept, December

1, 2014, https://theintercept.com/2014/12/01/justice-respect-ferguson-riots
-justified/.

16 **Francesca read the multiple press reports:** Benjamin Mullin, "The Intercept's Juan Thompson Fired for Fabrication," *Poynter*, February 2, 2016, https://www.poynter.org/archive/2016/the-intercepts-juan-thompson-fired-for-fabrication/; Julia Carrie Wong, "The Intercept Admits Reporter Fabricated Stories and Quotes," *The Guardian*, February 2, 2016, https://www.the guard ian.com/media/2016/feb/02/the-intercept-fires-reporter-juan-thompson.

17 **often the stalking began well before:** TK Logan, *Research on Partner Stalking: Putting the Pieces Together* (Lexington: University of Kentucky Department of Behavioral Science & Center on Drug and Alcohol Research, 2010), http://victimsofcrime.org/docs/Common%20Documents/Research %20on%20Partner%20Stalking%20Report.pdf.

17 **11 percent of victims have been stalked:** "Stalking Fact Sheet," National Center for Victims of Crime, August 2012, http://victimsofcrime.org/docs /src/stalking-fact-sheet_english.pdf.

17 **Stalking is one of the most effective ways for:** Logan, *Research on Partner Stalking*.

17 **More than 80 percent of women:** "Facts About Domestic Violence and Stalking," National Coalition Against Domestic Violence, 2015, https://www .speakcdn.com/assets/2497/domestic_violence_and_stalking_ncadv.pdf.

18 **stalking is generally defined:** "Analyzing Stalking Laws," National Center for Victims of Crime, 2015, http://victimsofcrime.org/docs/src/analyzing -stalking-statute.pdf.

18 **illegal in all fifty states:** "Stalking Fact Sheet," National Center for Victims of Crime.

18 **She died on her doorstep:** An excellent accounting of Schaeffer's murder can be found online at EW.com: Joe McGovern, "When Devotion Turns Deadly," *Entertainment Weekly*, June 12, 2017, http://rebeccaschaeffer .ew.com. See also: "How the Murder of Starlet Rebecca Schaeffer by Her Stalker 'Changed Hollywood,'" *People*, March 28, 2017, http://people.com /crime/rebecca-schaeffer-murder-by-her-stalker/; Andrea Ford, "Suspect on Tape Tells of Actress's Last Words," *Los Angeles Times*, October 22, 1991, http://articles.latimes.com/1991-10-22/local/me-114_1_bardo.

18 **Years later . . . Marcia Clark:** McGovern, "When Devotion Turns Deadly."

19 **Bardo was sentenced to life in prison:** Reuters, AP, "Actress' Killer Stabbed in Calif. Prison," *Hollywood Reporter*, July 30, 2007, https://www .hollywoodreporter.com/news/actress-killer-stabbed-calif-prison-145478.

19 **Senate Judiciary Committee hearing in 1992:** National Institute of Justice, *Domestic Violence, Stalking, and Antistalking Legislation: An Annual Report to Congress Under the Violence Against Women Act* (Washington, DC: April 1996), https://www.ncjrs.gov/pdffiles/stlkbook.pdf.

19 **Her story made national headlines:** National Institute of Justice, *Domestic Violence, Stalking, and Antistalking Legislation.*

19 **California was the first state:** National Institute of Justice, *Domestic Violence, Stalking, and Antistalking Legislation.*

19 **a history of stalking has been reported:** Logan, *Research on Partner Stalking.*

20 **Intimate partner stalking:** Logan, *Research on Partner Stalking.*

20 **Many of the deadliest mass shootings:** Hilary Brueck, "The Men Behind the US's Deadliest Mass Shootings Have Something in Common—and It's Not Mental Illness," Business Insider, November 7, 2017, http://www.busi nessinsider.com/deadliest-mass-shootings-almost-all-have-domestic -violence-connection-2017-11.

20 **Omar Mateen, who murdered forty-nine:** Suzanne Moore, "Omar Mateen's Domestic Violence Was a Clue to His Murderous Future," *The Guardian*, July 13, 2016, https://www.theguardian.com/commentisfree/2016/jun /13/omar-mateen-domestic-violence-clue-murderous-future.

20 **Devin P. Kelley, who, in 2017, entered a church:** Valentina Zarya, "5 Statistics That Explain the Link Between Domestic Violence and Mass Shootings," *Fortune*, November 7, 2017, http://fortune.com/2017/11/07/domestic -violence-shootings-statistics/.

20 **Nikolas Cruz, who opened fire:** Matthew Haag and Serge F. Kovaleski, "Nikolas Cruz, Florida Shooting Suspect, Described as 'Troubled Kid,'" *New York Times*, February 14, 2018, https://www.nytimes.com/2018/02/14 /us/nikolas-cruz-florida-shooting.html.

20 **After the shooting, it was reported that:** Haag and Kovaleski, "Nikolas Cruz, Florida Shooting Suspect, Described as 'Troubled Kid.'"

20 **the strongest predictor:** Soraya Chemaly, "America's Mass Shooting Problem Is a Domestic Violence Problem," *Village Voice*, November 8, 2017, https://www.villagevoice.com/2017/11/08/americas-mass-shooting -problem-is-a-domestic-violence-problem/.

28 **a rash of anti-Semitic bomb threats:** Mark Berman, "Trump Questions Who Is Really Behind Anti-Semitic Threats and Vandalism," *Washington Post*, March 1, 2017, https://www.washingtonpost.com/news/post-nation /wp/2017/02/28/trump-questioned-who-is-really-behind-anti-semitic- threats-and-vandalism-official-says/.

28 **The bomber "hates Jewish people":** Deposition of Christopher Mills, *United States of America v. Juan Thompson*, 17 U.S. 1532 (March 1, 2017), https://www.documentcloud.org/documents/3480376-U-S-v-Juan -Thompson-Complaint.html.

28 **In a separate email to a Jewish school:** Deposition of Christopher Mills, *USA v. Juan Thompson.*

28 **at least twelve different bomb threats:** Department of Justice, US Attorney's Office Southern District of New York, "Juan Thompson Sentenced in

Manhattan Federal Court to 60 Months in Prison for Cyberstalking and Making Hoax Bomb Threats to JCCs and Other Victim Organizations," news release, December 20, 2017, https://www.justice.gov/usao-sdny/pr/juan-thompson-sentenced-manhattan-federal-court-60-months-prison-cyberstalking-and; Mark Berman and Jake Zapotosky, "Former Journalist Arrested, Charged with Threats Against Jewish Facilities," *Washington Post*, March 3, 2017, https://www.washingtonpost.com/news/post-nation/wp/2017/03/03/missouri-man-arrested-charged-with-threats-against-jewish-facilities/.

29 **After a dispute over *Call of Duty*:** James Queally and Richard Winton, "L.A. 'Swatting' Suspect Charged with Manslaughter in Kansas over Hoax Call That Led to Fatal Police Shooting," *Los Angeles Times*, January 12, 2018, https://www.latimes.com/local/lanow/la-me-ln-kansas-swatting-20180112-story.html.

29 **Thompson, then thirty-one, was finally arrested:** Department of Justice, US Attorney's Office Southern District of New York, "Cyberstalking Charge Brought in Manhattan Federal Court Against Missouri Man for a Pattern of Harassment Involving Threats to Jewish Community Centers," news release, March 3, 2017, https://www.justice.gov/usao-sdny/pr/cyberstalking-charge-brought-manhattan-federal-court-against-missouri-man-pattern; *United States v. Juan Thompson* 1:17-cr-00165-PKC (United States District Court Southern District of New York, 2017).

29 **He was taken into custody in St. Louis:** Berman and Zapotosky, "Former Journalist Arrested."

30 **they confiscated twenty-five digital devices:** Van Syckle, "Cyberstalking Victim Calls Out NYPD."

30 **"an entire year to destroying":** Van Syckle, "Cyberstalking Victim Calls Out NYPD."

31 **"I screwed up royally":** Reuven Fenton, "Reporter Gets 5 Years in Prison for Threatening Jewish Centers," *New York Post*, December 20, 2017, https://nypost.com/2017/12/20/reporter-gets-5-years-in-prison-for-threatening-jewish-centers/.

31 **added an additional year:** Department of Justice, "Juan Thompson Sentenced."

CHAPTER 2: SWIPE RIGHT FOR STALKING

33 **It all started, he said:** The story of Matthew's abuse by his ex and his subsequent dealings with Grindr are detailed throughout this chapter. All information is based on my knowledge of the case, communications between Matthew and myself, or recollections Matthew shared directly with my co-writer, Jeannine Amber, during a series of interviews she conducted in January 2018. Details of Matthew's abuse are also described, in depth, in the following legal documents, which include accounts of Matthew's abuse and the

arguments against Grindr that appear in this chapter: First amended complaint, *Matthew Herrick v. Grindr, LLC, et al.*, No. 1:17-CV-00932 (VEC) (United States District Court Southern District of New York, March 31, 2017), http://www.cagoldberglaw.com/wp-content/uploads/2018/09/First-Amended-Complaint-2017.pdf. You can also read more about Matthew's case here: Andy Greenberg, "Spoofed Grindr Accounts Turned One Man's Life into a 'Living Hell,'" *Wired*, January 31, 2017, https://www.wired.com/2017/01/grinder-lawsuit-spoofed-accounts/.

35　**In 2009, a Wyoming woman:** DeeDee Correll, "Former Boyfriend Used Craigslist to Arrange Woman's Rape, Police Say," *Los Angeles Times*, January 11, 2010, http://articles.latimes.com/2010/jan/11/nation/la-na-rape-craigslist11-2010jan11.

37　**In their terms of service:** "Privacy Policy," Scruff, last revised October 14, 2018, https://www.scruff.com/en/info/privacy/; "Grindr Terms and Conditions of Service," Grindr, effective July 1, 2018, https://www.grindr.com/terms-of-service/.

38　**reportedly had more than three million:** Brian Latimer, "Grindr Security Flaw Exposes Users' Location Data," NBC News, March 28, 2018, https://www.nbcnews.com/feature/nbc-out/security-flaws-gay-dating-app-grindr-expose-users-location-data-n858446.

38　**Grindr . . . geolocative feature:** Sharif Mowlabocus, "Grindr's Locator 'Glitch' Was a Major Fail. It Revealed the Company's Lack of Empathy for Its Gay Users," *Washington Post*, September 8, 2014, https://www.washingtonpost.com/posteverything/wp/2014/09/08/grindrs-locator-glitch-was-a-major-fail-it-revealed-the-companys-lack-of-empathy-for-its-gay-users.

38　**Grindr's terms of service state:** Sara Ashley O'Brien, "1,100 Strangers Showed Up at His Home for Sex. He Blames Grindr," CNN Business, April 14, 2017, http://money.cnn.com/2017/04/14/technology/grindr-lawsuit/index.html.

39　**Free speech purists . . . hail the legislation:** "CDA 230: Legislative History," Electronic Frontier Foundation, accessed June 2017, https://www.eff.org/issues/cda230/legislative-history.

39　**When the law first came . . . a very different place:** Farhad Manjoo, "Jurassic Web," Slate, February 24, 2009, https://slate.com/technology/2009/02/the-unrecognizable-internet-of-1996.html.

39　**there was no Google:** "From the Garage to the Googleplex," Google, accessed December 25, 2018, https://www.google.com/about/our-story/; Christine Lagorio-Chafkin, "How Alexis Ohanian Built a Front Page of the Internet," *Inc.*, May 30, 2012, https://www.inc.com/magazine/201206/christine-lagorio/alexis-ohanian-reddit-how-i-did-it.html; Megan Rose Dickey, "The 22 Key Turning Points in the History of YouTube," Business Insider, February 15, 2013, https://www.businessinsider.com/key-turning-points

-history-of-youtube-2013-2; Nicholas Carlson, "The Real History of Twitter," Business Insider, April 13, 2011, https://www.businessinsider.com/how -twitter-was-founded-2011-4.

39 **Mark Zuckerberg was in middle school:** Ryan Mac, "Facebook's Mark Zuckerberg Turns 30: A Look Back," *Forbes*, May 14, 2014, https://www .forbes.com/sites/ryanmac/2014/05/14/facebooks-mark-zuckerberg-turns -30-a-look-back/.

39 **Amazon was an exciting new website:** Michael H. Martin, "The Next Big Thing: A Book Store?" *Fortune*, December 9, 1996, http://fortune.com /1996/12/09/amazon-bookstore-next-big-thing/.

39 **Cell phones could only make phone calls:** "Cellphone Ownership Soared Since 1998," *Wall Street Journal*, November 27, 2009, https://blogs.wsj.com /economics/2009/11/27/cellphone-ownership-soared-since-1998/.

39 **Internet access was even scarcer:** Eric C. Newburger, "Home Computers and Internet Use in the United States: August 2000," report no. P23-207, US Census Bureau, September 2001, https://www.census.gov/prod/2001pubs /p23-207.pdf.

40 **Prodigy Communications, featured:** Robert D. Shapiro, "This Is Not Your Father's Prodigy," *Wired*, June 1, 1993, https://www.wired.com/1993 /06/prodigy/.

40 **In 1992, users posted more than forty million messages:** Shapiro, "This Is Not Your Father's Prodigy."

40 **The company did its best to monitor:** Michael Banks, "Prodigy: The Pre-Internet Online Service That Didn't Live Up to Its Name," *Tech-Republic*, December 18, 2008, https://www.techrepublic.com/blog/classics -rock/prodigy-the-pre-internet-online-service-that-didnt-live-up-to-its -name/.

40 **In 1994, an anonymous user posted:** Conor Clarke, "How the Wolf of Wall Street Created the Internet," Slate, January 7, 2014, http://www.slate .com/articles/news_and_politics/jurisprudence/2014/01/the_wolf_of _wall_street_and_the_stratton_oakmont_ruling_that_helped_write.html.

40 **The poster claimed Stratton Oakmont was staffed:** Clarke, "How the Wolf of Wall Street."

40 **only two years later Stratton Oakmont:** Jay Mathews, "Stratton Oakmont Expelled from Securities Industry," *Washington Post,* December 6, 1996, https://www.washingtonpost.com/archive/business/1996/12/06/stratton -oakmont-expelled-from-securities-industry/bf70026a-2fd6-4b42-996e -9e9d815b609e.

40 *The Wolf of Wall Street*: David Haglund, "How Accurate Is *The Wolf of Wall Street*?" Slate, December 31, 2013, https://slate.com/culture/2013/12 /wolf-of-wall-street-true-story-jordan-belfort-and-other-real-people -in-dicaprio-scorsese-movie.html.

NOTES

40 **In a move that sent shock waves:** Jonathan Rosenoer, *CyberLaw: The Law of the Internet* (New York: Springer-Verlag, 1997), 123–126; Haglund, "How Accurate Is *The Wolf*."

40 **things start to get complicated:** Clarke, "How the Wolf of Wall Street"; Paul Ehrlich, "Communications Decency Act 230," *Berkeley Technology Law Journal* 17, no. 1 (January 2002): 401–419, https://scholarship.law.berkeley.edu/cgi/viewcontent.cgi?article=1358&context=btlj.

40 **the company should not be held liable:** Elizabeth Corcoran, "$200 Million Libel Suit Against Prodigy Dropped," *Washington Post*, October 25, 1995, https://www.washingtonpost.com/archive/business/1995/10/25/200-million-libel-suit-against-prodigy-dropped/d130d9d8-64ff-499e-9cd8-26f0304ceeba.

40 **New York Supreme Court judge:** *Stratton Oakmont, Inc. v. Prodigy Services Co.,* 1995 WL 323710 (New York Supreme Court, May 24, 1995), https://h2o.law.harvard.edu/cases/4540.

41 **After Prodigy issued a formal apology:** Corcoran, "$200 Million Libel Suit."

41 **They could simply distribute:** Ehrlich, "Communications Decency Act 230."

41 **What they worried about:** Robert Cannon, "The Legislative History of Senator Exon's Communications Decency Act: Regulating Barbarians on the Information Superhighway," *Federal Communications Law Journal* 49, no.1 (1996): 53–56, https://www.repository.law.indiana.edu/cgi/viewcontent.cgi?referer=&httpsredir=1&referer=&httpsredir=1&referer=https://www.google.com/&httpsredir=1&article=1115&context=fclj.

42 **swept the 1994 midterm elections:** Richard L. Berke, "The 1994 Election: The Voters; Religious-Right Candidates Gain as G.O.P. Turnout Rises," *New York Times*, November 12, 1994, https://www.nytimes.com/1994/11/12/us/1994-election-voters-religious-right-candidates-gain-gop-turnout-rises.html.

42 **focused on social issues:** James Traub, "Party Like It's 1994," *New York Times*, March 12, 2006, https://www.nytimes.com/2006/03/12/magazine/party-like-its-1994.html.

42 **many conservatives . . . regulate the internet:** Mike Godwin, *Cyber Rights: Defending Free Speech in the Digital Age* (Cambridge, MA: MIT Press, 2003), 323–325; John E. Semonche, *Censoring Sex: A Historical Journey Through American Media* (Lanham, MD: Rowman & Littlefield, 2007), 215–217.

42 **the same year Prodigy was sued for defamation:** John Zipperer, "Hard-Core Porn Technology Hits Home," *Christianity Today*, September 12, 1994, https://www.christianitytoday.com/ct/1994/september12/4ta042.html.

42 **the Senate chaplain took note:** Benjamin L. Riddle, "The Irony of the Communications Decency Act," *National Law Review*, July 26, 2012, https://www.natlawreview.com/article/irony-communications-decency

-act; Prayer of Lloyd John Ogilvie, *Congressional Record* vol. 141, no. 95 (June 12, 1995), https://www.gpo.gov/fdsys/pkg/CREC-1995-06-12/html/CREC -1995-06-12-pt1-PgS8127-2.htm.

43 **Senator Exon also introduced:** Cannon, "The Legislative History," 64.

43 **To bolster his case, Exon asked:** Cannon, "The Legislative History," 64.

43 **But what really sealed the deal:** Philip Elmer-Dewitt, "Finding Marty Rimm," *Time*, July 1, 2015, http://fortune.com/2015/07/01/cyberporn-time -marty-rimm/.

43 **The article inside spared no detail:** Elmer-Dewitt, "Finding Marty Rimm"; Philip Elmer-Dewitt, "On a Screen Near You," *Time*, June 24, 2001, http://content.time.com/time/magazine/article/0,9171,134361,00.html.

43 **was swiftly discredited:** Elmer-Dewitt, "Finding Marty Rimm"; Peter H. Lewis, "Tech: On the Net; The Internet Battles a Much-Disputed Study on Selling Pornography On Line," *New York Times*, July 17, 1995, http://www .nytimes.com/1995/07/17/business/tech-net-internet-battles-much -disputed-study-selling-pornography-line.html.

43 **Something had to be done:** Kathryn C. Montgomery, *Generation Digital: Politics, Commerce, and Childhood in the Age of the Internet* (Cambridge, MA: MIT Press, 2007), 39–41.

43 **the Communications Decency Act, aimed at protecting:** Pamela Mendels, "Supreme Court Throws Out Communications Decency Act," *New York Times*, June 26, 1997, https://archive.nytimes.com/www.nytimes.com /library/cyber/week/062697decency.html.

43 **The crime was punishable . . . up to $250,000 in fines:** Mendels, "Supreme Court Throws Out Communications Decency Act."

43 **But here's the crazy part:** Dan Brekke, "CDA Struck Down," *Wired*, June 26, 1997, https://www.wired.com/1997/06/cda-struck-down/; "Supreme Court Rules CDA Unconstitutional," CNN, June 26, 1997, http://www .cnn.com/US/9706/26/cda.overturned.hfr/; *Reno v. Am. Civil Liberties Union*, 521 U.S. 844 (1997).

45 **internet companies not only use:** Alina Selyukh, "Section 230: A Key Legal Shield for Facebook, Google Is About to Change," NPR *Morning Edition*, March 21, 2018, https://www.npr.org/sections/alltechconsidered/2018 /03/21/591622450/section-230-a-key-legal-shield-for-facebook-google-is-about -to-change; Christopher Zara, "The Most Important Law in Tech Has a Problem," *Wired*, January 3, 2017, https://www.wired.com/2017/01/the-most -important-law-in-tech-has-a-problem/; 47 U.S.C. § 230.

45 **all have terms of service:** "Terms of Service," Facebook, last revised April 19, 2018, https://www.facebook.com/terms.php; "Reddit User Agreement," Reddit, last revised March 21, 2018, https://www.reddit.com/wiki /useragreement; "Twitter Terms of Service," Twitter, last revised May 25, 2018, https://twitter.com/en/tos.

46 **reportedly valued at more than $245 million:** Ingrid Lunden, "Report: Grindr's Chinese Owner Kunlun Is Selling the Dating App after CFIUS Raised Personal Data Concerns," TechCrunch, March 27, 2019, https://tech crunch.com/2019/03/27/report-grindrs-chinese-owner-kunlun-is-selling -the-dating-app-after-cfius-raised-personal-data-concerns/.

46 **Facebook, Craigslist, Uber, Airbnb, Amazon:** Karen Turner, "Why Facebook and Other Big Sites Are Opposing This Rape Victim's Lawsuit," *Washington Post*, June 10, 2016, https://www.washingtonpost.com/news/the -switch/wp/2016/06/10/why-facebook-and-other-big-sites-are-opposing -this-rape-victims-lawsuit/; *Caraccioli v. Facebook, Inc.,* 167 F. Supp. 3d 1056 (NDCA 2016); *Chicago Lawyers' Committee for Civil Rights Under Law v. Craigslist, Inc.,* 519 F.3d 666 (7th Cir. 2008), as amended (May 2, 2008).

47 **In 2013, Mary Kay Beckman sued:** Suzanne Choney, "Woman Sues Match .com for $10 Million After Brutal Attack," NBC News, January 25, 2013, https://www.nbcnews.com/technology/woman-sues-match-com-10-million -after-brutal-attack-1C8119714; Eric Goldman, "Online Dating Websites Aren't Required to Warn That Some Members May Be Murderers," *Forbes*, June 3, 2013, https://www.forbes.com/sites/ericgoldman/2013/06/03/online -dating-websites-arent-required-to-warn-that-some-members-may-be -murderers/; Mealey's, "Match.com Had No Duty to Warn User of Attacker's Violent Tendencies, Judge Says," Lexis Legal News, March 15, 2017, https://www .lexislegalnews.com/articles/15609/match-com-had-no-duty-to-warn-user -of-attacker-s-violent-tendencies-judge-says; *Beckman v. Match.com, LLC,* 688 F. App'x 759 (9th Cir. 2016).

47 **until 2018, the courts' application:** Tom Jackman, "Bill Enabling Prosecutors, Victims to Pursue Websites That Host Sex Traffickers Heads to White House," *Washington Post*, March 21, 2018, https://www.washingtonpost .com/news/true-crime/wp/2018/03/21/bill-enabling-prosecutors-to-pursue -websites-that-host-sex-traffickers-heads-to-white-house/; *Jane Doe no. 1 et al. v. Backpage.com, LLC et al.,* No. 15-1724 (United States Court of Appeals for the First Circuit, March 14, 2016), http://media.ca1.uscourts .gov/pdf.opinions/15-1724P-01A.pdf.

47 **In January 2017, I filed our initial complaint:** Complaint, *Matthew Herrick v. Grindr, LLC, et al.,* No. 150903/17 (January 27, 2017), https://www .courthousenews.com/wp-content/uploads/2017/01/grindr.pdf.

48 **Matthew's story got picked up:** Greenberg, "Spoofed Grindr Accounts"; O'Brien, "1,100 Strangers"; Jackie Salo, "Man Sues Grindr over Alleged Fake Profile Scheme for Rape, Murder," *New York Post*, January 30, 2017, https:// nypost.com/2017/01/30/man-sues-grindr-over-alleged-fake-profile-scheme -for-rape-murder/.

48 **picked up in Canada and the UK:** Postmedia Network, "N.Y. Actor Sues Grindr After 1,100 Men Seek Him Out in 'Rape Fantasy,'" *Toronto Sun*,

April 16, 2017, https://torontosun.com/2017/04/16/ny-actor-sues-grindr
-after-1100-men-seek-him-out-in-rape-fantasy/wcm/26c7d1c0-4bcf-418c
-845d-9ea946bc8670; Anna Hopkins, "Actor Sues Gay Dating App Grindr
After His Ex-Lover 'Created Fake Profiles Impersonating Him and Invited
Men to His Home and Workplace Who Tried to Rape and Murder Him,'"
Daily Mail, January 30, 2017, https://www.dailymail.co.uk/news/article
-4173286/Grindr-sued-alleged-murder-rape-charges.html.

50 **liable for fourteen separate claims:** First amended complaint, *Matthew Herrick v. Grindr, LLC*, et al.

50 **By the time we filed our amended complaint:** First amended complaint, *Matthew Herrick v Grindr, LLC*, et al.

52 **A few months after Gutierrez's arrest:** Opinion and order, *Matthew Herrick v. Grindr, LLC, et al.*, No. 1:17-cv-00932-VEC slip op. at 63 (United States District Court Southern District of New York, January 25, 2018), https:// www.courthousenews.com/wp-content/uploads/2018/01/Grindr.pdf.

53 **On May 24, 2018, we filed an appeal:** Brief for plaintiff-appellant, *Matthew Herrick v. Grindr, LLC, et al.*, No. 18-396, (United States Court of Appeals for the Second Circuit, May 24, 2018), https://www.cagoldberglaw.com/wp -content/uploads/2018/09/Appellant-Brief-May-2018.pdf.

53 **More than twenty organizations . . . around the country:** Amicus curiae brief of Sanctuary for Families, Cyber Sexual Abuse Task Force, Day One, Domestic Violence Legal Empowerment and Appeals Project, HerJustice, Legal Momentum, My Sister's Place, New York Legal Assistance Group, https:// www.cagoldberglaw.com/wp-content/uploads/2018/09/Amicus-Brief -Sanctuary-for-Families-2018-05-30-Herrick-v-Grindr-540801.pdf; Amicus curiae brief of Electronic Privacy Information Center, https://www.cagold berglaw.com/wp-content/uploads/2018/09/Amicus-Brief-EPIC -Herrrick-v-Grindr-540801.pdf; Amicus curiae brief of Consumer Watchdog and Meaghan Barakett, https://www.cagoldberglaw.com/wp-content /uploads/2018/09/Consumer-Watchdog-Amicus-Brief-Herrick-v-Grindr .pdf; Amicus curiae brief of Break the Cycle, National Assistance of Women Lawyers, National Network to End Domestic Violence, Laura's House, Legal Aid Society of Orange County and Public Law Center, https://www.cagold berglaw.com/wp-content/uploads/2018/09/Amicus-Brief-Break-the-Cycle -2018-05-31-Herrrick-v-Grindr-540801.pdf; Amicus curiae brief of Consumer Watchdog, https://www.cagoldberglaw.com/wp-content/uploads /2018/09/Consumer-Watchdog-Amicus-Brief-Herrick-v-Grindr.pdf.

53 **most powerful lobbyists . . . filed amicus briefs:** Amicus Curiae Briefs in Support of Defendants prepared by Computer and Communications Industry Association, Match Group, Inc., Glassdoor, Inc., and Indeed, Inc., https:// www.cagoldberglaw.com/wp-content/uploads/2018/09/Amicus-for -Computer-Communications-Industry-Association-Match-Group

-Glassdoor-and-Indeed.pdf; Amicus Curiae Brief Urging Affirmance by Paul Alan Levy, https://www.cagoldberglaw.com/wp-content/uploads/2018/09 /Amicus-Brief-Paul-Alan-Levy.pdf; Amicus Curiae Brief in Support of Defendants Appellees prepared by Electronic Frontier Foundation and Center for Democracy and Technology, https://www.cagoldberglaw.com /wp-content/uploads/2018/09/Amicus-EFF-Appellee-Brief-Electronic -Frontier-Foundation-and-Center-for-Democracy-and-Technology.pdf.

53 **a copy of *Harper's*:** "Here Comes Everybody," *Harper's*, October 2017, https:// harpers.org/archive/2017/10/here-comes-everybody/.

CHAPTER 3: ASSHOLES IN CHARGE

57 **Texas . . . was one of the first states:** "Sexting Laws in Texas," Cyberbullying Research Center, January 2019, https://cyberbullying.org/sexting-laws /texas; Joe Holley and Austin Bureau, "State Senator's Bill Would Reduce Penalty for Teen Sexting," *Houston Chronicle*, February 7, 2011, https:// www.chron.com/news/houston-texas/article/State-senator-s-bill-would -reduce-penalty-for-1685811.php.

57 **In other jurisdictions, underage couples:** "Sexting Laws," Cyberbullying Research Center.

58 **In 2011, the state reduced:** "Sexting Laws," Cyberbullying Research Center.

58 **The online course "Before You Text":** "Before You Text: Sexting & Bullying Prevention, Education & Intervention Course," Texas State Texas School Safety Center, https://txssc.txstate.edu/tools/courses/before-you-text/.

58 **The brainchild of a trio of Stanford University bros:** Biz Carson, "The Rise of Snapchat from a Sexting App by Stanford Frat Bros to a $3 Billion IPO," Business Insider, February 5, 2017, https://www.businessinsider.com /the-rise-of-snapchat-from-a-stanford-frat-house-to-a-3-billion-ipo-2017-1.

59 **some dating experts credit Snapchat's:** Rachel Thompson, "Snapchat Has Revolutionized Sexting, but Not Necessarily for the Better," *Mashable*, February 7, 2017, https://mashable.com/2017/02/07/snapchat-sexting -revolution/.

59 **teenagers use Snapchat:** Maya Kosoff, "Snapchat Tells Underage Teens to Stop Sexting: 'Keep Your Clothes On!'" Business Insider, February 20, 2015, http://www.businessinsider.com/snapchat-tells-underage-teens-to-stop -sexting-2015-2.

59 **the most popular social media platform:** Brett Molina, "Teens Love Snapchat. Also Instagram," *USA Today*, April 14, 2016, https://www.usatoday .com/story/tech/news/2016/04/14/survey-snapchat-most-popular-app -among-teens/83021810/.

59 **"[Teenagers] are testing their level of appeal":** Randye Hoder, "Study Finds Most Teens Sext Before They're 18," *Time*, July 3, 2014, http://time .com/2948467/chances-are-your-teen-is-sexting/.

59 **Even Macie's mother notes:** Interview with Jeannine Amber, March 3, 2018.

60 **one out of every four teenagers:** Sheri Madigan, Anh Ly, and Christina L. Rash, et al., "Prevalence of Multiple Forms of Sexting Behavior Among Youth: A Systematic Review and Meta-Analysis," *JAMA Pediatrics* 172, no. 4 (April 2018), https://jamanetwork.com/journals/jamapediatrics/article-abstract/2673719.

60 **only 8 percent of teens:** Hoder, "Study Finds Most Teens"; Heidi Strohmaier, Megan Murphy, and David DeMatteo, "Youth Sexting: Prevalence Rates, Driving Motivations, and the Deterrent Effect of Legal Consequences," *Sexuality Research and Social Policy* 11, no. 3 (September 2014): 245–255, https://link.springer.com/article/10.1007/s13178-014-0162-9.

60 **Another study, authored by Bridgewater:** Elizabeth Englander, "Low Risk Associated with Most Teenage Sexting: A Study of 617 18-Year-Olds," *MARC Research Reports*, paper 6 (2012), http://vc.bridgew.edu/cgi/viewcontent.cgi?article=1003&context=marc_reports.

60 **almost a quarter of teens:** Englander, "Low Risk Associated."

61 **while boys and girls consensually sext:** Englander, "Low Risk Associated."

62 **In 2015, one Colorado high school:** Kassondra Cloos and Julie Turkewitz, "Hundreds of Nude Photos Jolt Colorado School," *New York Times*, November 6, 2015, https://www.nytimes.com/2015/11/07/us/colorado-students-caught-trading-nude-photos-by-the-hundreds.html.

62 **"because half the school was sexting":** Cloos and Turkewitz, "Hundreds of Nude Photos."

63 **In 2008 . . . Jessica Logan:** Mike Celizic, "Her Teen Committed Suicide over 'Sexting,'" *Today*, October 14, 2016, https://www.today.com/parents/her-teen-committed-suicide-over-sexting-2D80555048.

63 **Less than two years later . . . Hope Witsell:** Randi Kaye, "How a Cell Phone Picture Led to Girl's Suicide," CNN, October 7, 2010, http://www.cnn.com/2010/LIVING/10/07/hope.witsells.story/index.html.

64 **school administrators routinely single out:** Helin Jung, "Kindergarten Tells 5-Year-Old Her Dress Is Inappropriate, Dad Responds Like a Feminist Hero," *Cosmopolitan*, April 28, 2015, https://www.cosmopolitan.com/lifestyle/news/a39708/5-year-old-girl-violates-school-dress-code/.

64 **under the pretense of dress-code violations:** Kelly Wallace, "Do School Dress Codes End Up Body-Shaming Girls?" CNN, May 30, 2017, https://www.cnn.com/2017/05/30/health/school-dress-codes-body-shaming-girls-parenting/index.html; Talia Lakritz, "17 Times Students and Parents Said School Dress Codes Went Too Far," Insider, November 5, 2018, https://www.thisisinsider.com/school-dress-code-rules-controversy-2018-8.

65 **child pornography laws to adjudicate sexting teens:** Janet Burns, "14-Year-Old Charged with Felony Sex Crime for Sending a Dirty Selfie," *Forbes*,

January 3, 2018, https://www.forbes.com/sites/janetwburns/2018/01/03/14
-year-old-charged-with-felony-sex-crime-for-sending-a-dirty-selfie/.

65 **in response to the Meese Report:** Edwin McDowell, "Some Say Meese Report Rates an 'X,'" *New York Times*, October 21, 1986, https://www.nytimes
.com/1986/10/21/books/some-say-meese-report-rates-an-x.html.

65 **The resulting laws imposed serious penalties:** US Sentencing Commission, *The History of the Child Pornography Guidelines* (Washington, DC: October 2009), https://www.ussc.gov/sites/default/files/pdf/research-and
-publications/research-projects-and-surveys/sex-offenses/20091030_His
tory_Child_Pornography_Guidelines.pdf.

65 **Between 2009 and 2013, forty-two states:** Melissa R. Lorang, Dale E. McNiel, and Renée L. Binder, "Minors and Sexting: Legal Implications," *Journal of the American Academy of Psychiatry and the Law Online* 44, no. 1 (March 2016): 73–81, http://jaapl.org/content/44/1/73.

65 **in Georgia it is now a misdemeanor:** Lorang, McNiel, and Binder, "Minors and Sexting."

66 **teens get caught sexting in Georgia:** Representatives Neal of the 2nd, Atwood of the 179th, Nix of the 69th, Hitchens of the 161st, and Hightower of the 68th, House Bill 156 (as Passed House and Senate), http://www.legis
.ga.gov/Legislation/20132014/136927.pdf.

66 **Before this change, the same teens:** Lorang, McNiel, and Binder, "Minors and Sexting."

66 **But state laws vary widely:** Lorang, McNiel, and Binder, "Minors and Sexting."

66 **In 2015, North Carolina authorities:** Michael E. Miller, "N.C. Just Prosecuted a Teenage Couple for Making Child Porn—of Themselves," *Washington Post*, September 21, 2015, https://www.washingtonpost.com/news
/morning-mix/wp/2015/09/21/n-c-just-prosecuted-a-teenage-couple-for
-making-child-porn-of-themselves/.

66 **"We don't know where these pictures are going to go":** Cyrus Farivar, "2 North Carolina Teens Hit with Child Porn Charges After Consensual Sexting," Ars Technica, September 3, 2015, https://arstechnica.com/tech-policy
/2015/09/busted-in-north-carolina-you-can-have-sex-at-16-but-you-cant-sext/.

CHAPTER 4: GIRLS' LIVES MATTER

74 **A month and a half before:** All details of Vanessa's case outlined in this story are based on my years of extensive discussions with Vanessa and her mother, as well as my investigation into the handling of her case by her school administrators and the police. The story has also been covered extensively in press reports. See: Kate Taylor, "Schools Punished Teenagers for Being Victims of Sexual Assault, Complaints Say," *New York Times*, June 7, 2016, https://www.nytimes.com/2016/06/08/nyregion/schools-punished

-teenagers-for-being-victims-of-sexual-assault-complaints-say.html; Katie J. M. Baker, "Sent Home from Middle School After Reporting a Rape," BuzzFeed, March 14, 2016, https://www.buzzfeednews.com/article/katiejmbaker/sent-home-from-middle-school-after-reporting-a-rape; Gaby Del Valle, "Teen Allegedly Raped at School and Told to 'Move On,' Lawsuit Claims," *Teen Vogue*, July 19, 2018, https://www.teenvogue.com/story/teen-allegedly-raped-at-school-and-told-to-move-on-lawsuit-claims; Tyler Kingkade, "NYC Schools Suspended Sexual Assault Victims Because They're Black: Attorney," *HuffPost*, June 13, 2016, https://www.huffingtonpost.com/entry/nyc-schools-sexual-assault-victims_us_575ebf51e4b00f97fba8d405; Aviva Stahl, "'This Is an Epidemic': How NYC Public Schools Punish Girls for Being Raped," Broadly, June 8, 2016, https://broadly.vice.com/en_us/article/59mz3x/this-is-an-epidemic-how-nyc-public-schools-punish-girls-for-being-raped. I also co-authored an opinion piece about Vanessa's case and others outlined in this chapter in *HuffPost*, in September 2017. See: Carrie Goldberg and Servet Bayimli, "Back-to-School Advisory: K-12 Schools Must Address Sexual Violence," *HuffPost*, September 7, 2017, https://www.huffingtonpost.com/entry/k-12-sexual-violence_us_57d08623e4b06a74c9f2731f. In addition, I discuss Vanessa's case, and visit the site of the assault, in the excellent documentary *Netizens*, which was released in 2018. See: *Netizens*, directed by Cynthia Lowen (New York: Fork Films, 2018), DVD, https://www.netizensfilm.com/.

76 **For every report of sexual violation:** Robin McDowell, Reese Dunklin, Emily Schmall, and Justin Pritchard, "Hidden Horror of School Sex Assaults Revealed by AP," Associated Press, May 1, 2017, https://www.ap.org/explore/schoolhouse-sex-assault/hidden-horror-of-school-sex-assaults-revealed-by-ap.html.

76 **the vast majority of sexual assaults on children:** McDowell et al., "Hidden Horror of School Sex Assaults."

76 **Student-on-student sexual assaults:** McDowell et al., "Hidden Horror of School Sex Assaults."

76 **The impact of a sexual assault:** "Child Sexual Abuse Statistics," Darkness to Light, January 2017, https://www.d2l.org/wp-content/uploads/2017/01/all_statistics_20150619.pdf.

76 **In addition to the psychological symptoms:** "Sexual Violence: Consequences," Centers for Disease Control and Prevention, last updated April 10, 2018, https://www.cdc.gov/violenceprevention/sexualviolence/consequences.html.

76 **sexual assaults can also lead victims:** "Sexual Violence: Consequences," Centers for Disease Control and Prevention.

76 **fourteen times more likely:** "Child Sexual Abuse Statistics," National Center for Victims of Crime, 2018, http://victimsofcrime.org/media/reporting -on-child-sexual-abuse/child-sexual-abuse-statistics.

77 **Of the seventeen thousand incidents:** McDowell et al., "Hidden Horror of School Sex Assaults."

79 **Title IX of the Education Amendments:** US Department of Justice, "Equal Access to Education: Forty Years of Title IX," June 23, 2012, https:// www.justice.gov/sites/default/files/crt/legacy/2012/06/20/titleixreport.pdf; Title IX of the Educational Amendments, 20 U.S.C. §1681.

80 **Specifically, the thirty-seven-word clause:** US Department of Justice, "Equal Access to Education."

80 **only 8 percent of American women:** US Department of Justice, "Equal Access to Education."

80 **Some colleges refused to admit female students:** US Department of Justice, "Equal Access to Education."

80 **Title IX made these practices illegal:** US Department of Justice, "Equal Access to Education."

80 **By 2017, women were outpacing men:** Jon Marcus, "Why Men Are the New College Minority," *The Atlantic*, August 8, 2017, http://www.theatlantic.com /education/archive/2017/08/why-men-are-the-new-college-minority/536103/; "Percentage of Persons 25 to 29 Years Old with Selected Levels of Educational Attainment, by Race/Ethnicity and Sex: Selected Years, 1920 through 2017 (Table 104.20)," National Center for Education Statistics (NCES), 2017, https://nces.ed.gov/programs/digest/d17/tables/dt17_104.20.asp.

80 **Title IX also ensured:** Jaeah Lee and Maya Dusenbery, "Charts: The State of Women's Athletics, 40 Years After Title IX," *Mother Jones*, June 22, 2012, https://www.motherjones.com/politics/2012/06/charts-womens-athletics -title-nine-ncaa/.

80 **the only athletic program available to her:** Jackie Joyner-Kersee, "Jackie Joyner-Kersee's Winning Moment," ESPN, June 5, 2012, http://www.espn .com/espnw/title-ix/article/8011246/jackie-joyner-kersee-winning-moment; Jake Simpson, "How Title IX Sneakily Revolutionized Women's Sports," *The Atlantic*, June 21, 2012, https://www.theatlantic.com/entertainment/archive /2012/06/how-title-ix-sneakily-revolutionized-womens-sports/258708/.

80 ***Sports Illustrated* named Joyner-Kersee:** "Dreams Come True," *Sports Illustrated*, August 11, 2008, https://www.si.com/olympics/photos/2008/08 /11dreams-come-true----#1.

81 **took more than two decades:** "Know Your Rights: Title IX and Sexual Assault," American Civil Liberties Union, https://www.aclu.org/know -your-rights/title-ix-and-sexual-assault.

81 ***Davis v. Monroe County Board of Education***: *Davis v. Monroe County Board of Education* 529 U.S. 629 (1999), https://www.law.cornell.edu/supct/html/97-843.ZS.html.

81 **the University . . . could be held responsible:** "Know Your Rights," American Civil Liberties Union.

81 **The school was sued:** Howard Pankratz, "$2.8 Million Deal in CU Rape Case," *Denver Post*, December 5, 2007, https://www.denverpost.com/2007/12/05/2-8-million-deal-in-cu-rape-case/.

81 **The White House established:** White House Task Force to Protect Students from Sexual Assault, *Preventing and Addressing Campus Sexual Misconduct: A Guide for University and College Presidents, Chancellors, and Senior Administrators* (Washington, DC, 2017), https://www.whitehouse.gov/sites/whitehouse.gov/files/images/Documents/1.4.17.VAW%20Event.Guide%20for%20College%20Presidents.PDF.

81 **a nineteen-page "Dear Colleague" letter:** "Dear Colleague Letter: Sexual Violence Background, Summary, and Fast Facts," US Department of Education Office for Civil Rights, April 4, 2011, https://obamawhitehouse.archives.gov/sites/default/files/fact_sheet_sexual_violence.pdf.

82 **The letter also detailed:** "Dear Colleague" letter from United States Department of Education Office for Civil Rights.

82 **In 2011, the Association:** Anemona Hartocollis, "Colleges Spending Millions to Deal with Sexual Misconduct Complaints," *New York Times*, March 29, 2016, https://www.nytimes.com/2016/03/30/us/colleges-beef-up-bureaucracies-to-deal-with-sexual-misconduct.html; "About ATIXA and Title IX," Association of Title IX Administrators, https://atixa.org/about/.

82 **In 2017, only eighteen states:** McDowell et al., "Hidden Horror of School Sex Assaults."

82 **the majority . . . reported feeling ill-equipped:** "Resources for Parents & Educators," Break the Cycle, accessed on March 6, 2018, https://www.breakthecycle.org/back2school-adults.

82 **Dr. Bill Howe, a former K-12 teacher:** McDowell et al., "Hidden Horror of School Sex Assaults."

83 **the schools won't accommodate them:** "The Kids Aren't Alright," Reveal, May 27, 2017, https://www.revealnews.org/episodes/the-kids-arent-all-right/.

84 **out of 230 reported rapes:** "The Criminal Justice System: Statistics," RAINN, https://www.rainn.org/statistics/criminal-justice-system.

86 **I first met "Destiny":** The details of Destiny's case relayed in this chapter are based on many hours of discussion with Destiny and her mother. Her story has also been reported in the press. See: Kingkade, "NYC Schools Suspended"; Taylor, "Schools Punished Teenagers."

87 **in the *New York Daily News*:** Ben Chapman, "Brooklyn School Punished Intellectually Disabled Girl Who Was Gang Raped by Students and Tried Keeping It Secret: Lawsuit," *New York Daily News*, January 11, 2018, https://www.nydailynews.com/new-york/education/brooklyn-school-punished-gang-rape-victim-article-1.3750411; *L.W. as parent and guardian, on behalf of her infant daughter, K.M. v. New York City Department of Education*, United States District Court for the Southern District of New York, (17-CV-8415).

87 **another student's mother:** Ben Chapman, "Second Sexual Assault Victim at Brooklyn School Says Education Officials Failed to Keep Students Safe," *New York Daily News*, January 30, 2018, http://www.nydailynews .com/new-york/brooklyn/sexual-assault-victim-brooklyn-school-surfaces -article-1.3787058.

87 **In November of 2015, Kai:** Kai's case was also covered in multiple press reports. See: Taylor, "Schools Punished Teenagers"; Kingkade, "NYC Schools Suspended."

88 **Even when racial biases:** For an excellent overview of unconscious bias, see: "State of Science on Unconscious Bias," UCSF Office of Diversity and Outreach, https://diversity.ucsf.edu/resources/state-science-unconscious-bias.

88 **One famous study showed that résumés:** Marianne Bertrand and Sendhil Mullainathan, "Are Emily and Greg More Employable Than Lakisha and Jamal? A Field Experiment on Labor Market Discrimination," working paper no. 9873, National Bureau of Economic Research, July 2003, https://www.nber.org/papers/w9873.pdf; Katie Sanders, "Do Job-Seekers with 'White' Names Get More Callbacks Than 'Black' Names?" *Politifact*, March 15, 2015, https://www.politifact.com/punditfact/statements/2015/mar/15 /jalen-ross/black-name-resume-50-percent-less-likely-get-respo/.

88 **Other research found medical professionals assumed:** Ronald Wyatt, "Pain and Ethnicity," *AMA Journal of Ethics* 15, no. 5 (May 2013): 449–454, https://journalofethics.ama-assn.org/article/pain-and-ethnicity/2013-05; Sandhya Somashekhar, "The Disturbing Reason Some African American Patients May Be Undertreated for Pain," *Washington Post*, April 4, 2016, https://www.washingtonpost.com/news/to-your-health/wp/2016/04/04 /do-blacks-feel-less-pain-than-whites-their-doctors-may-think-so/.

88 **A meta-analysis of forty-two studies:** Yara Mekawi and Konrad Bresin, "Is the Evidence from Racial Bias Shooting Task Studies a Smoking Gun? Results from a Meta-Analysis," *Journal of Experimental Psychology* 61 (November 2015): 120–130, https://www.sciencedirect.com/science/article/pii/S002210 3115000992; Gabrielle Canon, "Study: People Are Quicker to Shoot a Black Target Than a White Target," *Mother Jones*, September 1, 2015, https://www .motherjones.com/politics/2015/09/study-shows-racial-bias-shootings/.

89 **teachers in K-12 schools were more likely:** "K-12 Education: Discipline Disparities for Black Students, Boys, and Students with Disabilities," US

Government Accountability Office (GAO), April 4, 2018, https://www.gao
.gov/products/GAO-18-258; German Lopez, "Black Kids Are Way More
Likely to Be Punished in School Than White Kids, Study Finds," Vox, April
5, 2018, https://www.vox.com/identities/2018/4/5/17199810/school
-discipline-race-racism-gao.

89 **This bias impacts children as soon as:** "Civil Rights Data Collection Data
Snapshot: School Discipline," Issue Brief no. 1, US Department of Education
Office for Civil Rights, March 2014, https://ocrdata.ed.gov/Downloads
/CRDC-School-Discipline-Snapshot.pdf.

89 **Georgetown Law Center on Poverty and Inequality's 2017 report:**
Rebecca Epstein, Jamilia J. Blake, and Thalia González, *Girlhood Interrupted: The Erasure of Black Girls' Childhood*, Georgetown Law Center
on Poverty and Inequality, June 27, 2017, https://www.law.georgetown.edu
/poverty-inequality-center/wp-content/uploads/sites/14/2017/08/girlhood
-interrupted.pdf.

89 **"adultification," can have a profound effect:** Epstein, Blake, and González,
Girlhood Interrupted.

89 **"adults see black girls as less innocent":** T. Rees Shapiro, "Study: Black
Girls Viewed as 'Less Innocent' Than White Girls," *Washington Post*, June
27, 2017, https://www.washingtonpost.com/local/education/study-black
-girls-viewed-as-less-innocent-than-white-girls/2017/06/27/3fbedc32-5ae1
-11e7-a9f6-7c3296387341_story.html.

90 *Washington Post's* **parenting blog:** Jonita Davis, "A Study Found Adults
See Black Girls as 'Less Innocent,' Shocking Everyone but Black Moms,"
Washington Post, July 13, 2017, https://www.washingtonpost.com/news
/parenting/wp/2017/07/13/a-study-found-adults-see-black-girls-as-less
-innocent-shocking-everyone-but-black-moms/.

90 **sent a letter home to Destiny's mother:** Kingkade, "NYC Schools Suspended."

90 **for every black woman who reports:** Brooke Axtell, "Black Women, Sexual
Assault and the Art of Resistance," *Forbes*, April 25, 2012, https://www
.forbes.com/sites/shenegotiates/2012/04/25/black-women-sexual-assault
-and-the-art-of-resistance/.

91 **even when black women do step forward:** "Black Women & Sexual Violence," National Organization of Women (NOW), February 2018, https://
now.org/wp-content/uploads/2018/02/Black-Women-and-Sexual
-Violence-6.pdf.

91 **the disparity is likely to continue ... Ethics Project:** Elizabeth Kennedy,
"Victim Race and Rape," Feminist Sexual Ethics Project, Brandeis University, September 26, 2003, https://www.brandeis.edu/projects/fse/slavery
/united-states/kennedy.html.

91 **Lifetime aired a scathing six-part docuseries:** *Surviving R. Kelly*, produced by Dream Hampton, aired January 3–5, 2019, on Lifetime, https://www.mylifetime.com/shows/surviving-r-kelly.

91 **Kelly's conduct had been the subject of credible press reports:** Jim DeRogatis, "Parents Told Police Their Daughter Is Being Held Against Her Will in R. Kelly's 'Cult,'" BuzzFeed, July 17, 2017, https://www.buzzfeed news.com/article/jimderogatis/parents-told-police-r-kelly-is-keeping -women-in-a-cult.

91 **finally dropped the multiplatinum-selling artist:** Jem Aswad and Shirley Halperin, "R. Kelly Dropped by Sony Music," *Variety*, January 18, 2019, https://variety.com/2019/biz/news/r-kelly-dropped-sony-music-12031 06180/.

92 **must designate at least one employee:** "Sex Discrimination: Frequently Asked Questions," US Department of Education Office for Civil Rights, last modified September 25, 2018, https://www2.ed.gov/about/offices/list/ocr /frontpage/faq/sex.html.

92 **Harvard University has one Title IX employee:** In 2016, Harvard had fifty Title IX employees and just under twenty thousand undergraduates and graduate students. See: Anemona Hartocollis, "Colleges Spend Millions to Deal with Sexual Misconduct Complaints," *New York Times*, March 29, 2016, https://www.nytimes.com/2016/03/30/us/colleges-beef-up-bureau cracies-to-deal-with-sexual-misconduct.html; "About Harvard/Harvard at a Glance," Harvard University, accessed January 2019, https://www.harvard .edu/about-harvard/harvard-glance.

93 **entire New York City Department of Education:** "Regulation of the Chancellor," NYC Department of Education, September 21, 2018, https://www .schools.nyc.gov/docs/default-source/default-document-library/a-830.

93 ***Brooklyn* magazine published an article:** Rebecca Jennings, "Talking to a Brooklyn Revenge Porn Lawyer," *Brooklyn*, February 28, 2014, http://www.bkmag.com/2014/02/28/talking-to-a-brooklyn-revenge-porn -lawyer/.

96 **the fastest growing in the country:** "2018 Honorees," Law Firm 500, 2018, https://lawfirm500.com/2018-award-honorees/.

96 **rescind Obama's Title IX guidelines:** Kathryn Joyce, "The Takedown of Title IX," *New York Times*, December 5, 2017, https://www.nytimes.com /2017/12/05/magazine/the-takedown-of-title-ix.html.

96 **met with various men's rights activists:** Erin Dooley, Janet Weinstein, and Meridith McGraw, "Betsy DeVos' Meetings with 'Men's Rights' Groups over Campus Sex Assault Policies Spark Controversy," ABC News, July 14, 2017, https://abcnews.go.com/Politics/betsy-devos-meetings-mens-rights-groups -sex-assault/story?id=48611688.

97 **false allegations account for less than:** Katie Heaney, "Almost No One Is Falsely Accused of Rape," The Cut, October 5, 2018, https://www.thecut .com/article/false-rape-accusations.html.

97 **Rape is the most underreported:** "Statistics About Sexual Violence," National Sexual Violence Resource Center.

97 **more than 90 percent:** "Statistics About Sexual Violence," National Sexual Violence Resource Center.

97 **a new set of Title IX guidelines:** Laura Meckler, "Betsy DeVos Set to Bolster Rights of Accused in Rewrite of Sexual Assault Rules," *Washington Post*, November 14, 2018, https://www.washingtonpost.com/local /education/betsy-devos-set-to-bolster-rights-of-accused-in-rewrite-of-sexual -assault-rules/2018/11/14/828ebd9c-e7d1-11e8-a939-9469f1166f9d_story .html.

97 **the city agreed to pay Destiny:** Ben Chapman, "Disabled Girl Who Said She Was Punished for Reporting School Gang Rape Wins Nearly $1 Million Settlement," *New York Daily News*, July 14, 2018, http://www.nydailynews .com/new-york/education/ny-metro-one-million-settlement-for-student -raped-at-school-and-punished-for-it-20180713-story.html.

98 **Three months after we sued the city, Vanessa spoke publicly:** Girls for Gender Equity (@GGENYC), "Today we are joined by organizations . . . ," Twitter, October 25, 2018, 8:19 a.m., https://twitter.com/GGENYC/status /1055478891144495104.

98 **Tarana Burke is the organization's senior director:** Tarana Burke, "Me Too Is a Movement, Not a Moment," filmed November 2018 in Palm Springs, CA, TEDWomen video, 16:15, https://blog.ted.com/watch-tarana-burkes -ted-talk-me-too-is-a-movement-not-a-moment/.

CHAPTER 5: GODWIN'S LAW

99 **Have you ever heard of Godwin's Law?:** Abby Ohlheiser "The Creator of Godwin's Law Explains Why Some Nazi Comparisons Don't Break His Famous Internet Rule," *The Washington Post*, August 14, 2017, https://www .washingtonpost.com/news/the-intersect/wp/2017/08/14/the-creator-of -godwins-law-explains-why-some-nazi-comparisons-dont-break-his-famous -internet-rule/.

108 **victims of Nazi persecution:** "What We Do," Claims Conference: The Conference on Jewish Material Claims Against Germany, accessed January 2019, http://www.claimscon.org/what-we-do/.

108 **Suddenly, there was money available:** "Holocaust Victim Assets Litigation," Swiss Bank Claims, last updated January 12, 2018, http://www.swiss bankclaims.com/overview.aspx; "Forced Labor in Austria," Fund for Reconciliation, Peace and Cooperation, accessed January 7, 2019, http://www .reconciliationfund.at/index-2.html.

108 **could get partial compensation:** "Holocaust Restitution: Compensation and Restitution, by Country," Jewish Virtual Library: A Project of AICE, last updated December 2005, https://www.jewishvirtuallibrary.org/holocaust-compensation-and-restitution-by-country.

108 **Hungarians, who'd previously been eligible:** "Holocaust Restitution," Jewish Virtual Library.

108 **credit forced labor toward social security:** Tony Helm, "Germany to Compensate Nazi Slave-Laborers," *The Telegraph*, May 31, 2001, https://www.telegraph.co.uk/news/worldnews/europe/germany/1332474/Germany-to-compensate-Nazi-slave-labourers.html; "German Forced Labor Compensation Programme," International Organization for Migration, https://www.iom.int/files/live/sites/iom/files/What-We-Do/docs/German-Forced-Labour-Compensation-Programme-GFLCP.pdf.

110 **a little write-up:** "In the Matter of the Application of Northern Manhattan Nursing Home, Petitioner, for the Appointment of Person and Property of A.M., an Incapacitated Person, 500080-08," *New York Law Journal*, May 26, 2011, https://www.law.com/newyorklawjournal/almID/1202495187880/.

CHAPTER 6: PROFITEERS OF PAIN

115 **In 2013, New York State:** "45 States + DC Now Have Revenge Porn Laws," Cyber Civil Rights Initiative, https://www.cybercivilrights.org/revenge-porn-laws/.

115 **Roughly one in twenty-five Americans:** Amanda Lenhart, Michele Ybarra, and Myeshia Price-Feeney, "Nonconsensual Image Sharing: One in 25 Americans Has Been a Victim of 'Revenge Porn,'" Data & Society Research Institute, December 13, 2016, https://datasociety.net/pubs/oh/Nonconsensual_Image_Sharing_2016.pdf.

116 **And more than 90 percent of victims:** Mudasir Kamal and William J. Newman, "Revenge Pornography: Mental Health Implications and Related Legislation," *Journal of the American Academy of Psychiatry and the Law Online* 44, no. 3 (September 2016): 359–367, http://jaapl.org/content/44/3/359; Mary Anne Franks, "Drafting an Effective 'Revenge Porn' Law: A Guide for Legislatures," Cyber Civil Rights, September 22, 2016, https://www.cybercivilrights.org/guide-to-legislation/.

117 **In January 2017 alone, Facebook:** Charlotte Alter, "'It's Like Having an Incurable Disease': Inside the Fight Against Revenge Porn," *Time*, June 13, 2017, http://time.com/4811561/revenge-porn/.

117 **before the term "revenge porn":** Ian Parker, "The Story of a Suicide," *New Yorker*, February 6, 2012, https://www.newyorker.com/magazine/2012/02/06/the-story-of-a-suicide.

117 **Clementi killed himself:** Parker, "The Story of a Suicide."

117 **Ravi would later tell Chris Cuomo:** Alice Gomstyn, "Rutgers' Ravi: 'I Wasn't the One Who Caused Him to Jump,'" ABC News, March 22, 2012, https://abcnews.go.com/blogs/headlines/2012/03/rutgers-ravi-i-wasnt-the-one-who-caused-him-to-jump/.

119 **In 2012, Moore:** Unless otherwise indicated, all information about Hunter Moore came primarily from Camille Dodero and Alex Morris's excellent reporting on the asshole, and from Charlotte Laws's detailed account of her experience battling Moore. See: Camille Dodero, "Hunter Moore Makes a Living Screwing You," *Village Voice*, April 4, 2012, https://www.villagevoice.com/2012/04/04/hunter-moore-makes-a-living-screwing-you/; Alex Morris, "Hunter Moore: The Most Hated Man on the Internet," *Rolling Stone*, November 13, 2012, https://www.rollingstone.com/culture/news/the-most-hated-man-on-the-internet-20121113; Charlotte Laws, "One Woman's Dangerous War Against the Most Hated Man on the Internet," Jezebel, November 22, 2013, https://jezebel.com/one-womans-dangerous-war-against-the-most-hated-man-on-1469240835.

121 **taken in a doctor's office:** Laws, "One Woman's Dangerous War."

121 **on ABC's *Nightline* in 2012:** Neal Karlinsky, Aude Soichet, and Lauren Effron, "Anti-Bullying Website Takes Over, Shuts Down 'Revenge Porn' Website," ABC News, April 19, 2012, http://abcnews.go.com/US/anti-bullying-website-takes-shuts-revenge-porn-website/story?id=16174425.

121 **three hundred thousand unique visitors a day:** Marlow Stern, "Hunter Moore, Creator of 'Revenge Porn' Website Is Anyone Up?, Is the Internet's Public Enemy No. 1," Daily Beast, March 13, 2012, https://www.thedailybeast.com/hunter-moore-creator-of-revenge-porn-website-is-anyone-up-is-the-internets-public-enemy-no-1.

121 **He received death threats:** Fidel Martinez, "Anonymous Hacks Hunter Moore.TV, Doxes Moore Again," Daily Dot, December 6, 2012, https://www.dailydot.com/news/hunter-moore-tv-hacked-anonymous-dox/.

122 **up to $30,000:** Morris, "Hunter Moore."

122 **The *Village Voice* feature:** Dodero, "Hunter Moore."

122 **A profile in *Rolling Stone*:** Morris, "Hunter Moore."

122 **A Daily Beast feature:** Stern, "Hunter Moore."

123 **from the Cyber Civil Rights Initiative:** Maureen O'Connor, "The Crusading Sisterhood of Revenge Porn Victims," The Cut, August 29, 2013, https://www.thecut.com/2013/08/crusading-sisterhood-of-revenge-porn-victims.html.

123 **friend and colleague Holly Jacobs:** Holly Jacobs, "Being a Victim of Revenge Porn Forced Me to Change My Name," *Thought Catalog*, November 27, 2013, https://thoughtcatalog.com/dr-holly-jacobs/2013/11/being-a-victim-of-revenge-porn-forced-me-to-change-my-name/.

123 **Within days of her ex posting:** Jacobs, "Being a Victim."

123 **incorporated in 2013:** "About CCRI," Cyber Civil Rights Initiative, accessed January 2019, https://www.cybercivilrights.org/welcome/.

123 **In 2017 . . . the first national survey:** Dr. Asia A. Eaton, Dr. Holly Jacobs, and Yanet Ruvalcaba, *2017 Nationwide Online Study of Nonconsensual Porn Victimization and Perpetration: A Summary Report*, Cyber Civil Rights Initiative, June 2017, https://www.cybercivilrights.org/wp-content/uploads /2017/06/CCRI-2017-Research-Report.pdf.

124 **More than 90 percent of victims:** Franks, "Drafting an Effective 'Revenge Porn' Law."

124 **In the first peer-reviewed study:** Samantha Bates, "Revenge Porn and Mental Health: A Qualitative Analysis of the Mental Health Effects of Revenge Porn on Female Survivors," *Feminist Criminology* 12, no. 1 (2016): 22– 42, https://journals.sagepub.com/doi/pdf/10.1177/1557085116654565.

124 **almost 50 percent of victims:** Franks, "Drafting an Effective 'Revenge Porn' Law."

125 **more than three thousand internet sites:** Franks, "Drafting an Effective 'Revenge Porn' Law."

125 **Craig Brittain ran the revenge porn site:** Chase Hoffberger, "Revenge Porn Site Creator Buys ObamaNudes.com," Daily Dot, April 5, 2013, https:// www.dailydot.com/news/revenge-porn-obama-nudes-isanybodydown/; Federal Trade Commission, "Website Operator Banned from the 'Revenge Porn' Business After FTC Charges He Unfairly Posted Nude Photos," news release, January 29, 2015, https://www.ftc.gov/news-events/press-releases /2015/01/website-operator-banned-revenge-porn-business-after-ftc-charges.

125 **Kevin Bollaert ran a:** Dana Littlefield, "SD 'Revenge Porn' Case a Landmark," *San Diego Union-Tribune*, February 7, 2015, http://www.sandiegouniontribune .com/sdut-revenge-porn-california-law-bollaert-2015feb07-story.html.

125 **middle-aged, married mother of two teenagers:** Littlefield, "SD 'Revenge Porn' Case."

125 **"This was not porn":** Littlefield, "SD 'Revenge Porn' Case."

125 **At least one teacher lost her job:** Laws, "One Woman's Dangerous War."

125 **Craig Brittain instituted a "bounty system":** Federal Trade Commission, "Website Operator Banned."

126 **referred to these ill-gotten images as "wins":** State of California Department of Justice, Office of the Attorney General, "Attorney General Kamala D. Harris Announces Arrest of Revenge Porn Operator in Oklahoma," news release, February 14, 2014, https://oag.ca.gov/news/press-releases/attorney -general-kamala-d-harris-announces-arrest-revenge-porn-operator-oklahoma.

126 **Digital Millennium Copyright Act of 1998:** The Digital Millennium Copyright Act of 1998, Pub. L. No. 105-304, 112 Stat. 2860 (Oct. 28, 1998), US Copyright Office, December 1998, https://www.copyright.gov/legislation/dmca .pdf; Digital Millennium Copyright Act (DMCA) of 1998, 17 U.S.C. §512.

126 **filing DMCA notifications became a full-time job:** Margaret Talbot, "The Attorney Fighting Revenge Porn," *New Yorker*, December 5, 2016, https://www.newyorker.com/magazine/2016/12/05/the-attorney-fighting -revenge-porn.

126 **notorious for posting takedown notifications:** Caitlin Dewey, "How Copyright Became the Best Defense Against Revenge Porn," *Washington Post*, September 8, 2014, https://www.washingtonpost.com/news/the -intersect/wp/2014/09/08/how-copyright-became-the-best-defense-against -revenge-porn/.

126 **submit DMCA notices to Chilling Effects:** "Project Lumen," Berkman Klein Center for Internet & Society at Harvard University, last updated June 21, 2018, https://cyber.harvard.edu/research/lumen.

127 **one of the most-trafficked sites:** Christine Cassis and Justin Bassett, "Reddit's Year in Review: 2018," Reddit, December 4, 2018, https://redditblog .com/2018/12/04/reddit-year-in-review-2018/.

127 **the platform's "anything goes" ethos:** Katie Notopoulos, "Re-Rank the Order of Which NSFW Subreddit Creeps You Out the Most," BuzzFeed, June 3, 2015, https://www.buzzfeed.com/katienotopoulos/rank-the-order -of-which-nsfw-subreddit-creeps-you-out-the.

127 **the now infamous /r/creepshot subreddit:** Notopoulos, "Re-Rank the Order."

127 **Anderson Cooper did a segment:** Kevin Morris, "Anderson Cooper Boosts Visibility of Teen-Girl Pics," Daily Dot, October 3, 2011, https://www.daily dot.com/society/anderson-cooper-reddit-jailbait-traffic/.

127 **Reddit's general manager:** Adi Robertson, "Longtime Reddit General Manager Erik Martin Steps Down," The Verge, October 13, 2014, https:// www.theverge.com/2014/10/13/6969101/longtime-reddit-general-manager -erik-martin-steps-down.

128 **every major social media platform:** Roger Cheng, "Women in Tech: The Numbers Don't Add Up," CNET, May 6, 2015, https://www.cnet.com /news/women-in-tech-the-numbers-dont-add-up/.

128 **In 2014, only 10 percent:** Cheng, "Woman in Tech."

128 **Then came "the Fappening":** Timothy McLaughlin, "Hacker Who Stole Nude Photos of Jennifer Lawrence and Other Celebrities Jailed for Nine Months," *Independent*, January 25, 2017, https://www.independent.co.uk /news/world/americas/hacker-celebrity-nude-pictures-videos-jennifer -lawrence-kate-upton-kirsten-dunst-edward-majerczyk-a7544626.html.

128 **A subreddit devoted to the leak:** Kelsey McKinney, "Reddit Made over $100,000 Off Stolen Celebrity Nudes," Vox, September 11, 2014, https:// www.vox.com/jennifer-lawrence-celebrities-nude-photo-hack-crime/2014 /9/11/6135345/reddit-money-celebrity-hacking.

128 **$150,000 in additional revenue:** Jeff Stone, "Reddit Fappening Ban Triggers Outraged Response from Nude Photo Distributor," *International Business Times*, September 8, 2014, http://www.ibtimes.com/reddit-fappening-ban -triggers-outraged-response-nude-photo-distributor-1681708.

129 **November 2014 issue of *Vanity Fair*:** "Cover Exclusive: Jennifer Lawrence Calls Photo Hacking a 'Sex Crime,'" *Vanity Fair*, October 8, 2014, https:// www.vanityfair.com/hollywood/2014/10/jennifer-lawrence-cover.

129 **"It's my body":** "Cover Exclusive: Jennifer Lawrence," *Vanity Fair.*

129 **"You're perpetuating a sexual offense":** "Cover Exclusive: Jennifer Lawrence," *Vanity Fair.*

129 **Lawrence's Wikipedia page:** Zachary Volkert, "Jennifer Lawrence's Wikipedia Slammed with the Fappening Photos Same Day She Breaks Silence," Inquisitr, October 2, 2014, https://www.inquisitr.com/1525888/jennifer -lawrences-wikipedia-slammed-with-nude-the-fappening-photos-same-day -she-breaks-silence/.

129 **Norma, a nineteen-year-old fashion student:** You can read more about Norma's case in the *New Yorker*. See: Talbot, "The Attorney Fighting."

130 **operation since 2007:** Seung Lee, "Pornhub Joins Fight Against Revenge Porn," *Newsweek*, October 14, 2015, http://www.newsweek.com /pornhub-revenge-porn-help-victims-383160.

130 **was entertaining eighty-one million visitors per day:** "2017 Year in Review," Pornhub, January 9, 2018, https://www.pornhub.com/insights/2017 -year-in-review.

130 **organized into porn-specific genres:** Maureen O'Connor, "Pornhub Is the Kinsey Report of Our Time," The Cut, June 12, 2017, https://www .thecut.com/2017/06/pornhub-and-the-american-sexual-imagination.html; "Pornhub Categories: Find Your Favorite Free Hardcore Porn Videos," Pornhub, accessed November 13, 2018, https://www.pornhub.com/cate gories.

130 **In 2004, New Jersey:** Senate Committee Substitute for Senate, No. 2366, P.L. 2003, Chapter 206, January 8, 2004, ftp://www.njleg.state.nj.us /20022003/AL03/206_.PDF.

130 **the invasion of privacy statute:** *State of New Jersey v. Dharun Ravi*, 2016 N.J. App. Docket No. A-4667-11T1 (2016), https://law.justia.com/cases/new -jersey/appellate-division-published/2016/a4667-11.html.

130 **a copy of Section 2C: 14-9:** Senate Committee Substitute for Senate, No. 2366, P.L. 2003, Chapter 206.

131 **C.M. was charged:** Kathianne Boniello, "Man Ordered to Attend Counseling After Revenge Porn Confession," *New York Post*, March 27, 2016, https:// nypost.com/2016/03/27/revenge-porn-confession-leads-young-man-to -counseling/.

132 **banning nonconsensual porn:** Aja Romano, "Reddit Banned Revenge Porn and Users Are Mad About It," Daily Dot, December 11, 2015, https://www.dailydot.com/layer8/reddit-ban-on-revenge-porn/.

132 **a site-wide announcement:** Jessica Moreno, Ellen Pao, and Alexis Ohanian, "From 1 to 9,000 Communities, Now Taking Steps to Grow Reddit to 90,000 Communities (and Beyond!)," Reddit, February 24, 2015, https://www.reddit.com/r/announcements/comments/2x0g9v/from_1_to_9000_communities_now_taking_steps_to/.

132 **banning revenge porn from the platform:** David Goldman, "Embarrassed Twitter Bans Revenge Porn," CNN Money, March 12, 2015, http://money.cnn.com/2015/03/12/technology/twitter-revenge-porn/index.html.

132 **Google, Yahoo, and Bing:** Talbot, "The Attorney Fighting"; Stassa Edwards, "Google Will Remove 'Revenge Porn' from Its Search Results," Jezebel, June 20, 2015, https://jezebel.com/google-will-remove-revenge-porn-from-its-search-results-1712783324.

133 **even Pornhub got on board:** Amar Toor, "Pornhub Makes It Easier to Report Revenge Porn," The Verge, October 13, 2015, https://www.theverge.com/2015/10/13/9518029/pornhub-revenge-porn-reporting-page.

134 **like Kevin Bollaert:** Complaint, *The People of the State of California v. Kevin Christopher Bollaert* (Superior Court of the State of California, San Diego Superior Court, December 10, 2013), https://oag.ca.gov/system/files/attachments/press_releases/Complaint_3.pdf.

134 **The felony arrest warrant:** Arrest warrant, *People of the State of California v. Kevin Christopher Bollaert* (Superior Court of the State of California, San Diego Superior Court, December 10, 2013), https://oag.ca.gov/system/files/attachments/press_releases/Arrest%20warrant_0.pdf.

134 **At Bollaert's sentencing:** Littlefield, "SD 'Revenge Porn' Case."

134 **"My life has just gone through":** Littlefield, "SD 'Revenge Porn' Case."

134 **the judge read aloud a portion:** Littlefield, "SD 'Revenge Porn' Case."

134 **"Like, it was just fun":** Littlefield, "SD 'Revenge Porn' Case."

134 **listing a post office box number:** Littlefield, "SD 'Revenge Porn' Case."

135 **was sentenced to eighteen years:** Littlefield, "SD 'Revenge Porn' Case."

135 **In 2015, Craig Brittain:** Federal Trade Commission, "Website Operator Banned."

135 **The FTC's complaint noted:** Federal Trade Commission, "Website Operator Banned."

135 **nonprofit Without My Consent:** "Who We Are," Without My Consent, https://withoutmyconsent.org/who-we-are.

135 **The FTC charged Brittain:** Federal Trade Commission, "Website Operator Banned"; *In the Matter of Craig Brittain, individually*—Federal Trade Communication Docket c-a4564, Issued December 28, 2015.

135 **It was the first time the commission:** Danielle Citron and Woodrow Hartzog, "The Decision That Could Finally Kill the Revenge-Porn Business," *The Atlantic*, February 3, 2015, https://www.theatlantic.com/technology/archive/2015/02/the -decision-that-could-finally-kill-the-revenge-porn-business/385113/.

135 **In December 2015, he went down:** Department of Justice, US Attorney's Office Central District of California, "Man Who Operated 'Revenge Porn' Website Pleads Guilty in Hacking Scheme That Yielded Nude Photos from Google Email Accounts," news release, February 25, 2015, https://www.jus tice.gov/usao-cdca/pr/man-who-operated-revenge-porn-website-pleads -guilty-hacking-scheme-yielded-nude-photos.

135 **The warrior responsible for Moore's demise:** Laws, "One Woman's Dangerous War."

136 **FBI launched its own investigation:** Laurie Segall, "Revenge Porn Hacker: 'Scary How Quickly I Would Drop My Morals,'" CNN Money, April 28, 2015, https://money.cnn.com/2015/04/26/technology/charlie-evens -revenge-porn-hacker/index.html.

136 **were arrested and indicted:** Department of Justice, US Attorney's Office Central District of California, "Two California Men Arrested in E-Mail Hacking Scheme That Yielded Nude Photos That Were Posted on 'Revenge Porn' Website," news release, January 23, 2014, https://archives.fbi.gov/ar chives/losangeles/press-releases/2014/two-california-men-arrested-in-e-mail -hacking-scheme-that-yielded-nude-photos-that-were-posted-on-revenge -porn-website; Neal Karlinsky and Lauren Effron, "Revenge Porn Mogul Indicted on Federal Conspiracy Charges," ABC News, January 23, 2014, https://abcnews.go.com/Technology/revenge-porn-mogul-hunter-moore -indicted-federal-conspiracy/story?id=21641397.

136 **Evens pleaded guilty:** Abby Ohlheiser, "Revenge Porn Purveyor Hunter Moore Is Sentenced to Prison," *Washington Post*, December 3, 2015, https:// www.washingtonpost.com/news/the-intersect/wp/2015/12/03/revenge -porn-purveyor-hunter-moore-is-sentenced-to-prison/.

136 **In 2010, when dickhead Hunter Moore:** Heather Kelly, "New California 'Re venge Porn' Law May Miss Some Victims," CNN, October 3, 2013, https:// www.cnn.com/2013/10/03/tech/web/revenge-porn-law-california/index.html.

136 **thirty-four states and the District of Columbia:** "45 States + DC," Cyber Civil Rights Initiative.

136 **there were still five states that refused:** "45 States + DC," Cyber Civil Rights Initiative.

137 **a piracy law that makes it illegal:** Rachel Stilwell and Makenna Cox, "Phone Recordings of Concerts Are More Than Just Annoying, They're Potentially Illegal: Guest Post," *Billboard*, March 17, 2017, https://www.bill board.com/articles/business/7724330/phone-recordings-concerts-illegal -federal-bootlegging-laws.

137 **the Intimate Privacy Protection Act:** Intimate Privacy Protection Act of 2016, H.R. 5896, 114th Congress, https://www.congress.gov/bill/114th-congress/house-bill/5896/text.

138 **the Ending Nonconsensual Online User Graphic Harassment (ENOUGH) Act:** ENOUGH Act, S. 2162, 115th Congress, https://www.congress.gov/bill/115th-congress/senate-bill/2162/text.

CHAPTER 7: WHEN TROLLS ARMIES ATTACK

140 **In 2013, web game developer Zoë Quinn:** Sean Illing, "The Woman at the Center of #Gamergate Gives Zero Fucks about Her Haters," Vox, September 19, 2017, https://www.vox.com/culture/2017/9/19/16301682/gamergate-alt-right-zoe-quinn-crash-override-interview.

140 **"If I ever see you are doing a panel":** Noreen Malone, "Zoë and the Trolls," *New York*, July 24, 2017, http://nymag.com/intelligencer/2017/07/zoe-quinn-surviving-gamergate.html.

140 **the handle Death to Brianna:** Michael McWhertor, "Game Developer Brianna Wu Flees Home After Death Threats, Mass. Police Investigating," Polygon, October 11, 2014, https://www.polygon.com/2014/10/11/6963279/brianna-wu-death-threats-police-harassment.

140 **"I'm going to rape your filthy ass":** Peter Andrew Hart, "Game Developer Brianna Wu Flees Her Home After Death Threats," *HuffPost*, October 11, 2014, https://www.huffingtonpost.com/2014/10/11/game-developer-death-threats_n_5970966.html.

140 **Wu and her husband fled their home:** Hart, "Game Developer Brianna Wu Flees."

141 **Brilliant writer Jessica Valenti:** Catherine Piner, "Feminist Writer Jessica Valenti Takes a Break from Social Media After Threat Against Her Daughter," Slate, July 28, 2016, https://slate.com/human-interest/2016/07/feminist-writer-jessica-valenti-takes-a-break-from-social-media-after-threat-against-her-daughter.html.

141 **the 2018 documentary *Netizens*:** *Netizens*, directed by Lowen.

141 **her project *Tropes vs. Women*:** Jordan Erica Webber, "Anita Sarkeesian: 'It's Frustrating to Be Known as the Woman Who Survived #Gamergate,'" *The Guardian*, October 16, 2017, https://www.theguardian.com/lifeandstyle/2017/oct/16/anita-sarkeesian-its-frustrating-to-be-known-as-the-woman-who-survived-gamergate.

141 **created *Beat Up Anita Sarkeesian*:** Sarah O'Meara, "Internet Trolls Up Their Harassment Game with 'Beat Up Anita Sarkeesian,'" *HuffPost*, June 7, 2012, https://www.huffingtonpost.co.uk/2012/07/06/internet-trolls-online-beat-up-anita-sarkeesian-game_n_1653473.html.

141 **Almost 50 percent of Americans:** Amanda Lenhart et al., "Online Harassment, Digital Abuse, and CyberStalking in America," Data & Society, November 21, 2016, https://datasociety.net/pubs/oh/Online_Harassment _2016.pdf.

141 **"You could be sitting at home":** Laura Bates, "Violence Against Women Online," Amnesty International, March 21, 2018, https://www.amnesty.org /en/latest/research/2018/03/laura-bates-online-violence-against-women/.

141 **More than 80 percent of women:** "Toxic Twitter—The Silencing Effect," Amnesty International, March 2017, https://www.amnesty.org/en/latest /research/2018/03/online-violence-against-women-chapter-5/.

142 **organization considers online harassment:** Shiromi Pinto, "What Is Online Violence and Abuse Against Women?" Amnesty International, November 20, 2017, https://www.amnesty.org/en/latest/campaigns/2017/11/what -is-online-violence-and-abuse-against-women/.

142 **Jessica Valenti called the FBI:** Amanda Hess, "Why Women Aren't Welcome on the Internet," Pacific Standard, January 6, 2014, https://psmag .com/social-justice/women-arent-welcome-internet-72170.

142 **"It was totally impossible advice":** Hess, "Why Women Aren't Welcome."

142 **As Hess puts it:** Hess, "Why Women Aren't Welcome."

142 **In 1993, a Usenet poster:** Jamie Bartlett, "A Life Ruin: Inside the Digital Underworld," *Medium*, November 30, 2015, https://medium.com/@PRH Digital/a-life-ruin-inside-the-digital-underworld-590a23b14981.

143 **described it to the *New York Times*:** Mattathias Schwartz, "The Trolls Among Us," *New York Times Magazine*, August 3, 2008, https://www.ny times.com/2008/08/03/magazine/03trolls-t.html.

143 **attacked the Epilepsy Foundation website:** Schwartz, "The Trolls Among Us."

143 **In *The Dark Net*:** Jamie Bartlett, *The Dark Net: Inside the Digital Underworld* (Brooklyn: Melville House, 2015).

143 **In 2006, Mitchell Henderson:** Mattathias Schwartz, "The Rise of Malwebolence," *New York Times*, August 1, 2008, https://www.nytimes.com/2008 /08/04/technology/04iht-troll04.1.14949386.html.

144 **documented on Encyclopedia Dramatica:** "Mitchell Henderson," Encyclopedia Dramatica, April 16, 2011, https://encyclopediadramatica.rs/Mitch ell_Henderson.

144 **the description of Mitchell's suicide:** "Mitchell Henderson," Encyclopedia Dramatica.

144 **defacing the pages with sick comments:** Whitney Phillips, "LOLing at Tragedy: Facebook Trolls, Memorial Pages, and Resistance to Grief Online," *First Monday* 16, no. 12 (December 5, 2011), http://firstmonday.org/article /view/3168/3115.

144 **In 2011, British RIP troll Sean Duffy:** Steven Morris, "Internet Troll Jailed After Mocking Deaths of Teenagers," *The Guardian*, September 13, 2011, https://www.theguardian.com/uk/2011/sep/13/internet-troll-jailed -mocking-teenagers.

144 **Duffy wrote on the tribute Facebook page:** Morris, "Internet Troll Jailed."

144 **Britain's Malicious Communications Act:** "Who, What, Why: What Laws Currently Cover Trolling?" BBC News, October 20, 2014, http:// www.bbc.com/news/blogs-magazine-monitor-29686865.

144 **research on the effects of online anonymity:** John Suler, "The Online Disinhibition Effect," *CyberPsychology & Behavior* 7, no. 3 (July 2004): 321– 326, https://www.researchgate.net/publication/8451443_The_Online_Dis inhibition_Effect.

145 **In a process of dissociation:** Suler, "The Online Disinhibition Effect."

145 **In 2012, journalist Adrian Chen:** Adrian Chen, "Unmasking Reddit's Violentacrez: The Biggest Troll on the Web," Gawker, October 12, 2012, http://gawker.com/5950981/unmasking-reddits-violentacrez-the-biggest -troll-on-the-web.

145 **the mastermind behind /r/jailbait:** Fernando Alfonso III, "Redditors Declare War on Gawker Media," Daily Dot, October 11, 2012, https://www .dailydot.com/news/gawker-reddit-banned-adrian-chen-violentacrez/.

146 **the second most frequently used:** Chen, "Unmasking Reddit's Violenta- crez."

146 **Violentacrez's real name:** Chen, "Unmasking Reddit's Violentacrez."

146 **But when Chen told Brutsch:** Chen, "Unmasking Reddit's Violentacrez."

146 **he was fired:** "Violentacrez Fired: Michael Brutsch Loses Job After Reddit Troll Identity Exposed by Gawker," *HuffPost*, October 15, 2012, https:// www.huffingtonpost.com/2012/10/15/michael-brutsch-reddits-biggest -loses-job-identity-gawker_n_1967727.html.

146 **earliest studies of troll psychology:** Erin E. Buckels, Paul D. Trapnell, and Delroy L. Paulhus, "Trolls Just Want to Have Fun," *Personality and Individual Differences* (2014), https://scottbarrykaufman.com/wp-content /uploads/2014/02/trolls-just-want-to-have-fun.pdf.

147 **"In fact," wrote the researchers:** Buckels, Trapnell, and Paulhus, "Trolls Just Want to Have Fun."

147 **distinct similarities between troll behavior:** Stephanie Smith-Strickland, "The Psychology of Internet Trolls" (episode 7), May 19, 2016, in *Conversations* podcast, Highsnobiety, https://www.highsnobiety.com/2016/05/19 /internet-trolls-podcast/.

147 **the online name Obnoxious:** Unless otherwise indicated, all information pertaining to Obnoxious can be found in Jason Fagone's *New York Times Magazine* feature. See: Jason Fagone, "The Serial Swatter," *New York Times*

Magazine, November 24, 2015, https://www.nytimes.com/2015/11/29/magazine/the-serial-swatter.html.

147 **in 2018, Twitch averaged:** Ben Gilbert, "Amazon's Streaming Service Twitch Is Pulling in as Many Viewers as CNN and MSNBC," Business Insider, February 13, 2018, https://www.businessinsider.com/twitch-is-bigger-than-cnn-msnbc-2018-2.

149 **One of his victims was so shaken:** "Lizard Squad Member Pleads Guilty over 23 Counts Related to 'Swatting,'" *The Guardian*, May 22, 2015, https://www.theguardian.com/technology/2015/may/22/lizard-squad-canadian-pleads-guilty-over-23-counts-related-to-swatting.

149 **Obnoxious was eventually arrested:** Fagone, "The Serial Swatter."

149 **Lin answered a Craigslist ad:** The details included about Lin's harassment are based on my personal knowledge of the case. You can read more about the case here: Department of Justice, US Attorney's Office District of Massachusetts, "Newton Man Sentenced to Over 17 Years in Prison for Extensive Cyberstalking Campaign," news release, October 3, 2018, https://www.justice.gov/usao-ma/pr/newton-man-sentenced-over-17-years-prison-extensive-cyberstalking-campaign; Jason Murdock, "Massachusetts Man Gets 17 Years in Prison for Cyberstalking, Hacking, Child Porn, Bomb Threats," *Newsweek*, October 4, 2018, https://www.newsweek.com/massachusetts-man-gets-17-years-prison-cyberstalking-hacking-child-porn-hoax-1152787; Kim Tunnicliffe, "Man Charged with Cyberstalking Ex-Roommate Also Tied to Waltham School Threats," WBZ NewsRadio (Boston, MA), October 6, 2017, https://boston.cbslocal.com/2017/10/06/cyberstalking-charges-ryan-lin-waltham-school-threats/.

150 **Lin pleaded guilty:** Department of Justice, Office of Public Affairs, "Massachusetts Man Pleads Guilty to 25 Offenses Associated with Cyberstalking Former Housemate and Others," news release, May 9, 2018, https://www.justice.gov/opa/pr/massachusetts-man-pleads-guilty-25-offenses-associated-cyberstalking-former-housemate-and; *United States v. Ryan Lin* No. 1:18-cr-10092-WGY (Mass. 2018).

151 **Journalist Amy Guth found herself:** Karis Hustad, "Amy Guth Takes on the Trolls with a Documentary Series on Online Harassment," Chicago Inno, April 18, 2016, https://www.americaninno.com/chicago/amy-guth-takes-on-trolls-doxing-in-online-harassment-documentary/.

151 **Professional athletes and referees:** Joel Stein, "How Trolls Are Ruining the Internet," *Time*, August 18, 2016, http://time.com/4457110/internet-trolls/; John Shammas, "Police Probe Sick Twitter Threats by Trolls to Rape Jamie Vardy's Young Daughter," *Mirror*, April 4, 2016, https://www.mirror.co.uk/news/uk-news/police-probe-sick-twitter-threats-7686918.

151 **YouTube makeup artist Em Ford:** Stein, "How Trolls Are Ruining."

151 **When comedian Leslie Jones starred:** Casey Cipriani, "Sexism and Misogyny Plague 'Ghostbusters' Trailer Proving Even Male Directors Aren't Immune," Women and Hollywood, May 3, 2016, https://womenandhollywood.com/sexism-and-misogyny-plague-ghostbusters-trailer-proving-even-male-directors-arent-immune-1cdabe3f16cb/; Adam Howard, "Sexist 'Ghostbusters' Backlash Coincides with 2016 Gender Divide," NBC News, May 26, 2016, https://www.nbcnews.com/news/nbcblk/sexist-ghostbusters-backlash-coincides-2016-gender-divide-n580921.

151 **One troll sent an image:** Katie Rogers, "Leslie Jones, Star of 'Ghostbusters,' Becomes a Target of Online Trolls," *New York Times*, July 19, 2016, https://www.nytimes.com/2016/07/20/movies/leslie-jones-star-of-ghostbusters-becomes-a-target-of-online-trolls.html; Anna Silman, "A Timeline of Leslie Jones's Horrific Online Abuse," The Cut, August 24, 2016, https://www.thecut.com/2016/08/a-timeline-of-leslie-joness-horrific-online-abuse.html.

152 **for people of color to be targeted:** Terrell Jermaine Starr, "The Unbelievable Harassment Black Women Face Daily on Twitter," AlterNet, September 16, 2014, https://www.alternet.org/unbelievable-harassment-black-women-face-daily-twitter.

152 **In another case, my firm filed a federal suit:** *National Network of Abortion Funds, et al., v. Does 1–15* (1:18-cv-10596-GAO) District Court of Massachusetts 2018.

153 **French psychologist Gustave Le Bon:** Gustave Le Bon, *The Crowd: A Study of the Popular Mind* (1896; repr., Kitchener, Ont.: Batoche Books, 2001), https://socialsciences.mcmaster.ca/econ/ugcm/3ll3/lebon/Crowds.pdf; International Encyclopedia of the Social Sciences, s.v. "Le Bon, Gustav," https://www.encyclopedia.com/people/social-sciences-and-law/sociology-biographies/gustave-le-bon.

153 **crowds display more "primitive" behaviors:** Le Bon, *The Crowd*, 19.

153 **mob behavior is contagious:** Le Bon, *The Crowd*, 18, 23, 73.

153 **By Le Bon's reckoning:** Encyclopaedia Britannica, s.v. "Deindividuation," by Karen M. Douglas, last updated January 4, 2019, https://www.britannica.com/topic/deindividuation.

153 **A study on trolling behavior:** Stanford University, "Stanford Research Shows That Anyone Can Become an Internet Troll," news release via EurekAlert!, February 7, 2017, https://www.eurekalert.org/pub_releases/2017-02/su-srs020717.php. See also: Justin Cheng, Michael Bernstein, Cristian Danescu-Niculescu-Mizil, and Jure Leskovec, "Anyone Can Become a Troll: Causes of Trolling Behavior in Online Discussions," *Proceedings of the 2017 ACM Conference on Computer Supported Cooperative Work and Social Computing* (February/March 2017), http://www.cs.cornell.edu/~cristian/Anyone_Can_Become_a_Troll_files/anyone_can_become_a_troll.pdf; Justin

Cheng, Cristian Danescu-Niculescu-Mizil, Jure Leskovec, and Michael Bernstein, "Our Experiments Taught Us Why People Troll," The Conversation, March 1, 2017, https://theconversation.com/our-experiments-taught-us-why-people-troll-72798.

153 **"spiral of negativity"**: Taylor Kubota, "Under the Right Circumstances, Anyone Can Become an Internet Troll," *Stanford Engineering*, February 9, 2017, https://engineering.stanford.edu/magazine/article/under-right-circumstances-anyone-can-become-internet-troll.

154 **Andrew Anglin had a pretty normal childhood:** Unless otherwise indicated, all details pertaining to Andrew Anglin can be found in Luke O'Brien's excellent profile in *The Atlantic*: Luke O'Brien, "The Making of an American Nazi," *The Atlantic*, December 2017, https://www.theat lantic.com/magazine/archive/2017/12/the-making-of-an-american-nazi/544119/.

154 **On July 4, 2013, Anglin launched:** "Andrew Anglin: Five Things to Know," Anti-Defamation League, April 25, 2018, https://www.adl.org/news/article/andrew-anglin-five-things-to-know.

154 **With Daily Stormer:** "Andrew Anglin," Southern Poverty Law Center (SPLC), https://www.splcenter.org/fighting-hate/extremist-files/individual/andrew-anglin.

155 **Anglin published an article:** Andrew Anglin, "Heather Heyer: Woman Killed in Road Rage Incident Was a Fat, Childless 32-Year-Old Slut," Daily Stormer, August 13, 2017, https://dailystormer.name/heather-heyer-woman-killed-in-road-rage-incident-was-a-fat-childless-32-year-old-slut/.

155 **Anglin is one of the most prominent:** "Andrew Anglin," SPLC.

155 **Dylann Roof, who, in 2015:** O'Brien, "The Making of an American Nazi."

155 **In 2017 . . . Jackson boarded a bus:** N. R. Kleinfield, "A Man Who Hated Black Men Found a Victim Who Cared for Others," *New York Times*, March 23, 2017, https://www.nytimes.com/2017/03/23/nyregion/james-harris-jackson-timothy-caughman.html; Ashley Southall, "White Suspect in Black Man's Killing Is Indicted on Terror Charges," *New York Times*, March 27, 2017, https://www.nytimes.com/2017/03/27/nyregion/timothy-caughman-james-harris-jackson-terrorism.html.

155 **according to O'Brien:** O'Brien, "The Making of an American Nazi."

155 **sicced his troll army on Tanya Gersh:** O'Brien, "The Making of an American Nazi"; Michael Kunzelman, "Target of Online Trolls Suing Neo-Nazi Website's Publisher," *Chicago Tribune*, April 16, 2017, https://www.chicagotribune.com/news/nationworld/ct-daily-stormer-intimidation-lawsuit-20170418-story.html; Allie Conti, "Does Unleashing a Neo-Nazi 'Troll Army' Count as Free Speech?" Vice, April 10, 2018, https://www.vice.com/en_us/article/kzx3n9/does-unleashing-a-neo-nazi-troll-army-count-as-free-speech.

155 **You may recall Spencer:** Aleem Maqbool, "Hail Trump: White National- ists Mark Trump Win with Nazi Salute," BBC News, November 22, 2016, https://www.bbc.com/news/av/world-us-canada-38057104/hail-trump -white-nationalists-mark-trump-win-with-nazi-salute.

156 **Spencer . . . punched on camera:** Kaitlyn Tiffany, "Right-Wing Extremist Richard Spencer Got Punched, but It Was Memes That Bruised His Ego," The Verge, January 23, 2017, https://www.theverge.com/2017/1/23/14356306 /richard-spencer-punch-internet-memes-alt-right.

156 **left a voicemail for Gersh:** Rachel Gutman, "Who Is Weev, and Why Did He Derail a Journalist's Career?" *The Atlantic*, February 14, 2018, https:// www.theatlantic.com/technology/archive/2018/02/who-is-weev/553295/.

156 **In 2017, the Nazi also:** Sarah Larimer, "After Bananas and Nooses on Cam- pus, Here's How a Student Body President Copes," *Washington Post*, June 26, 2017, https://www.washingtonpost.com/local/education/after-bananas -and-nooses-on-campus-heres-how-a-student-body-president-copes/2017/06 /26/b8bdf706-5791-11e7-a204-ad70646f1a4f_story.html; Sarah Larimer, "Former AU Student Government President Sues over 'Troll Storm' After Bananas Incident," *Washington Post*, May 2, 2018, https://www.washington post.com/news/grade-point/wp/2018/05/02/former-au-student-government -president-sues-over-troll-storm-after-bananas-incident/; Michael Harriot, "White Supremacist Troll Forced to Publicly Apologize to Black Student He Harassed," The Root, December 19, 2018, https://www.theroot.com/white -supremacist-troll-forced-to-publicly-apologize-to-1831204622.

157 **When Anglin discovered that campus police:** Harriot, "White Suprema- cist Troll Forced to Publicly Apologize."

157 **Dumpson was diagnosed with PTSD:** Karen Zraick, "Student Targeted by 'Troll Storm' Hopes Settlement Will Send a Message to White Suprema- cists," *New York Times*, December 21, 2018, https://www.nytimes.com/2018 /12/21/us/american-university-racist-hate-training.html.

157 **Melania met with tech company:** Stephen Balkam, "Forget Donald Trump's Tweets, Melania Could Be a Great Crusader Against Cyberbullying," *USA Today*, March 28, 2018, https://www.usatoday.com/story/opinion/2018/03 /28/melania-ideal-cyberbullying-crusader-despite-donald-trump -tweets-column/464062002/.

157 **the *New York Times* published:** Jasmine C. Lee and Kevin Quealy, "The 487 People, Places, and Things Donald Trump Has Insulted on Twitter: A Complete List," *New York Times*, July 10, 2018, accessed on July 10, 2018, https://www.ny times.com/interactive/2016/01/28/upshot/donald-trump-twitter-insults.html.

157 **Cheri Jacobus noted wryly:** Lorraine Bailey, "Pundit Called 'Dummy' by Trump Can't Sue for Defamation," Courthouse News Service, December 12, 2017, https://www.courthousenews.com/pundit-called-dummy-by-trump -cant-sue-for-defamation/.

157 **"because I am a Trump critic:"** Cheri Jacobus, "From 'Little Marco' to 'Cryin' Chuck,' All Hail Melania Trump's Cyberbullying Campaign," *USA Today*, March 22, 2016, https://www.usatoday.com/story/opinion/2018/03 /22/melania-trump-cyberbullying-campaign-cold-comfort-donald-targets -column/445448002/.

157 **Cyberstalking . . . requires that the offender:** Joey L. Blanch and Wesley L. Hsu, "An Introduction to Violent Crime on the Internet," *Cyber Misbehavior* 64, no. 3 (May 2016), https://www.justice.gov/usao/file/851856/download.

158 **assaulted by a swarm of angry bees:** O'Brien, "The Making of an American Nazi."

158 **The chaos started in late October:** Unless otherwise indicated, details relating to Pizzagate can be found in Amanda Robb's excellent *Rolling Stone* feature story. See: Amanda Robb, "Anatomy of a Fake News Scandal," *Rolling Stone*, June 25, 2018, https://www.rollingstone.com/politics/news/piz zagate-anatomy-of-a-fake-news-scandal-w511904; Laura Starcheski and Amanda Robb, "Pizzagate: A Slice of Fake News," Reveal, November 18, 2017, https://www.revealnews.org/episodes/pizzagate-a-slice-of-fake-news/; Gregor Aisch, Jon Huang, and Cecilia Kang, "Dissecting the #PizzaGate Conspiracy Theories," *New York Times*, December 10, 2016, https://www .nytimes.com/interactive/2016/12/10/business/media/pizzagate.html.

159 **tweeted about Pizzagate:** Robb, "Anatomy of a Fake News Scandal"; Jay Michaelson, "#Pizzagate Is the 'Satanic Panic' of Our Age—but This Time, the President's Men Believe It," Daily Beast, December 6, 2016, https://www .thedailybeast.com/pizzagate-is-the-satanic-panic-of-our-agebut-this-time -the-presidents-men-believe-it.

159 **discussed Pizzagate on Breitbart Radio:** Robb, "Anatomy of a Fake News Scandal."

159 **Jones ran a YouTube channel:** Zack Beauchamp, "Alex Jones, Pizzagate Booster and America's Most Famous Conspiracy Theorist, Explained," Vox, December 7, 2016, https://www.vox.com/policy-and-politics/2016/10/28 /13424848/alex-jones-infowars-prisonplanet.

159 **Jones's media empire was built on bizarre conspiracies:** Eric Killelea, "Alex Jones' Mis-Infowars: 7 Bat-Sh*t Conspiracy Theories," *Rolling Stone*, February 21, 2017, https://www.rollingstone.com/culture/lists/alex-jones -mis-infowars-7-bat-sht-conspiracy-theories-w467509/the-government -is-controlling-the-weather-w467722.

159 **"I mean it's fake!"** Aaron Cooper, "Six More Sandy Hook Families Sue Broadcaster Alex Jones," CNN, August 6, 2018, https://www.cnn.com /2018/05/23/us/alex-jones-sandy-hook-suit/index.html.

159 **In 2013, Jones was reportedly:** Beauchamp, "Alex Jones."

159 **For years after Sandy Hook:** Jorge Milian, "Sandy Hook Parent Hopes Arrest in Threat Case Stops Talk of 'Hoax,'" *Palm Beach Post*, December 23,

2016, https://www.palmbeachpost.com/news/crime-law/sandy-hook
-parent-hopes-arrest-threat-case-stops-talk-hoax/Fayp5d0Eib2W56smBbJgsK/.

159 **"Did you hide your imaginary son":** Bethania Palma, "Sandy Hook Parents Sue Conspiracy Troll Alex Jones for Defamation," Snopes, April 17, 2017, https://www.snopes.com/news/2018/04/17/sandy-hook-parents-sue -conspiracy-troll-alex-jones/.

160 **a condition of her parole:** Elizabeth Williamson, "Alex Jones, Pursued over Infowars Falsehoods, Faces a Legal Crossroads," *New York Times*, July 31, 2018, https://www.nytimes.com/2018/07/31/us/politics/alex-jones-defama tion-suit-sandy-hook.html.

160 **Noah's parents were forced to move:** Williamson, "Alex Jones, Pursued over Infowars Falsehoods."

160 **Jones raged about Clinton and Pizzagate:** Marc Fisher, John Woodrow Cox, and Peter Hermann, "Pizzagate: From Rumor, to Hashtag, to Gunfire in DC," *Washington Post*, December 6, 2016, https://www.washingtonpost .com/local/pizzagate-from-rumor-to-hashtag-to-gunfire-in-dc/2016/12/06 /4c7def50-bbd4-11e6-94ac-3d324840106c_story.html.

160 **YouTube post from November 27:** Eric Hananoki, "Alex Jones Deletes Video in Which He Had Told His Audience to Personally 'Investigate' 'Pizzagate' Restaurant," Media Matters for America, December 16, 2016, https://www .mediamatters.org/blog/2016/12/16/alex-jones-deletes-video-which-he-had -told-his-audience-personally-investigate-pizzagate-restaurant/214846.

160 **Less than two weeks later, Edgar Maddison Welch:** Faiz Siddiqui and Susan Svrluga, "N.C. Man Told Police He Went to D.C. Pizzeria with Gun to Investigate Conspiracy Theory," *Washington Post*, December 5, 2016, https://www.washingtonpost.com/news/local/wp/2016/12/04/d-c-police -respond-to-report-of-a-man-with-a-gun-at-comet-ping-pong-restaurant/.

160 **Welch spent December 1 binge-watching:** Spencer Hsu, "'Pizzagate' Gun-man Says He Was Foolish, Reckless, Mistaken—and Sorry," *Washington Post*, June 14, 2017, https://www.washingtonpost.com/local/public-safety /pizzagate-shooter-apologizes-in-handwritten-letter-for-his-mistakes -ahead-of-sentencing/2017/06/13/f35126b6-5086-11e7-be25-3a519335381c _story.html.

160 **Welch loaded up his car with:** Robb, "Anatomy of a Fake News Scandal."

161 **Welch found a closet with cooking supplies:** Robb, "Anatomy of a Fake News Scandal."

161 **he'd gone to "self investigate" the child sex ring:** Siddiqui and Svrluga, "N.C. Man Told Police."

161 **In June 2017, Welch was sentenced:** Eric Ortiz, "'Pizzagate' Gunman Sentenced to Four Years in Prison," NBC News, June 22, 2017, https://www

.nbcnews.com/news/us-news/pizzagate-gunman-edgar-maddison-welch
-sentenced-four-years-prison-n775621.

161 **Alek Minassian was struggling:** Les Perreaux, Josh O'Kane, Patrick
White, and Becca Clarkson, "Suspect in Toronto Van Attack Publicly
Embraced Misogynist Ideology," *Globe and Mail*, April 24, 2018, https://
www.theglobeandmail.com/canada/article-facebook-post-connected
-to-suspect-in-van-rampage-cites-incel/.

161 **Elliot Rodger who, in 2014:** "Elliot Roger: How Misogynist Killer Became
'Incel Hero,'" BBC News, April 26, 2018, https://www.bbc.com/news/world
-us-canada-43892189.

161 **On April 23, 2018, Alek Minassian:** Perreaux et al., "Suspect in Toronto
Van Attack."

162 **Gersh sued Anglin:** Kunzelman, "Target of Online Trolls"; Carter Sherman,
"Suing the Trolls," Vice, April 27, 2017, https://news.vice.com/en_ca/article
/xwv3j4/troll-storm-lawsuit-against-neo-nazi-may-provide-blueprint-for
-fighting-online-harassment; Karen Zraick, "Neo-Nazis Have No First Amendment Right to Harassment, Judge Rules," *New York Times*, November 15, 2018,
https://www.nytimes.com/2018/11/15/us/daily-stormer-anti-semitic-lawsuit
.html.

162 **The following month, Taylor Dumpson:** Larimer, "Former AU Student";
Harriot, "White Supremacist Troll"; Zraick, "Student Targeted by 'Troll
Storm.'"

162 **In April 2018, the parents:** Plaintiffs' original petition and request for dis-
closure, *Leonard Pozner and Veronique de la Rosa v. Alex E. Jones, Infowars,
LLC, and Free Speech Systems, LLC*, No. D-1-GN-18-001842 (District
Court of Travis County, Texas, April 16, 2018), https://www.scribd.com
/document/376707398/Pozner-v-Jones-Et-Al.

162 **six more Sandy Hook families:** Cooper, "Six More Sandy Hook Families."

162 **all imposed sanctions on Jones:** Jane Coaston, "YouTube, Facebook, and
Apple's Ban on Alex Jones, Explained," Vox, August 6, 2018, https://www.vox
.com/2018/8/6/17655658/alex-jones-facebook-youtube-conspiracy-theories.

163 **In September 2018, Twitter permanently banned:** Tony Romm, "Twitter
Has Permanently Banned Alex Jones and Infowars," *Washington Post*,
September 6, 2018, https://www.washingtonpost.com/technology/2018/09
/06/twitter-has-permanently-banned-alex-jones-infowars/.

163 **Jones's supporters cried "censorship":** Alan Feuer, "Free Speech Scholars to
Alex Jones: You're Not Protected," *New York Times*, August 7, 2018, https://
www.nytimes.com/2018/08/07/business/media/alex-jones-free-speech-not
-protected.html; Coaston, "YouTube, Facebook, and Apple's Ban."

NOTES

CHAPTER 8: PORN TROLL SEX POLICE

165 **I've never asked Anna:** The identifying details of Anna's story have been changed to protect her privacy.

168 **incels and Men Going Their Own Way:** Alex Brook Lynn, "The Women of the Men's Rights Movement," Vice, August 4, 2014, https://www.vice .com/en_us/article/8gdd8a/the-women-of-the-mens-rights-movement-804.

168 **to red pillers:** Amelia Tait, "Spitting Out the Red Pill: Former Misogynists Reveal How They Were Radicalised Online," *New Statesman*, February 28, 2017, https://www.newstatesman.com/science-tech/internet/2017/02/red dit-the-red-pill-interview-how-misogyny-spreads-online.

168 **and pickup artists:** "Male Supremacy," Southern Poverty Law Center, https:// www.splcenter.org/fighting-hate/extremist-files/ideology/male-supremacy.

169 **Fans upload their favorite porn clips:** Cade Metz, "The Porn Business Isn't Anything Like You Think It Is," *Wired*, October 15, 2015, https://www .wired.com/2015/10/the-porn-business-isnt-anything-like-you-think-it-is/.

169 **In 2017 alone, users uploaded:** "2017 Year in Review," Pornhub, January 9, 2018, https://www.pornhub.com/insights/2017-year-in-review.

169 **data transferred through Pornhub in a year:** "2017 Year in Review," Pornhub.

169 **Netflix's 2015 documentary *Hot Girls Wanted*:** *Hot Girls Wanted*, directed by Jill Bauer and Ronna Gradus (Los Gatos, CA: Netflix, 2015), DVD.

170 **For decades, starting in the 1970s:** Melia Robinson, "How LA's 'Porn Valley' Became the Adult Entertainment Capital of the World," Business Insider, September 29, 2017, https://www.businessinsider.com/history-of -porn-valley-hugh-hefner-2017-9.

170 **California's San Fernando Valley:** Sue Chan, "San Fernando's Open Secret," CBS News, November 26, 2002, https://www.cbsnews.com/news /san-fernandos-open-secret/.

170 **ran like old-school Hollywood studios:** For good information on the early days of pornography, see: Katrina Forrester, "Making Sense of Modern Por- nography," *New Yorker*, September 26, 2016, https://www.newyorker.com /magazine/2016/09/26/making-sense-of-modern-pornography.

171 **In 1995 . . . newcomer Jenna Jameson:** Matthew Miller, "The Celebrity 100: The (Porn) Player," *Forbes*, July 4, 2005, https://www.forbes.com/free _forbes/2005/0704/124.html.

171 **Jameson famously never did an anal scene:** Forrester, "Making Sense."

171 **In 2000, Jameson launched Club Jenna:** Miller, "The Celebrity 100."

171 **revenues of $30 million:** Miller, "The Celebrity 100."

171 **cover model Tera Patrick:** Andrew Vontz, "A Day in the Life of Porn Star Tera Patrick," Andrew Vontz (personal website), 2005, http://www.an drewvontz.com/terapatrick/.

171 **Adult actress Stormy Daniels:** Catherine Pearson, "Meet the Powerful Women Directors Working in Porn," *HuffPost*, August 27, 2015, https://www .huffingtonpost.com/entry/meet-the-powerful-women-directors-working-in -porn_us_55ca50a7e4b0f1cbf1e68c13; Lissa Townsend Rodgers, "The Female Porn Director Winning All the Awards," The Cut, February 9, 2016, https:// www.thecut.com/2016/02/stormy-daniels-wanted.html.

172 **group of college-bro tech-nerds in Montreal:** Benjamin Wallace, "The Geek-Kings of Smut," *New York*, January 30, 2011, http://nymag.com/news /features/70985/.

172 **The dudes launched Pornhub the same year:** All information about the history of Pornhub is from Jon Ronson's excellent podcast. See: Jon Ronson, "A Nondescript Building in Montreal" (episode 1), November 2, 2017, in *The Butterfly Effect with Jon Ronson* podcast, https://www.stitcher.com/pod cast/audible/the-butterfly-effect-with-jon-ronson/e/52096344.

172 **the first generation of iPhones hit the market:** Annys Shin, "When Apple Introduced the iPhone," *Washington Post Magazine*, June 22, 2017, https:// www.washingtonpost.com/lifestyle/magazine/when-apple-introduced-the -iphone/2017/06/20/7f2e968a-3cde-11e7-9e48-c4f199710b69_story.html.

172 **Online distribution puts billions:** David Auerbach, "Vampire Porn," Slate, October 23, 2014, http://www.slate.com/articles/technology/technology /2014/10/mindgeek_porn_monopoly_its_dominance_is_a_cautionary _tale_for_other_industries.html.

172 **Critics compare . . . to a sweatshop:** Gail Dines and David L. Levy, "Porn 'Disruption' Makes Stormy Daniels a Rare Success in Increasingly Abusive Industry," The Conversation, April 9, 2018, https://theconversation.com /porn-disruption-makes-stormy-daniels-a-rare-success-in-increasingly -abusive-industry-94534.

172 **one of the most trafficked websites:** Ruqayyah Moynihan, "Internet Users Access Porn Websites More Than Twitter, Wikipedia, and Netflix," Insider, September 30, 2018, https://www.thisisinsider.com/internet-users-access -porn-more-than-twitter-wikipedia-and-netflix-2018-9.

172 **with ninety-two million visitors per day:** "2018 Year in Review," Porn-Hub Insights, December 11, 2018, https://www.pornhub.com/insights/2018 -year-in-review.

172 **a generation of independent pornographers emerged:** Alexander Bisley, "How Free Porn Enriched the Tech Industry—and Ruined the Lives of Ac-tors," Vox, October 6, 2017, https://www.vox.com/conversations/2017/10/6 /16435742/jon-ronson-butterfly-effect-internet-free-porn.

173 **Their specialty is amateur porn:** Dorian Hargrove, "San Diego's Porn Stu-dios," *San Diego Reader*, January 4, 2017, https://www.sandiegoreader.com /news/2017/jan/04/cover-san-diegos-porn-studios/.

173 **a performer might be paid anywhere:** Forrester, "Making Sense."

173 **In the free-porn economy:** Jon Ronson, "The Fallow Years Between Teen & MILF" (episode 2), November 3, 2017, in *The Butterfly Effect with Jon Ronson* podcast, https://www.stitcher.com/podcast/audible/the-butterfly -effect-with-jon-ronson/e/52105434; *Hot Girls Wanted*, directed by Bauer and Gradus.

174 **more than sixty thousand views:** Nippon HD, "The New Girl at Work Blows Her Bosses for a Raise," Pornhub video, 7:04, https://www.pornhub .com/video/search?search=the+new+girl+at+work+blows+her+bosses +for+a+raise.

174 **"Exxtra small teen gets punished":** Danika Mori, "Exxtra Small Teen Gets Punished After She Cheated on Her Boyfriend," Pornhub video, 21:41, https://www.pornhub.com/video/search?search=exxtra+small+teen+get+ punished+after+she+cheated+on+her+boyfriend.

174 **videos depicting men choking and slapping women:** "Facials," Pornhub, https://www.pornhub.com/video/search?search=facials.

174 **also known as "facial abuse":** "Facial Abuse," Pornhub, https://www.porn hub.com/video/search?search=facial+abuse.

174 **90 percent of the most popular porn:** "How Consuming Porn Can Lead to Violence," Fight the New Drug, August 23, 2017, https://fightthenew drug.org/how-consuming-porn-can-lead-to-violence/.

174 **She famously described pornography:** Andrea Dworkin, *Pornography: Men Possessing Women* (New York: Putnam, 1981).

174 **a man-hating agenda and derided:** Katharine Viner, "'She Never Hated Men,'" *The Guardian*, April 12, 2005, https://www.theguardian.com/books /2005/apr/12/gender.highereducation.

174 **definitive work on the matter:** Dworkin, *Pornography*.

174 **a meta-analysis of twenty-two different studies:** Paul J. Wright, Robert Tokunaga, and Ashley Kraus, "A Meta-Analysis of Pornography Consumption and Actual Acts of Sexual Aggression in General Population Studies," *Journal of Communication* 66, no. 1 (December 2015), https://www .researchgate.net/publication/288905229_A_Meta-Analysis_of_Pornogra phy_Consumption_and_Actual_Acts_of_Sexual_Aggression_in_Gen eral_Population.

175 **Still, there is a body of research:** "How Consuming Porn Can Lead to Violence," Fight the New Drug.

175 **films like *Deep Throat*:** Roger Ebert, review of *The Devil in Miss Jones*, directed by Gerard Damiano, *Chicago Sun-Times*, June 13, 1973, https:// www.rogerebert.com/reviews/the-devil-in-miss-jones-1973.

175 **reviewed by mainstream film critics:** Ralph Blumenthal, "'Hard-Core' Grows Fashionable—and Very Profitable," *New York Times*, January 21, 1973, https://www.nytimes.com/1973/01/21/archives/pornochic-hardcore -grows-fashionableand-very-profitable.html.

175 **nine minutes and fifty-nine seconds:** "2017 Year in Review," Pornhub.

176 **For $29.99 a month:** "Real Amateur Girls Having Sex on Video for the Very First Time," Girls Do Porn, accessed January 7, 2019, http://www.girlsdo porn.com/page1.php.

176 **"these girls on any other website":** "Real Amateur Girls," Girls Do Porn.

176 **a dozen women . . . suing Girls Do Porn:** Don Debenedictis, "Women Call SoCal Pornographers Brutal Liars," Courthouse News Service, June 9, 2016, https://www.courthousenews.com/women-call-socal-pornographers -brutal-liars/; *Jane Does 1–22 v. GirlsDoPorn.com, et al.*, Superior Court of California, County of San Diego, case number 37-2016-19027-CU-FR-CTL; Hargrove, "San Diego's Porn Studios."

180 **Since the earliest days of Usenet groups:** Megan Garber, "Doxing: An Etymology," *The Atlantic*, March 6, 2014, https://www.theatlantic.com /technology/archive/2014/03/doxing-an-etymology/284283/.

180 **"Dox" is a neologism:** Caitlin Dewey, "How Doxing Went from a Cheap Hacker Trick to a Presidential Campaign Tactic," *Washington Post*, August 12, 2015, https://www.washingtonpost.com/news/the-intersect/wp/2015 /08/12/how-doxing-went-from-a-cheap-hacker-trick-to-a-presidential -campaign-tactic/.

180 **Anonymous doxed . . . the Church of Scientology:** Dewey, "How Doxing Went."

180 **In 2015, Walter Palmer:** Megan Condis, "Cecil the Lion's Hunter Becomes the Hunted," Al Jazeera America, August 1, 2015, http://america.aljazeera .com/opinions/2015/8/cecil-the-lions-hunter-becomes-the-hunted.html.

180 **He received death threats:** Meghan Holden and Danika Fears, "Lion-Killing Dentist Hides as Protesters Swarm His Office," *New York Post*, July 30, 2015, https://nypost.com/2015/07/30/lion-killing-dentist-hides-as-protesters -swarm-his-office/; Chris Perez, "Lion-Killing Dentist Hires Ex-Cops to Pro-tect His Vacation Home," *New York Post*, August 5, 2015, https://nypost.com /2015/08/05/lion-killing-dentist-hires-ex-cops-to-protect-vacation-home/; Caroline Mortimer, "Cecil the Lion Death: Police Step Up Patrols at Office of US Dentist Walter Palmer After 'Terroristic Threats,'" *Independent*, July 30, 2015, https://www.independent.co.uk/news/world/americas/cecil-the-lion -death-police-step-up-patrols-at-office-of-us-dentist-walter-palmer-after -terroristic-10426168.html.

180 **forbid users from posting other people's:** Kate Knibbs, "Twitter Just Banned Revenge Porn and Doxxing," Gizmodo, March 11, 2015, https://giz modo.com/twitter-just-banned-revenge-porn-and-doxxing-1690916107; "The Twitter Rules," Twitter Help Center, accessed in January 2019, https:// help.twitter.com/en/rules-and-policies/twitter-rules; Todd Haselton, "Here's Facebook's Once-Secret List of Content That Can Get You Banned,"

CNBC, April 24, 2018, https://www.cnbc.com/2018/04/24/facebook-content-that-gets-you-banned-according-to-community-standards.html; "Community Standards," Facebook, accessed in January 2019, https://www.facebook.com/communitystandards/introduction/.

180 **doxing as a weapon:** Decca Muldowney, "Doxx Racists: How Antifa Uses Cyber Shaming to Combat the Alt-Right," Pacific Standard, November 2, 2017, https://psmag.com/news/doxxing-the-alt-right-racists.

180 **white supremacist rally:** Emma Grey Ellis, "Whatever Your Side, Doxing Is a Perilous Form of Justice," *Wired*, August 17, 2017, https://www.wired.com/story/doxing-charlottesville/; Muldowney, "Doxx Racists."

180 **several left-leaning activists:** Micah Lee, "How Right-Wing Extremists Stalk, Dox, and Harass Their Enemies," The Intercept, September 6, 2017, https://theintercept.com/2017/09/06/how-right-wing-extremists-stalk-dox-and-harass-their-enemies/.

180 **Nazi trolls launched:** Lee, "How Right-Wing Extremists."

181 **In June 2017, Massachusetts representative Katherine Clark:** Joshua Miller, "Police Swarm Katherine Clark's Home After Apparent Hoax," *Boston Globe*, February 1, 2016, https://www.bostonglobe.com/metro/2016/02/01/cops-swarm-rep-katherine-clark-melrose-home-after-apparent-hoax/yqEpcpWmKtN6bOOAj8FZXJ/story.html.

181 **the Online Safety Modernization Act:** US Congress, House of Representatives, "Online Safety Modernization Act," H.R. 3067 (2017), https://katherineclark.house.gov/_cache/files/b1841244-4daa-49ce-bb95-2cdcf16bc5b2/online-safety-modernization-act.pdf.

181 **The bill was referred to:** Online Safety Modernization Act of 2017, H.R. 3067, 115th Congress, https://www.congress.gov/bill/115th-congress/house-bill/3067/all-actions.

182 **they'll scour the internet tirelessly:** Darren Orf, "Creeps Are Using a Neural Network to Dox Porn Actresses," Gizmodo, April 26, 2016, https://gizmodo.com/creeps-are-using-neural-networks-to-dox-porn-actresses-1773130390.

182 **created Porn Wikileaks:** Tracy Clark-Flory, "The Twisted World of Porn WikiLeaks," Salon, April 1, 2011, https://www.salon.com/2011/03/31/porn_wikileaks/.

182 **complained to the Daily Beast:** Richard Abowitz, "Porn Wikileaks: The Person Behind the Website Scaring Porn Stars," Daily Beast, March 31, 2011, https://www.thedailybeast.com/porn-wikileaks-the-person-behind-the-website-scaring-porn-stars.

183 **In seventeenth-century colonial America:** Encyclopaedia Britannica, s.v. "Cucking and Ducking Stools," by Geoffrey Abbott, August 9, 2007, www.britannica.com/topic/cucking-stool.

183 **Historians note that some men of the day:** Jenny Paull, "The Scold's Bridle," Lancaster Castle, http://www.lancastercastle.com/history-heritage /further-articles/the-scolds-bridle/.

183 **"pioneer in the field of sexual privacy":** Talbot, "The Attorney Fighting."

185 **XXXLaw in the URL:** J.D. Odenberger and Associates, "A Law Firm Devoted to Liberty," XXX Law, http://www.xxxlaw.com.

CHAPTER 9: POWER PERVS

188 **Department of Justice would identify sextortion:** US Department of Justice, *The National Strategy for Child Exploitation Prevention and Interdiction: A Report to Congress* (Washington, DC: April 2016), https://www .justice.gov/psc/file/842411/download.

188 **In 2012, fifteen-year-old Amanda Todd:** *Vancouver Sun*, "Amanda Todd's Heart-Breaking YouTube Video of Cyberbullying," YouTube video, 8:52, February 28, 2018, https://youtu.be/FS95zvN5MiI.

189 **He created a Facebook account:** CBC News, "The Sextortion of Amanda Todd," *The Fifth Estate*, YouTube video, 42:19, August 11, 2014, https:// youtu.be/uQRnSIa-qQM.

189 **She suffered depression:** CBC News, "The Sextortion of Amanda Todd."

189 **"I can never get that photo back":** *Vancouver Sun*, "Amanda Todd's YouTube."

189 **Less than two months after:** Michelle Dean, "The Story of Amanda Todd," *New Yorker*, October 18, 2012, https://www.newyorker.com/culture/cul ture-desk/the-story-of-amanda-todd.

189 **After her death, the video was shared:** Naomi Woolf, "Amanda Todd's Suicide and Social Media's Sexualisation of Youth Culture," *The Guardian*, October 26, 2012, https://www.theguardian.com/commentisfree/2012/oct/26 /amanda-todd-suicide-social-media-sexualisation; Katinka Dufour, "Amanda Todd Case Highlights Issue of Online Bullying," *The Telegraph*, October 16, 2012, https://www.telegraph.co.uk/news/worldnews/northamerica/usa /9612030/Amanda-Todd-case-highlights-issue-of-online-bullying.html.

189 **Sextortionists will spend:** Quinta Jurecic, Clara Spera, Benjamin Wittes, and Cody Poplin, "Sextortion: The Problem and the Solution," Brookings Institution, May 11, 2016, https://www.brookings.edu/blog/techtank/2016 /05/11/sextortion-the-problem-and-solutions/; US Department of Justice, *The National Strategy for Child Exploitation Prevention*.

190 **thirty-two-year-old Mijangos lived:** David Kushner, "The Hacker Is Watching," *GQ*, January 11, 2012, https://www.gq.com/story/luis-mijangos -hacker-webcam-virus-internet.

191 **Mijangos was finally arrested in June 2010:** Richard Winton, "6 Years for O.C. Hacker Who Victimized Women, Girls," *Los Angeles Times*, Septem-

ber 1, 2011, https://latimesblogs.latimes.com/lanow/2011/09/sextortion-six
-years-for-oc-hacker-who-forced-women-to-give-up-naked-pics-.html.

191 **Brookings Institution's groundbreaking report:** Benjamin Wittes, Cody
Poplin, Quinta Jurecic, and Clara Spera, "Sextortion: Cybersecurity, Teenagers, and Remote Sexual Assault," Center for Technology Innovation at
Brookings, May 2016, https://www.brookings.edu/wp-content/uploads
/2016/05/sextortion1-1.pdf.

192 **In 2015, the FBI analyzed:** US Department of Justice, *The National Strategy for Child Exploitation Prevention*.

192 **According to a 2016 Department of Justice report:** US Department of
Justice, *The National Strategy for Child Exploitation Prevention*.

193 **In 2017, Coban . . . was sentenced:** Andrea Woo, "Dutch Court Hands
Amanda Todd's Cyberbully Maximum Sentence," *Globe and Mail*, March
16, 2017, https://www.theglobeandmail.com/news/national/man
-charged-in-amanda-todd-case-sentenced-to-11-years-in-dutch-prison
/article34318268/; Mike Corder, "Aydin C. Trial: Cyberbully Accused in
Amanda Todd Case Could Face 11 Years in Dutch Prison," *HuffPost*, February 9, 2017, https://www.huffingtonpost.ca/2017/02/09/aydin-c-trial_n
_14658116.html.

193 **In 2015, a twenty-five-year-old:** Jesse Paul, "Ohio Man Sentenced in Jef-
ferson County for Sexually Exploiting Teen," *Denver Post*, January 12, 2015,
https://www.denverpost.com/2015/01/12/ohio-man-sentenced-in-jefferson
-county-for-sexually-exploiting-teen/.

194 **Internet Crime Complaint Center:** Federal Bureau of Investigation
Internet Crime Complaint Center (IC3), https://www.ic3.gov/default.aspx.

196 **drafting a bill to help combat:** Rachel Martin and Katherine Clark, "Latest 'Swatting' Incident Keeps Rep. Clark Pushing for Legislation," NPR
Morning Edition, January 2, 2018, https://www.npr.org/2018/01/02
/575043357/latest-swatting-incident-keeps-rep-clark-pushing-for-legislation.

196 **The Interstate Sextortion Prevention Act:** Interstate Sextortion Prevention Act of 2016, H.R. 5749, 114th Congress, https://www.congress.gov
/bill/114th-congress/house-bill/5749/text.

196 **the Online Safety Modernization Act:** Online Safety Modernization Act
of 2017, H.R. 3067, 115th Congress, https://www.congress.gov/bill/115th
-congress/house-bill/3067/text.

197 **In 1975, Carmita Wood:** Raina Lipsitz, "Sexual Harassment Law Was
Shaped by the Battles of Black Women," *The Nation*, October 20, 2016,
https://www.thenation.com/article/sexual-harassment-law-was-shaped
-by-the-battles-of-black-women/; Jessica Campbell, "The First Brave Woman
Who Alleged 'Sexual Harassment,'" Legacy, February 5, 2016, http://www
.legacy.com/news/culture-and-trends/article/the-first-brave-woman-who
-alleged-sexual-harassment.

197 **coined the term "sexual harassment":** Sascha Cohen, "A Brief History of Sexual Harassment in America Before Anita Hill," *Time*, April 11, 2016, http://time.com/4286575/sexual-harassment-before-anita-hill/.

198 **the *New York Times* used the phrase:** Enid Nemy, "Women Begin to Speak Out Against Sexual Harassment at Work," *New York Times*, August 19, 1975, https://www.nytimes.com/1975/08/19/archives/women-begin-to-speak-out-against-sexual-harassment-at-work.html.

198 **"Patients were there":** Nemy, "Women Begin to Speak Out."

198 **"It was just devastating to me":** Nemy, "Women Begin to Speak Out."

198 **a 1986 *Time*/Yankelovich Clancy Shulman poll:** Janie Velencia, "Americans Didn't Believe Anita Hill. How Will They Respond to Kavanaugh's Accuser?" FiveThirtyEight, September 17, 2018, https://fivethirtyeight.com/features/americans-didnt-believe-anita-hill-how-will-they-respond-to-kavanaughs-accuser/.

198 **Multiple women had witnessed Thomas's bad behavior:** Jill Abramson, "Do You Believe Her Now?" *New York*, February 19, 2018, http://nymag.com/intelligencer/2018/02/the-case-for-impeaching-clarence-thomas.html.

199 **Hill recounted in vivid detail:** Elizabeth Mitchell, "Anita Hill's Afterlife," *O, The Oprah Magazine*, July 2005, https://www.oprah.com/omagazine/anita-hills-afterlife/all.

199 **Hill told the committee that Thomas:** Abramson, "Do You Believe Her Now?"

199 **Twenty million people tuned in:** Mitchell, "Anita Hill's Afterlife."

199 **A psychologist invited to testify:** Shannon Carlin, "The Claims Against Anita Hill During the Clarence Thomas Hearings Were Harsh, Strange & All Over the Place," Bustle, April 15, 2016, https://www.bustle.com/articles/154735-the-claims-against-anita-hill-during-the-clarence-thomas-hearings-were-harsh-strange-all-over.

199 **David Brock, who at the time:** Alex Kuczynski and William Glaberson, "Book Author Says He Lied in His Attacks on Anita Hill in Bid to Aid Justice Thomas," *New York Times*, June 27, 2001, https://www.nytimes.com/2001/06/27/us/book-author-says-he-lied-his-attacks-anita-hill-bid-aid-justice-thomas.html.

199 **Brock confessed that he'd:** Kuczynski and Glaberson, "Book Author Says."

199 **intimidating the woman into silence:** Margaret Carlson, "Smearing Anita Hill: A Writer Confesses," *Time,* July 9, 2001, http://content.time.com/time/nation/article/0,8599,167355,00.html.

199 **voted in favor of tightening the definition:** Abramson, "Do You Believe Her Now?"

200 **"let a lot of people off the hook":** Abramson, "Do You Believe Her Now?"

201 **Enduring repeated sexual harassment:** Elyse Shaw, Ariane Hegewisch, and Cynthia Hess, "Sexual Harassment and Assault at Work: Understand-

ing the Cost," Institute for Women's Policy Research, October 15, 2018, https://iwpr.org/publications/sexual-harassment-work-cost/.

201 **as many as eight in ten women:** Amy Blackstone, Heather McLaughlin, and Christopher Uggen, "Workplace Sexual Harassment," *State of the Union 2018*, Stanford Center on Poverty and Inequality, 2018, https://inequality .stanford.edu/sites/default/files/Pathways_SOTU_2018_harassment.pdf.

201 **Even when they stay in their positions:** Blackstone, McLaughlin, and Uggen, "Workplace Sexual Harassment."

202 **The Standford study found:** Blackstone, McLaughlin, and Uggen, "Workplace Sexual Harassment."

202 **Weinstein's . . . misconduct exploded into the mainstream:** Ronan Farrow, "From Aggressive Overtures to Sexual Assault: Harvey Weinstein's Accusers Tell Their Stories," *New Yorker*, October 10, 2017, https://www .newyorker.com/news/news-desk/from-aggressive-overtures-to-sexual -assault-harvey-weinsteins-accusers-tell-their-stories; Jodi Kantor and Megan Twohey, "Harvey Weinstein Paid Off Sexual Harassment Accusers for Decades," *New York Times*, October 5, 2017, https://www.nytimes.com /2017/10/05/us/harvey-weinstein-harassment-allegations.html.

202 **the women were blacklisted:** Brooks Barnes, "Ashley Judd Sues Harvey Weinstein, Saying He Harmed Her Career," *New York Times*, April 30, 2018, https://www.nytimes.com/2018/04/30/business/media/ashley-judd-harvey -weinstein-lawsuit.html; Yohana Desta, "How Actresses Allegedly Blacklisted by Harvey Weinstein Are Making Big Comebacks," *Vanity Fair*, January 5, 2018, https://www.vanityfair.com/hollywood/2018/01/blacklisted-actresses -comeback-weinstein.

202 **Peter Jackson, the director:** Marwa Eltagouri, "Peter Jackson Recalls Weinstein's Company Warned That Ashley Judd and Mira Sorvino Were 'a Nightmare,'" *Washington Post*, December 15, 2017, https://www.washing tonpost.com/news/arts-and-entertainment/wp/2017/12/15/oscar-winning -director-says-weinstein-company-warned-against-hiring-ashley-judd-and -mira-sorvino/.

203 **In May 2018, Weinstein:** *People v. Harvey Weinstein* (New York Supreme Court—Criminal Term) Case No. 023335-2018.

203 **"used his money . . . to violate them sexually":** Benjamin Mueller and Alan Feuer, "Arrested on Rape Charges, Weinstein Posts $1 Million Bail," *New York Times*, May 25, 2018, https://www.nytimes.com/2018/05/25 /nyregion/harvey-weinstein-arrested.html.

204 **Within weeks . . . dozens more women:** Sara M. Moniuszko and Cara Kelly, "Harvey Weinstein Scandal: A Complete List of the 87 Accusers," *USA Today*, October 27, 2017, https://www.usatoday.com/story/life/people /2017/10/27/weinstein-scandal-complete-list-accusers/804663001/.

205 **Within a year of Weinstein's . . . more than 250:** Anna North, Constance Grady, Laura McGann, and Aja Romano, "252 Celebrities, Politicians, CEOs, and Others Who Have Been Accused Since April 2017," edited by Michelle Garcia, Susannah Locke, and Eleanor Barkhorn, Vox, accessed on October 8, 2018, https://www.vox.com/a/sexual-harassment-assault -allegations-list.

205 **In fact, the movement had existed:** Sandra E. Garcia, "The Woman Who Created #MeToo Long Before Hashtags," *New York Times*, October 20, 2017, https://www.nytimes.com/2017/10/20/us/me-too-movement-tarana -burke.html.

205 **Alyssa Milano tweeted:** Garcia, "The Woman Who Created #MeToo."

205 **Esteemed NBC newsman Matt Lauer:** Erik Wemple, "Just How Did Matt Lauer's Famous Desk Button Work?" *Washington Post*, May 11, 2018, https:// www.washingtonpost.com/blogs/erik-wemple/wp/2018/05/11/just-how -did-matt-lauers-famous-desk-button-work/.

206 **Lauer is alleged to have bent:** Jessica Simeone and David Mack, "Matt Lauer Says He's 'Embarrassed and Ashamed' in His First Statement Since Being Fired from NBC News," BuzzFeed, November 29, 2017, https://www .buzzfeednews.com/article/jessicasimeone/matt-lauer-has-been-fired-from -nbc-news-amid-report-of.

206 **Lauer was fired, and later issued:** Simeone and Mack, "Matt Lauer Says."

206 **federal judge Alex Kozinski:** Matt Zapotosky, "Prominent Appeals Court Judge Alex Kozinski Accused of Sexual Misconduct," *Washington Post*, December 8, 2017, https://www.washingtonpost.com/world/national -security/prominent-appeals-court-judge-alex-kozinski-accused-of -sexual-misconduct/2017/12/08/1763e2b8-d913-11e7-a841-2066faf731ef _story.html.

206 **Kozinski resigned within weeks:** Dan Berman and Laura Jarrett, "Judge Alex Kozinski, Accused of Sexual Misconduct, Resigns," CNN, December 18, 2017, https://www.cnn.com/2017/12/18/politics/alex-kozinski-resigns /index.html.

206 **respected journalist Charlie Rose:** Irin Carmon and Amy Brittain, "Eight Women Say Charlie Rose Sexually Harassed Them—with Nudity, Groping, and Lewd Calls," *Washington Post*, November 20, 2017, https://www .washingtonpost.com/investigations/eight-women-say-charlie-rose-sexually -harassed-them--with-nudity-groping-and-lewd-calls/2017/11/20/9b168de8 -caec-11e7-8321-481fd63f174d_story.html.

206 **"pursuing shared feelings":** Carmon and Brittain, "Eight Women Say."

206 **professor Dacher Keltner:** Dacher Keltner, curriculum vitae, https:// greatergood.berkeley.edu/dacherkeltner/docs/vita_dacherkeltner.pdf; Dacher Keltner, Deborah H. Gruenfeld, and Cameron Anderson,

"Power, Approach, and Inhibition," *Psychological Review* 10, no. 2 (2003): 265–284, http://www.ajhepworth.yolasite.com/resources/9822-a2.pdf.

206 **being powerful leads men to overestimate:** Dacher Keltner, "Sex, Power, and the Systems That Enable Men Like Harvey Weinstein," *Harvard Business Review*, October 13, 2017, https://hbr.org/2017/10/sex-power-and-the-systems -that-enable-men-like-harvey-weinstein; Jonathan W. Kunstman and Jon K. Maner, "Sexual Overperception: Power, Mating Motives, and Biases in Social Judgment," *Journal of Personality and Social Psychology* 100, no. 2 (February 2011), https://static1.squarespace.com/static/56cf3dd4b6aa60904403973f/t /5717de91356fb08915fab22f/1461182098198/sexual-overperception.pdf.

206 **reduces empathy and diminishes:** Keltner, "Sex, Power and the Systems."

207 **sexualize their work environments:** Keltner, "Sex, Power and the Systems."

207 **Keltner, author of *The Power Paradox*:** Dacher Keltner, *The Power Paradox: How We Gain and Lose Influence* (New York: Penguin Books, 2016).

207 **abuses of power are "predictable and reoccurring":** Keltner, "Sex, Power and the Systems."

207 **differences when comparing the brains:** Jeremy Hogeveen, Michael Inzlicht, and Sukhvinder S. Obhi, "Power Changes How the Brain Responds to Others," *Journal of Experimental Psychology: General* 143, no. 2 (2014), https://www.oveo.org/fichiers/power-changes-how-the-brain-responds -to-others.pdf.

207 **"mirroring" functions differently in the two groups:** Hogeveen, Inzlicht, and Obhi, "Power Changes."

207 **instrumental in empathy:** Lea Winerman, "The Mind's Mirror," *Monitor on Psychology* 36, no. 9 (October 2005): 48, https://www.apa.org/monitor /oct05/mirror.aspx.

207 **the 2009 issue of *Brain*:** David Owen and Jonathan Davidson, "Hubris Syndrome: An Acquired Personality Disorder? A Study of US Presidents and UK Prime Ministers over the Last 100 Years," *Brain* 132, no. 5 (May 2009): 1396– 1406, https://academic.oup.com/brain/article/132/5/1396/354862.

208 **The authors warn:** Owen and Davidson, "Hubris Syndrome."

209 **actors Ashley Judd and Rose McGowan:** Kantor and Twohey, "Harvey Weinstein Paid."

209 **who don't have the financial freedom:** Shaw, Hegewisch, and Hess, "Sexual Harassment and Assault at Work."

209 **32 percent of women:** Blackstone et al., "Workplace Sexual Harassment."

209 **serial sexual abuse of migrant farmworkers:** Ariel Ramchandani, "There's a Sexual Harassment Epidemic on America's Farms," *The Atlantic*, January 29, 2018, https://www.theatlantic.com/business/archive/2018/01/agricul ture-sexual-harassment/550109/.

209 **hotel workers:** Samantha Raphelson, "Advocates Push for Stronger Measures to Protect Hotel Workers from Sexual Harassment," NPR, June 29,

2018, https://www.npr.org/2018/06/29/624373308/advocates-push-for
-stronger-measures-to-protect-hotel-workers-from-sexual-harass.

209 **restaurant staff:** Maura Judkis and Emily Heil, "Rape in the Storage Room. Groping at the Bar. Why Is the Restaurant Industry So Terrible for Women?" *Washington Post*, November 17, 2017, https://www.washingtonpost.com /lifestyle/food/rape-in-the-storage-room-groping-at-the-bar-why-is-the -restaurant-industry-so-terrible-for-women/2017/11/17/54a1d0f2-c993-11e7 -b0cf-7689a9f2d84e_story.html.

209 **automotive assembly line workers:** Susan Chira and Catrin Einhorn, "How Tough Is It to Change a Culture of Harassment? Ask Women at Ford," *New York Times*, December 19, 2017, https://www.nytimes.com/in teractive/2017/12/19/us/ford-chicago-sexual-harassment.html.

209 **In September 2018, female employees at the country's:** Kim Elsesser, "McDonald's Workers Are Striking over Sexual Harassment, but Will the Company Act?" *Forbes*, September 17, 2018, https://www.forbes.com/sites /kimelsesser/2018/09/17/mcdonalds-workers-strike-over-sexual-harassment -but-will-mcdonalds-act/.

209 **Breauna Morrow . . . complained to her supervisor:** Danielle Paquette, "McDonald's Workers Describe Rampant Harassment, Workplace Groping and Suggestive Comments," *Washington Post*, May 22, 2018, https://www .washingtonpost.com/news/wonk/wp/2018/05/22/mcdonalds-workers -describe-rampant-harassment-workplace-groping-and-suggestive -comments/.

210 **experienced verbal and physical sexual harassment:** Gillian Thomas, "McDonald's Is Serving Up Sexual Harassment," ACLU Women's Rights Project, January 14, 2019, https://www.aclu.org/blog/womens-rights/wom ens-rights-workplace/mcdonalds-serving-sexual-harassment.

210 **with almost 400,000 workers:** Jennifer Calfas, "The 6 Biggest Employers in the U.S. Right Now," *Money*, April 27, 2017, http://money.com/money /4754123/biggest-us-companies/.

ACKNOWLEDGMENTS

Jeannine Amber, I will live my life in gratitude for all the love and care, intensity and nuance you poured into this book and the stories we tell. Your determination to figure stuff out, put the pieces together, sculpt all these parts into something real, to help me figure out if I really wanted to "go there," and to call me out when I started going off the rails is just hard to describe. You are a phenomenal journalist and have one of the most disciplined brains I know.

To my agent, Adriann Ranta Zurhellen, and the crew at Foundry Media—you came into my life, Adriann, on a day I couldn't make payroll and was desperately trying to figure out a supplement. I thought: book advance. (In retrospect, LOL!) Forget the fact that I didn't have a book proposal or even an idea, I researched the best feminist writers and their agents and all roads led to you. I still marvel at my good fortune that you emailed me back. You had faith in me and this book before either one of us (me or the book) had come into being. I will forever be grateful for your gamble on me so early on.

To my editor, Maya Ziv, at Penguin Random House, it's been such a joy working with you. You've been a constant source of positivity and girl power during this entire process. And OMG, thank you to the skill and expertise of the rest of my team at Penguin: Kayleigh George in marketing, Alice Dalrymple in production editorial, and Jill Schwartzman, the editorial director of Plume. Linda Huang, the designer of my cover, you are so good at your job! Thank you to Eva Allen for all your hard work!

Thank you, T., for being the best lawyer, friend, and man. Individually we are powerful but together we are unstoppable. I love you madly and I love you calmly.

To Susan Crumiller, she who has always steered toward the deepest waters. My best friend. "A ship in harbor is safe, but that's not what ships are built for." You've kept me afloat all these years. Without you, I'd be sunken, capsized, at the bottom of the ocean or at least somebody's toilet. #BDVictories!!! Oh, and readers, if you're being screwed by your employer, check out Crumiller.com. Susan will fight the bejesus against any asshole employer trying to take you down.

There are some people you owe a debt to in anything you do because they have formed you into you: Larry and Jane Goldberg—I love you, Mom and Dad—Heesok and Sophia Chang, Amy Rowley, David, and Lauren. Thank you, Mom—the best sections were written beside you in bed. Long live my lovely ladies from the Selfhelp days and beyond—Wendy Rota, Meredith Gemeiner, and Rhona Kaplan. Oh, the hijinks we got up to at 620 Fort Washington. And my deepest love to the talented women who found me worthy for their projects—Cynthia Lowen, Margaret Talbot, Michelle Sy, Joy Gorman, Brian Yorkey, Marissa Jo Cerar, Sophia Chang, Sasha Erwitt—and changed my life in the process.

For those who were with me during the darkest hours of my life, you will never know the extent of my gratitude. You gave me a bed to sleep on, supplied boxes of Kleenex, sat next to me in court, brought me home from jail, helped me move, listened to me, and didn't turn your back—Heesok and Sophia, Julia Kaminsky, Melissa Paige, Kaminsky family, Rebecca Symes, Erin Tobin, Tara Dziezic, Sasha Lehman, Scott Harding, Jessie Kilguss, Will Carlough, Brooke Belisle, P.W., and Barry Agulnick, Esq.—I'll never forget your kindness.

This wouldn't be possible without my clients putting their trust in me. I dedicate this book to every client who has ever hired me. I'm so proud to have gotten to work with you all. Huge extra love to M.J.B., Francesca Rossi, Matthew Herrick, L.V., Norma Buster, K.M., M.M., K., Lucia Evans, S.M., Michelle Hadley, and M.K.

I have the best team in the world. The goal is to have staff members who are better at their jobs than I could ever dream of being—and jeez, I've got that in Adam Massey, Norma Buster, Lindsay Lieberman, Carrie Sophia Zoubul, Aurore DeCarlo, Elizabeth Dehaan, Amna Khalid, Deborah Shapiro, Caroline Knaught, Edward Williams, Annie Seiffulah, and Marline Etienne. This is your book you guys. Adam, what would life even be without you? You are the bedrock of this firm and have been since month three. And, g-d, thank you for the eleventh-hour citations! Thank you also to Carlie Tise, Sophie Kravet, Carla Cain-Walther, and Shi Jian Hong.

Grampy Jay and Grammy Doc, I miss you both so much. It's a mean trick of time that the people who root for us the hardest won't live to see who they've helped us become.

Thank you, Aron Schulz, for the sage advice.

T.E. and S.E., I love you both, and I'm so excited to help you not become—or cross paths with—psychos, assholes, pervs, or trolls.

My work wife, Elisa D'Amico, you are such a talented hell-on-wheels attorney. Your kindness and tenacity are an inspiration. I'm most mesmerized by how singular a person you are. Erica Johnstone, you are such an incredible lawyer and you were litigating the shit outta the enemies of privacy long before most of us came along. Your work paved the way for the rest of us.

ACKNOWLEDGMENTS

Holly Jacobs, Mary Anne Franks, and Danielle Citron—in my darkest moments, reading about you guys gave me hope. How you welcomed me into the fold changed my life. I've never experienced that kind of professional kindness. For the first time in my career, you made me feel smart, useful, and purposeful. To my tribe of lady-lawyer bosses, I adore you—Kristen Marcroft, Meghan Freed, Maggie McLetchie, Marni Jo Snyder, Jill Zuccardy, Ellaretha Coleman, Clare Corado. TAYE ASTUOP to Susan Crumiller, Jessica Stein, Jennifer Gore-Cuthbert, and Holly Moore.

My biggest love and gratitude to caseworkers and attorneys at non-profits. Your work is really important. To all the people toiling away in law school, please appreciate the artistic tool and violent weapon your degree is. Don't squander it on unworthy agendas somebody imposes upon you.

This book is in honor of the community I came from in Aberdeen, Washington, and the community I plopped into in Brooklyn, New York. And finally, love to a few others who shaped, supported, and taught me in big ways: Lindsay Lunnum, James McGeveran, Alysha Trautman, Karinna Jones, Beverly Smith, Helen Quinn, Louise Lipman, Jay Blass Cohen, Lazlow Jones, Paul and Leisa Goldberg, Valerie Bogart, Julie Stoil-Fernandez, Jean Wilson, Grampy Kenneth Fales, and my survivors at Selfhelp, RIP.

To all the assholes, psychos, pervs, trolls, and stalkers who've crossed my path over the years, I will stop short of thanking you here. But I acknowledge the field of research you've provided.

INDEX

ABOUT THE AUTHORS

Carrie Goldberg is a victims' rights lawyer born and raised in Aberdeen, Washington. Her law firm, C.A. Goldberg, PLLC, litigates nationally for targets of online harassment, stalking, and sexual assault. Before starting her law firm, Carrie provided social services to Nazi victims and went on to become a lawyer for the Vera Institute of Justice. Her major litigations include *Herrick v. Grindr, NNAF v. John Doe, Hadley v. City of Anaheim*, and *L.W. as parent/guardian of K.M. v. New York City Department of Education*. Her work was featured in the documentary *Netizens*. Carrie attended Vassar College and Brooklyn Law School. She resides in Brooklyn, New York.

Jeannine Amber is the former senior writer for *Essence* magazine and the recipient of more than a dozen awards for her investigative journalism and feature writing focusing on crime, race, and gender. Jeannine is also the coauthor of *Rabbit: A Memoir,* listed as one of Amazon's best books of 2017, and a finalist for an NAACP Image Award for Outstanding Literary Work. Jeannine lives in Brooklyn with her daughter and their dog. You can read more of her work at JeannineAmber.com or reach her on Twitter @jamberstar.